Growing Up Old School

Introduction

✍ Everybody has stories to tell; maybe I've got a few more than most. I feel as though I've led a fairly normal life, but the more I tell stories about my childhood, the more people tell me that I should write a book. Well, here it is.

I'll admit to being a little reckless and a little wild as a kid, but there were certainly guys a heck of a lot more reckless and a heck of a lot wilder than myself. This book is not about times that we TRIED to be wild and reckless, it is about the things we did as kids that were normal, everyday things for us back in the sixties and seventies. They weren't at all out of the ordinary. These are the collective events that all of us shared together in one way or another in what I can only imagine as the greatest time in the history of our country to be a kid!

I've been blessed with the gift of a great memory. I don't know if you'd call it a photographic memory, but I am certainly able to recall trivial events from thirty or forty years ago very easily. I think the main reason that I can relive those times so readily is because the past means so much to me. When I recall those events with the people who were there, they really seem to enjoy the flashback in time. I suppose the re-telling of these tales makes us young again, or allows us to forget some of our current problems, or maybe we just sit back and marvel at how we survived it all.

✍ I grew up in Cambridge, a small Eastern Ohio town of about 12,000. We were a very diverse community: whites, blacks, wealthy, poor, blue collar, and white collar. All of which I can easily sit back and recognize now, but as kids, we didn't know or care about our differences. It's amazing that as little kids we have no concept of prejudice, but as we *grow up*, we have different categories for everyone. Doesn't that seem contradictory as to how it should be? Anyways.

We were primarily city kids, not like Chicago or New York, but we didn't live on farms like many of our parents had when

2

they were kids. Our parents grew up in much harder times than we had to. Many of them grew up on farms where they put in long, tough hours, at very young ages. Many of them had also lived through The Great Depression and World War II or the Korean Conflict. Basically, our elders had earned whatever wrinkles and scars that shown on their faces. We heard a lot of, "When I was a kid..." stories and looking back, they had every right to use those stories on us.

As children of the sixties and seventies we were allowed to just be kids. I assume that our parents wanted to give us opportunities that they didn't have when they were young. They had suffered through difficult times and one of the best ways for them to give us something that they hadn't had was to tell us these two words, "Go play." We knew exactly what that meant and you didn't have to tell us twice, we were out the door, doing what we were told, PLAYING.

Unlike our parents, there really wasn't anything for us to do around the house anyways, we lived in the city; there were no fields to plow or cows to milk, our family's financial existence didn't rely on us kids reaping the back forty. I'm sure we felt bad every once in a blue moon because it seemed like we were just never home, we were always outside just goofing around while our parents were going to work, doing housework, or complaining about the bills, but I don't think we felt bad for very long, we were too busy, we had stuff to do. We were professional kids and we took our jobs of playing and goofing off very seriously. I think I'd match our ability to play and invent ways to keep occupied with that of any generation.

To the parents of the children of the sixties and seventies, I'd just like to say, "Thanks." Thanks for allowing us to just be kids, and I'll tell you what, we were pretty darn good at it too; being a kid that is. You always told us that we had our whole lives to work and that we should just go out and have fun. Well, you'll be amazed at some of the ways that we made that happen.

✍   I watch how kids entertain themselves today and it's no wonder that we live in the most obese and out of shape society in the world. PlayStation, Xbox, and Nintendo have taken the place of imagination and activity. Cell phones, texting, Facebook, Twitter, and Instagram have eliminated the idea of walking to a friend's house to see what they are doing. Today's parents have to actually make play date appointments for their kids. Ha, I can just imagine my old man calling someone else's dad and asking when it would be a good time for me to come over and play. Just wouldn't have happened. Matter-of-fact, I've gotta believe that I probably would've got smacked in the back of the head for even bringing it up. For an age group of kids that dominated the concept of just going outside and playing for hours at a time, we have really dropped the ball when it comes to how our kids entertain themselves. We should all be a little bit ashamed.

✍   I've been working on this book for quite a number of years and in truth I probably could've finished it five or six years ago, but by not finishing it, I've been able to... I don't know, hold on to those years a little longer. I guess I figured if I was able to sit down and write a little bit every day, and re-write, and edit, and add more and more to the book, it would never leave me; but by not publishing it, I have been withholding those memories for others who deserve the chance to read the book and hit rewind to relive those years as I have.

This book is like a time machine; it will take you back to a time and place that we all cherished, a time when we were as free and unburdened as we would ever be. Enjoy your journey back home.

Chapter 1
The Elementary School Days

Kindergarten, first, second, and third grade teachers always seemed to be motherly-types who were pretty quick with a hug. They had to control a variety of attitudes and abilities. They had to mold us little "squirmers" into future students. We learned the alphabet, shapes, colors, how to read and write, how to add and subtract, how to get along with others, how to share, and how to sit in our seats for what seemed like weeks at a time. When you look back at it, we were just like little sponges, soaking up tons of information every day. I only wish that I could now learn in a year, all of the things that I absorbed in a year of early elementary school; I'd have an I.Q. of 200. Bottom line was that we were ready to learn and we were eager workers, at least as long as they could hold our attention. We didn't have medical labels giving us built-in excuses of why we couldn't sit still; our labels were "ornery" or "rambunctious" and for the most part a little bit of rigid discipline put us back on target without a handful of pills for breakfast and a fidget spinner to calm us down. I can guarantee that most of the dad's I knew of that era would've bounced a fidget spinner off our foreheads like a Kung-Fu throwing star if we told them we needed that to control our actions.

It was probably important that our early elementary teachers were motherly or grandmotherly-types because here we were five, six, seven, maybe eight years old and we had been stripped away from our mothers and sent to school. In the 1960's, it wasn't like we had spent three years at a daycare center and then another year or two at pre-school. For the most part many of our mothers did not work outside of the home, WE were their jobs and they were our sole providers, we hadn't really left their sight for five or six years. I can't tell you how I remember, but I definitely remember my mom walking me up the alley and across the street to Park School for my first day of kindergarten. I was crying like I was being dragged to the gas chamber and before it was all over with; she was balling just as badly as I was. In today's world, Children's Services would have been called in to find out why all of these kids were crying like beaten, red-haired step-children. In those days I don't even think there was such a thing as Children's Services. You had whatever rights your mom and dad told you that you had and if some uppity lady came knocking on the door inquiring about why little Johnny got his butt spanked; it would have only earn you another beating, and that uppity lady would've gotten told off in a loud and expletive filled manner.

✍ I know that in kindergarten and maybe even in first grade, we were given cookies and milk and then we all lay down and took a nap. We had no State academic standards that we had to have forced down our throats, we had no governmental nutritional standards; we just had teachers who knew we were hungry and needed a nap. Amazingly, our daily cookie didn't create obesity problems and the nap we took didn't take away from valuable learning opportunities, we awoke with vigor and newly charged energy. Aren't there still days that it feels pretty good to get a half hour nap in? I say, absolutely.

✍ We started every day of school with the Pledge of Allegiance called out over the intercom. We would all put our right hand over our hearts and recite The Pledge out loud. No one dared to screw around during The Pledge; the teachers would always be glancing around out of the corner of their eye, and honestly it would have cost you a trip to the office and earned a call to your parents. There was no one calling in and telling the school that their kid wasn't going to say The Pledge; whatever problems existed during this time, being un-American wasn't one of them. There certainly wasn't an issue of "One Nation Under God" either, in fact I don't think anyone even thought about it, and I know that no one worried about it. We still proudly say the Pledge of Allegiance at the school I work at and our kids do a great job with it. There are actually hundreds of countries that you can move to if you don't like this one, (sorry, soap box moment).

✍ I also remember all of us standing in line in the cafeteria waiting to get vaccinations. Anyone born in the late 50's and early 60's still carries the pock mark on their upper left arm. They used a gun to shoot us with the vaccine, I think to prevent smallpox although it could've been polio; anyways, the thing made a loud sound and kicked enough to scare the ever living crap out of all of the little kids. If you were standing towards the back of the line you got to watch several of your classmates take one in the arm and potentially start screaming and crying. At that point in our lives trying to act tough in front of our friends wasn't something that we concerned ourselves with. In elementary school if you felt the urge to cry, well... then you cried.

✍ When I walk through the elementary hallways of the school I work at, I am reminded of many of the art projects that apparently have recycled throughout history: The super-realistic looking Hand Turkey, a snowman scene using cotton, a Spring flower scene, and of course our tiny little hands forever cast in Plaster-of-Paris mementos. Just to show how our society has changed, forty years ago we all made ashtrays as gifts for our dads at Christmas-time or Father's Day; can you imagine doing that today?

✍ Today I see girls from kindergarten to college-age, wearing rain boots. They range from polka dots to leopard prints to the popular houndstooth pattern. In the sixties and seventies, especially as little elementary kids, our wardrobes served 100% for function and 0% for fashion; so with that functionality in mind, we wore "galoshes". Just the name of them is unattractive and probably has a hidden German meaning of "more work than they're worth." The idea behind these rubber boots was simple: you pull them over your shoes and protect your feet from the cold and wet weather. But the reality of these five buckle torture contraptions was a little different; first of all it was hard for us to distinguish the right from left boot (remember, we were little), secondly they had a pretty good shelf life which meant that we would have the same boots for quite a few years, so you had kids who wore size eight tennis shoes and were trying to get a size five pair of galoshes over them. I can remember working up a tremendous sweat trying to get my ever-growing foot into what seemed to be an ever-shrinking rubber boot. Getting them off was no better, we could never just get the boot off and leave our tennis shoes on; we would have to kick the whole unit off and then reach in and fish out our shoe (and sometimes your sock.) The worst part was that the kids who didn't wear the boots for school either got to go to recess five minutes earlier than you or Heaven Forbid the class had to wait for you to get your boots on before they could go out to recess. Talk about peer pressure, no wonder we later had no problems performing in front of crowds.

✍ Teachers became stricter as we moved through the grades. We could no longer get away with breaking the rules and have the teacher smooth it over with, "Johnny, please don't do that again."

You could actually get in trouble: you could be made to stay after school, you could get sent to the office, you could have your parents called in, you could stand against the wall at recess, or if you were really bad you could get paddled. Whacks (as we called them) didn't happen very often in elementary school, but I can remember a couple guys who got heated up back in fifth and sixth grade. The guys who got whacked always came back crying and nothing much was ever discussed about it. I know personally, I didn't want any part of it. I tried to disassociate myself from anyone who got whacked; I didn't want the teachers thinking that I was a trouble-maker too. (Maybe a good strategy in adult life.)

We grew up in a double-indemnity era. Whatever punishment you got at school, you usually got double that at home. I got more than enough beatings at home so I sure in the heck wasn't going to compound my problems by getting in trouble at school. I'm not sure if I was afraid of getting knocked around by my old man, or if I was afraid of my teachers, or if I sincerely respected my elders, but the rules that the teachers gave us seemed plenty fair enough in my book and I had no reason to buck the system.

Back in those days it wasn't anything out of the norm for a parent to walk into the school and give their kid a pretty decent slap. As a matter-of-fact, if your parent was called into school, you could probably bank on some kind of rabbit-punch to the back of the head as the kid was being dragged out to the car. This wasn't the "my kid is holier than thou, he certainly wouldn't have done that, it must be the teacher's fault" society that we live in today. Teachers were respected and the kids had no say in the verdict. Actually parents didn't even want to hear their kid's side of the story, they listened to what the teachers had to say and then doled out punishment as they saw fit.

As we went through the years, the teachers showed a little bit more of their true personalities. We figured out that they weren't the Saints that we thought they were. Although this chapter is primarily about our elementary days, I still vividly remember the first time I heard a teacher say the "F" word, it happened in freshman gym class and I thought that it was by far the coolest thing I had ever witnessed throughout my then ten years of education.

It wasn't like I had never heard that word before, as a matter-of-fact, my old man and most of my friend's dads could rattle off a twenty-five or thirty-word sentence and use that particular word fifteen or sixteen times when they were on a full roll, but we for some reason we didn't think that our teachers did those things. I was in seventh grade before I saw my first teacher at Bargain City, I was amazed. I really didn't think that they shopped at the same stores we went to. The elementary kids I teach today still have that same awed reaction whenever they see me at Walmart. I try to make a big deal out of seeing them, like I'm impressed and of course I always get the comment the next day mixed in with a sly little grin, "I saw you at Walmart last night."

Those elementary teachers would lose their cool, just like we do now with our own kids and they would definitely let us know about it. Obviously, times have changed since then, but I can tell you that forty-years ago the teachers would get mad and grab a kid by the scruff of the neck or yank them by the arm and drag them all the way down the hallway to the office. Remember, we were still under twelve years old and none of us were very big yet, so when you took a 200+ pound male teacher (or female teacher for that matter), and you added anger, and a sixty-five pound eleven year old running his mouth, you definitely had the ingredients for flight. There were a lot of times I witnessed some of our future high school hellions, make the entire 150-foot trek to the office with their feet only touching the ground three or four times.

✍ I don't remember too many classroom lessons from elementary school, but seeing that I can read, write, and do my "rithmatic", I guess things went fairly well. We didn't have a clue as to what time we did Reading, we didn't know what time Math class was, and they could have taken Social Studies and thrown it out the window for all we cared, but I can tell you that we all knew exactly what time recess started, when it ended, how many recesses we got for each grade, what the weather was supposed to be like during those periods, who was the line leader, and who's turn it was to bring the football.

✍ Recess was the ultimate incentive. Teachers held recess over our heads in the same manner that our parents held Christmas over our heads. They could have threatened to drop our grades by a letter or two and that would have been fine with us, but just don't screw up our recess. We would suffer through our academic classes with 90% of our focus on trying to calculate exactly how many minutes until recess. As a matter-of-fact, we all had it counted down and knew exactly what second the bell would ring for recess. When we had occasional power outages and the clocks were off by a minute or two, it would have us all screwed up.

A lot of times we had to have all of our desks cleaned off or we had to be sitting quietly before we could go to recess; every once in a while someone would be lagging behind which would hold us up from our appointed play time. You could then hear the rough whispers of, "Hurry Up!" start to rotate around the room. As a teacher now, I do the same thing, if there is a kid who is being a jerk and wants to operate on their own agenda, I simply hold the rest of the class back until the little rebel does what I ask. Nothing is more effective than peer group justice.

When it was finally time to go to recess, we would hit that playground like Allied troops hitting the beaches of Normandy. Our single-file, perfectly silent march to freedom quickly turned into thirty little electrons bouncing wildly outside the shell of an unstable plutonium atom as soon as we got onto that playground blacktop; we were scattered everywhere within five seconds. I've seen poor little fat kids and dainty little girls in $50 dresses get run over by the herd. Never underestimate the power of the herd. Trust me, Darwin never had to go into the jungle to come up with *Survival of the Fittest*, five minutes of watching fifth or sixth-grade recess and anyone could have come up with that concept.

Schools spent entirely too much money on playground equipment, sure there was always a group of girls who merrily went back and forth on the swings, but all of that other stuff like slides, teeter totters, and monkey bars were only useful to weave in and out of while being pursued by various assailants. As a matter-of-fact, to demonstrate how much we disliked using the playground equipment, one time when we had our footballs and basketballs taken away from us for a couple days, (probably for tearing up our clothes on picture day, or hitting a substitute teacher in the head with a football), we all met down by the old, giant oak tree and played a game in which we would run as fast as we could up the side of the tree and jump up and see who could reach up the furthest on the tree. If you slipped, you ate tree bark. We loved it. But there was no way we were going to use the playground equipment, and even when we did use it, we didn't use it correctly. The slide, which seems pretty self-explanatory, only seemed any fun if we crawled up the slide or tried to slide down it on our feet like the Silver Surfer. The merry-go-round was basically off limits to us boys; about once a year we would all meet at the whirling "Ring of Death" and try to spin it so fast that someone threw up, or try to jump on it while it was spinning and it would throw us ten or fifteen feet into the fence or onto the concrete. And of course there were always the swings which were only useful to "Parachute" from, which meant to swing as high as possible and then jump out at the absolute apex, trying to beat each other's records for both distance and height. (You could not play that game and actually try to win without at least spraining your ankle.) There was also the urban legend of some elementary kid from some other school, who supposedly swung all the way around the top bar; I think we can now all see how this act would negate the actual laws of physics, but as twelve-year old boys we didn't understand the laws of physics anyways so we tried like crazy to swing so high that we looped over the top bar.

All we really needed was a big field or patch of asphalt, a basketball hoop (of which a net was a bonus, a luxury really), and maybe a wall (we liked to play On the Wall Dodgeball). The girls didn't seem to need much of anything, like I said, a few swings and a place where they could stand around in a circle and talk and they seemed pretty content. The idea of girls joining in our recess athletic contests just wasn't fathomable. This was the 1960's and there wasn't much in the line of Women's Rights, or women's sports, or a Women's Movement. I'm sure I sound sexist right now as you read this, but honestly, girls weren't asking to play sports with the boys; it was a completely foreign concept. Don't get me wrong, if they had asked, we would have whined and complained and would have come up with a hundred different reasons why they couldn't play with us, but bottom line was that I just don't think it even crossed their minds to want to join in. What girl would have wanted to join in anyways? We were a hybrid of a group of wild wolves fighting for the same bone, a hornet's nest just hit by a stick, and a dozen blood-crazed sharks.

As kids, we played sports pretty much every waking hour. Football, basketball, baseball, whiffleball, dodgeball, basically anything involving a ball (or even sometimes things that we turned into a ball, like a ball of tape, or a pinecone, or maybe even a good nicely-formed rock), we could invent a way to turn it into a competitive sport. In our world winning did matter. We weren't gung-ho about trophies and such, mainly because trophies were rare prizes back in those days (unlike today's society that give out trophies and medals and certificates to everyone with enough stamina to fill out an entry form). Our prizes were bragging rights; at least for that day, which gave incentive to keep those bragging rights for the next day and gave incentive to others to take those bragging rights away from you tomorrow.

All games started with the choice of captains, usually this was the two toughest guys in class, the alpha males if you will, (which usually closely coincided with the fastest rate of maturity or the guy whom had been held back and was a year or two older than everybody else). Every once in a while someone would say, "Hey, why don't we let such and such pick today." Of which, he would immediately pick one of the guys that were always the captain and then would take *advice* from his first round draft choice and pick the exact same team anyways. I'm sure that most of the guys have outgrown any complexes that they developed through those years, but there were a few poor unathletic souls who were picked last or next to last from first through twelfth grades. It was like volunteering to eat cat puke when one of the captains had to pick certain players; they would often make up reasons why they couldn't draft some of these players for their team:

"I can't take him; it'll make the teams uneven."

"I ain't gonna take him, I've had him two days in a row."

"If I take him today, I get first pick tomorrow."

"I just ain't taking him, if you want him, you can have him."

Now mind you, these conversations were announced directly in front of these boys. We didn't have therapy or counseling back then, but if we did, I can name three or four guys right off the top of my head that would have been lying on a couch somewhere.

We played football more than any other recess sport, I don't know if we liked it the best, if we could get more people involved, or if we just liked the rough and tumble aspect of giving someone a free pop in the mouth, shove to the back, or slap to the side of the head.

The game was two-hand touch below the neck, three catches for a first down, on a 150 x 60-foot slab of asphalt. Touchdowns were at the edge of the pea gravel parking lot on one end and the edge of the bike rack at the other end. Of course there was an 8% incline to deal with, so one team always had a definite advantage of being able to build up speed and the other team always had the advantage of being able to stop before they ran into the fence or out into the street. I'm sure all elementary playgrounds were different but they all had their own built in obstacles.

Obstacles were any teachers that strayed onto the playing field (mostly substitutes, the regular teachers knew to stand near the doorway), any kid who wasn't playing football, and anyone who was playing basketball (of which the basketball court sat at what would be equivalent to the fifty yard line). A sidewalk clearly marked the out-of-bounds for one of the sidelines, but the other sideline was never clearly defined. In four-years of playing football at Park School, I could have never told you where the other out-of-bounds marker was. That roaming sideline was based on a lot of things: how nice was the catch? Did it go for a first down? Did it go for a touchdown? Was it intercepted? What was the score? And how much time was left in the recess? But the two main questions were who caught the ball? And who was disputing the call? If an alpha male caught the ball or threw the pass, the play was going to stand. If an alpha male was disputing the call, the play was going to be overturned, simple as that. Former N.F.L. Commissioner Paul Tagliabue couldn't overrule these guys. The only other scenario that could possibly take place was when both alpha males got involved in the ruling, and then there was going to be some fireworks. At some point the ball either was going to be knocked out of someone's hand followed by a shove to the chest or the ball was going to be thrown at someone's head. Recesses were occasionally shut down early (albeit probably thirty or forty seconds early) because the alpha males couldn't come to some kind of resolution. The ball was taken away from us and we were left standing there staring at each other, wondering who would be the first person to walk over and start using the playground equipment.

At least a dozen times during one of these alpha male showdowns, we all stood there and watched as the ball was tossed into the street and either got ran over by a car, or made it directly into the sewer hole across the street, or other times when it was thrown onto the roof of the school. Most of the time the ball was one that was brought in by a student and I can tell you from experience that when you didn't come home with the ball that you took to school, you were interrogated by your parents as to the whereabouts of said football. (Remember, this wasn't an Age of Excess, as it is today. Your parents had a detailed inventory of your belongings and if something came up missing or broken, they wanted some answers). When you told them about the ball being thrown on the roof, here were two of the more common responses:

"Why didn't you stop him?" or "What's that little son-of-a-bitches phone number?"

At that point you went into some very dramatic and often tear-laced pleading, "Don't call! I can get it back tomorrow. The janitor goes up there every day and he'll get it down for me. I already talked to him and he said he'd get it down tomorrow." All of which were lies, but you knew you were seven dialed digits away from a beating if your old man called up and got one of the school bullies in trouble with their dad.

✍ It was funny because at Park School it was possible to climb up the window sills to the roof even though the sills only stuck out about an inch and a half. It was about fifteen-feet to the roof and I'm sure there was always the possibility of crashing your leg through the glass, or getting caught by the police or principal, but none of that seemed nearly as harmful as the possible sanctions that could play out from not coming home with your football or basketball, so up we climbed, clinging to the glass like Spiderman. Once you were up on the roof it was like a smorgasbord of awesome things that little boys liked to play with; a variety of balls, cool-shaped rocks, an occasional nickel, doll's heads, a few G.I. Joes, maybe a Hot Wheel or two. You were a hero when you started tossing those things down to their rightful owners, always sure to stick some of the better bounty into your own pocket first. Of course getting down from the roof was always dramatic as you now had to try to scale back down the windows which never worked nearly as well as going up them. You had to use the *hang and drop method* which was always a fifty-fifty coin flip as to getting hurt or not, not hospital hurt, but limping around on a sprained ankle for the next couple days hurt for sure.

In later years we would send our best Spiderman up to the roof, have him go through a skylight or some other kind of venting system (I don't really know what it was because I was the shakiest of all Spidermen and only went up there a couple times in absolute desperation to make sure I had a ball to take home), drop down into the school, open the doors for the rest of us and we would go in and play basketball until we either actually heard the cops at the front door or just thought we heard the cops. I think about it now and doubt if it was ever the police, it was probably just another one of our gang of hobo's and street riff-raff that wanted to come in and shoot some baskets with us. At no point did we ever destroy anything or steal anything, we just wanted a place to come in out of the cold and shoot some baskets. I suppose if we wanted to get technical, yeah sure it was probably breaking and entering, but we were only eleven or twelve, we weren't destroying anything, and if we are gonna keep track of all of the "little crimes" we may or may not have committed during those years, I should stop typing right now. Statute of limitations ran out on that stuff decades ago, (maybe that's why it took so long for me to write this book.)

✍ Back to the epic elementary football games: The football games were all pass and three completions out of the four downs was a first down. If you could catch and you were fast you were a pretty hot commodity. The ability to throw short accurate passes for some reason wasn't much of a selling point. The long ball was all that most quarterbacks wanted to throw, even though the team that threw the most short passes would almost always win the game. There apparently wasn't a lot of aesthetic beauty in the art of piecing together a bunch of pinpoint short passes, not when you could just rear back and wing it as far as you could and have every play resemble the Flutie Miracle Throw (which was more than a decade from even happening yet.) Those long full-court heaves probably had less than a five-percent chance of actually connecting with a player from your own team, but that didn't stop us from trying them on almost every play.

Tackling was always an adventure on the asphalt. If you pushed someone too hard, they would go flying, if you missed a tackle you would go flying. Once you were heading to the asphalt at top speed, it was sometimes hard to fall gracefully, at some point you were going to have to pay your tax to the Asphalt God. If you didn't tap someone hard enough you started the daily debate, "You didn't get me." Every day, every single day that we ever played recess football we fought that war. The outcome of many games rested in your ability to defend your statement of, "I got you."

"No you didn't."

"Yes I did, right in the middle of your back."

"No you didn't, you only got me with one hand."

"Yes I did, my left hand was on your sleeve and my right hand was in the middle of your back."

"I felt the one in the middle of my back, but my sleeve is just hanging there, it's not even part of me, that don't count."

Being that we had no instant replay or registered officials to help us work this out, we handled it the best way we could. There would be absolutely, positively no debate on the next play, the next tackle would without a doubt be with two hands and the receiver would without a doubt, for sure, feel it this time. It was not going to be pretty and there was for sure going to be some blood coming from a knee, elbow, or palm. Sometimes the offense would even repent after looking at the anger in the defensive player's faces, anticipating the retaliation tackles that would ensue and give in by saying, "Fine, I don't know, maybe you did get me, let's just play."

Personally, I would try my darndest not to be open on the next play, because I wasn't big on getting drilled; I was built for speed not punishment.

Speaking of blood on the knees, the only way for that to happen was for us to fall on the asphalt and tear our pants. Torn pants were much worse than not bringing home your football (most of us didn't even have money for a football, but we all wore pants). You could make up a story about the lost football; the hole in the pants was non-negotiable. You tried to hide the hole for as long as you could, but the only thing that happened then was that the hole got bigger. I remember seeing my old man come into the living room unexpectedly one time and I hurriedly threw a blanket across my legs so he wouldn't see the hole in the knee of my pants. Well it might have worked if it hadn't been early September.

"What the hell are you trying to hide? It's a hundred degrees in here what do you have that blanket on for?"

As I recall, I got one smack for the blanket and another one for the hole in the knee. Oh well, it was worth a try.

Some of us had moms that would do sneaky things to help us out of a jam so our dads wouldn't find out about the dumb things that we had done, and some of us had dads that would go out of their way to avoid our mom finding out about certain brain dead things that we had done. My mother was a Saint as far as trying to save me from getting in trouble; I think I learned all of my good lying skills from her. She would tell some real whoppers right to my old man's face to take the blame for something I did. Thanks mom.

My mom would try to patch my pants with these little denim (and mind you, it didn't matter if the pants were denim or not, you were still getting the denim patches), iron-on patches that looked like hell and wouldn't stick for crap. I am positive that the gaping hole and bloody scabbed up knee looked way better than the patch. After about a week, when the patch fell off (because it didn't stick and because boys can't leave anything alone without picking at it, scabs were the best!), you were left with two possible alternatives:

1. Sew a big Frankenstein-looking seam across the hole which was noticeable from outer space like the Great Wall of China or

2. Cut them into shorts. (I can tell you that I never owned a pair of shorts that were not cut-offs until I went into junior high and we had to buy school gym shorts). Some of you are probably wondering, "Well, why didn't you just go buy a new pair of pants?"

You bought new clothes the week before school started and those lasted all year and often times a couple years after that. We didn't have the money to be buying school clothes more than once a year. If you had a growth spurt, you wore floods, if they got torn up; they got repaired, if a new style came out mid-year, tough crap! There was no style, there was what fit you and what your mom and dad could afford and what they believed would last the longest. All clothes started out as school clothes and then got labeled as play clothes. You would immediately change out of your school clothes as soon as you walked in the door from school. The only advantage to tearing your pants at school was that they turned into an extra pair of play clothes. There were many times when I saw parents drive up to an after school football game, get out of the car and drag their sons into the car, the whole time yelling, "Are those your school clothes? Are you retarded? How many times do you have to be told not to play in your school clothes? Get your ass in that car!"

At no point. Never, ever, ever did the kid mouth off, retaliate, or try to get their say in. The most they might've gotten out was, "I'm sorry" or a possible, "I won't do it again."

Both of which were always followed by something resembling, "You bet your ass you won't do it again."

The other kids watched for a few seconds and then went right back to playing. They didn't run home and tell their parents what took place; there were no interventions, or counseling sessions. The witnesses were just glad it hadn't happened to them. A lot of families were so close with their cousins and in-laws and such that people outside of your immediate family had a right to pull over and publicly discipline you as they saw fit, of which you would then get another dose once you got home and your dad heard the story from your aunt or uncle.

At some point though the Old Man was going to find out about the hole in the pants and you were in deep trouble.

"I just bought them damn pants (*just bought* could range from two days ago to a little over a year), what in the hell was you doing?"

"Playing football at recess, I fell down trying for a pass." I sure in the heck wasn't going to tell him I was pushed to the ground by the school bully.

"Well if I see you out there playing football anymore I'm gonna pull over and beat your ass, you got that? I mean it, if I drive by that school and you are out there playing that damn football again, I'm pulling over and beating your ass in front of everyone."

"Yea", would be all that you could dejectedly utter as you walked away looking at the ground as you sulked back to your room, glad that you didn't take more of a smacking.

So for the next two or three days you played basketball, or got stuck playing some other recess activity that you really didn't want to be involved in. It was horrible telling your buddies in near tears, "Remember guys, don't pick me today, I can't play for a while."

"Oh yeah, you ripped your pants, man that's gotta be tough. Hang in there buddy; I'll catch a touchdown for ya."

You were treated like they had just heard that you only had a couple days left to live. No one felt sorry for guys who stubbed their thumb or got a knot on their head from running into the basketball pole; but not being able to play because of torn pants. "Darn man, I feel for you."

You'd watch the game being played out of the corner of your eye and pretend like you were having fun doing something else, then it got to be too much, you would get to a point where you just couldn't take it anymore and you just had to start playing football again; usually to a round of applause from your cronies, "Hey, Johnny's back. Alright."

I know that I did that one time and sure enough, here comes my old man in the Cadillac, driving down the street right past the playground, and there I was holding the football over my head ready to spike it after a glorious touchdown catch, I froze, waived at him with the football in my hand and he just waived back and drove right on down the street. He had probably completely forgotten about our heated football conversation ten minutes after it happened. I know that my heart stopped working for a couple seconds when I saw that sky blue Caddy roll right past me.

On one exceptionally warm spring recess, I remember all of us meeting down at the furthest part of the playground dreaming up an escape plan. So we gathered up whatever money we had; a collection of dimes and nickels and pennies and gave them to our bravest leader. We threw a kickball across the street and watched it as it rolled further and further down the road before we sent this brave leader to ask permission to cross the street and retrieve it. He looked both ways, crossed the street, picked up the ball, and continued walking away from the school directly to the corner market, (The Victory Market, every other corner in town had a similar mom and pop-run operation.) We all watched with baited breath to see if he was going to make it without being noticed by the teachers on recess duty, and he did. He casually strolled back with a bag of confections that would make any pre-teen boy go into a sugar high for a week. He handed us the bag, gave us the kickball, and climbed the fence with the teachers never the wiser. We all sat behind the big oak tree eating a smorgasbord of sunflower seeds, Smarties, Pixie Stix, malted milk balls, Sixlets, and finished them all off with a big ole bubble gum cigar. We thought we had planned the Brinks robbery; never had so many 12-year old boys walked around with bigger smirks on their faces as we walked into school that day; thank you girls, for not telling on us.

✍️   The recess basketball games were always pretty competitive; if you didn't have some real basketball skills then there was no reason to step onto the court. Elementary recess basketball was less than scintillating, but the youth program that existed in Cambridge was very, very good. It consisted of the seven elementary schools that were in Cambridge at that time, (Park, Oakland, Garfield, Lincoln, Glass Plant, Washington, and Liberty) and we all played each other. It was a great way to get a lot of kids involved in basketball. It's amazing that we started with probably over 100 kids all playing basketball as fifth and sixth graders and the numbers started dwindling down until as seniors there were probably only five or six guys still playing.

Attrition. It's really that way in everything we do isn't it? People just get weeded out. The strong do find a way to survive. We all start out with the same exact chances when we are first graders and then because of circumstances, environment, abilities, and choices we all go our separate ways. 300 of us all started school together, yet only one ended up as valedictorian. In America we are all given opportunities, (some more than others) and then it's ultimately a series of coin flips as to how things turn out.

Anyways, back to elementary basketball. Like I mentioned, Cambridge had seven elementary schools and we all had our own basketball programs, with a couple of the larger elementary schools even having two teams. It would be unheard of in today's society to not include a girl's program, but back in the late sixties and early seventies, there was no such animal.

As fifth graders we played our games at the junior high and in sixth grade we played at the high school. It was a great feeder system for the high school because nearly every boy in the Cambridge City School system was playing for one of the elementary teams.

We would practice two or three nights a week and always play our games on Saturday mornings. As a varsity basketball coach today, I can only imagine how difficult it would have been to get fifteen to twenty kids into a basketball game, but give those elementary coaches credit; they did a nice job of trying to not only contain and manage us, but teach us the game of basketball and keep everyone interested in the sport.

There aren't a lot of fantastic stories concerning the elementary basketball league, but let me explain some of the idiosyncrasies of playing basketball in our early childhood days. Here are a few of the things we had to deal with: We practiced in tile-floored cafeterias that doubled as gyms and just happened to have hoops on each end. Most gyms had a stage very close to the end line and had walls that served as a very immediate out-of-bounds. So in other words we played arena basketball. Throw in the fact that we were eleven or twelve years old and usually were trying to play at Mach five, and you always had players who were literally bouncing off of the walls.

Our sports apparel was... Well, it wasn't exactly what we have today. Let's start with our shorts; they were exactly that, short. They were tight, they were made of cloth, and they could rip out at a moment's notice. Most of us practiced in cut-off jeans, (albeit ripped from recess football). And that's not saying that a lot of us didn't practice in regular length jeans. It wasn't until they passed out uniforms that we actually had a pair of green gym shorts (Park Panther colors). We also practiced and played every day in button up shirts; most of us would strip down to a white t-shirt that we always wore underneath. Button up plaid dress shirts didn't exactly allow a full-range of motion for a jump shot.

Let's move to the number one reason we didn't score more points, the number one reason we traveled, the number one reason we ran into walls, the number one reason we fouled the other team, and basically the number one reason why our game was played completely differently than it is today, was because of OUR SHOES!

We, and when I say we, I'm talking about 90% of the players in the elementary league; had to wear Bargain City Specials. Bargain City was our equivalent to Wal-Mart; if you needed something, anything, you went to Bargain City. Need school clothes? Off to Bargain City. Need a bike tire or a basketball? Go to Bargain City. You want paint, BBs, screws, school supplies, or a Halloween mask? Whatever it was, you went to Bargain City to get it. Unfortunately, this also included tennis shoes. And Bargain City sold a crap ton of tennis shoes! These shoes were affectionately called, "Slip and Slides", or "Bargain City Specials." They sold these high quality tennis shoes to the tune of two pair for five dollars. Oh you definitely heard me right; I said two pair of shoes for five dollars! That is $1.25 per shoe!

I'm looking at what I've written and I've thrown in four exclamation points into this small little section. That should tell you something.

How on Earth could a store sell two pair of tennis shoes for the price of five dollars, even in the sixties? I'll tell you how; they probably only had thirty cents of raw material in each pair. The upper part of the shoe was a fake canvas material sewn together with four-pound test fishing string and then there were the bottoms. The soles of these shoes were unbelievable; although they correctly copied the diagram of the bottom of a pair of Converse, that's where the similarities ended. They were made of some of the hardest plastic known to man. In case of war with the Russians, we were instructed to hold the shoes up as shields to ward off the incoming bullets. Not only were the shoe bottoms hard, but they were also razor-thin, so after about three weeks of wearing them you could begin to see where the first hole was going to expose itself, (always at the ball of the foot.)

So try to imagine playing basketball on a slippery tile floor with rock-hard slippery-soled shoes; sort of a combination of trying to roller-skate on the slipperiest ice you've ever stood on. We however adjusted and adapted and learned how to stop prematurely so as not to collide with other players or referees or the wall. Stops were impossible and starts were just as bad; we often looked like cartoon characters whose legs would churn wildly for a couple seconds before taking off like a flash. It seems funny now, but it was frustrating as hell at the time. To this day, no matter how much money I have, I always make sure my kids wear good gym shoes.

Remember the percentage I gave of players in the league who wore Bargain City Specials; there was however that 10% of players who actually could stop and start on a dime because they were the ones lucky enough to own a pair of Converse. Converse in the sixties and seventies were the absolute Ferrari of tennis shoes. To own a pair of Converse in those days was an immeasurable advantage; you could not only start and stop, but you probably didn't have a hole in the sole of your shoe, or have a cardboard cut-out as an insole, or a blowout on the side of the shoe, or have electrical tape around your shoe trying to hold your foot inside. It also meant that your family probably had a little bit of money, which wasn't the most common thing for families back in those days; at least not where I grew up.

We also had an annual elementary track meet that would throw all of the schools together. A few teachers who may or may not have known anything about track, stayed after school for about three days preparing us for the meet. As a State Champion track coach, former collegiate decathlete, and father of a Division I track athlete, I think back to how much of a clusterbang that whole thing must've been. There were however a lot of great people in my hometown who loved sports and tried like the dickens to expose us to as many positive things as possible.

I think every boy in Cambridge played Little League baseball. We started in Prep League which was probably seven and eight-year olds, then there was Midget League which was nine and ten-year olds, and then came Little League which was the eleven and twelve-year olds. Of course there was a lot of moving around within the league and younger kids could play up a division if they were good enough but older kids couldn't play down a division. We didn't have T-Ball at that time or coach pitch. We didn't have a count of how many pitches a kid could throw or any other limitations on play. Every kid had to play a little bit, but no one was keeping track of it too closely. A dad or two usually did the coaching but there were a few passionate souls who coached just to coach and were out there every year coaching teams like Tom Bruney Chevrolet, and the Kiwanis Braves, and Tip Top Drilling, and Dick's Phillips 66, and the ever strong Ken Bender Motors. Those father/coaches lugged that catcher's equipment and bat bag around in the back of their trucks and in the trunks of their cars all summer long.

We had four little league diamonds and always had enough teams to fill them every night during the summer. Our umpires usually consisted of one adult ump and one high school baseball player who umped the bases and thought he could earn some easy summer money. I did it one summer and I can tell you there wasn't anything easy about it. There was someone mad at the end of every call and it wasn't anything for some coach or even a parent to start to walk out onto the field and state their case and end up subdued by one of the more rational dads or the other coach. Mothers would sometimes leave the stands and go wait in the car because their husbands were making such asses of themselves.

If you were the winning team you had earned the right to go to the concession stand and get a free pop, (that the coaches paid for). I think most of us always ordered "suicides" (a mix of all of the flavors, which as I remember was Coke, Sprite, and orange soda). I can remember a couple losses where the only thing I was mad about was the fact that I wasn't going to be able to go get my "suicide", and at least one win in which the pop machine was broken and we got screwed out of our reward. If you had an extra dime you bought a Chick-O-Stick (of which I couldn't tell you what they were made of, but as ten-year olds we would've done just about anything to get a bite of one).

The uniforms were made of some kind of industrial strength flannel that was probably some sort of Army Surplus material made to withstand small mortar fire and keep soldiers warm in battles against the Soviets in Siberia. How we could run and throw and bat in them was as unbelievable as how none of us ever had a heat stroke. Games were occasionally called for rain, games were called for lightning, I think one time the game was called because wasps (I remember my dad called them mud daubers) were crawling out of the infield and stinging the kids, but under no circumstance were games ever postponed because of heat. 100°, not a problem, hurry up and get your two-inch thick flannel uniform on and let's go play some ball. And by the way (kids of today), when you get a new baseball cap, you curve the brim, or even bend it directly in half, but you never leave it flat and straight. Even the absolute worst player on the team would know enough to curve the brim of their hat and then write their name on the inside of the bill.

We always had a lot of infield chatter, "Swing batter, batter" and stuff like that. I can remember playing first base and going through the motions of our regular infield chatter and in between each pitch I would spit in the same spot, over, and over, and over until there was a stagnate bubbling pond of spit, right where the other team's first baseman had to stand. They would always hate coming over to their base after I was there.

We watched a lot of baseball on tv and we all had our favorite players. As 11 and 12-year olds we probably had ten kids who used a Willie Stargell-type swing (which included a lot of arm motions and flapping your arm, all unneeded); it used to drive our coaches crazy and they'd yell at us to just bat normal. We were actually pretty good little baseball players. I remember we had a kid in our league, who was light years ahead of all of us in every category; he would start each game by throwing a wild pitch to put all of us on edge. Now I'm not talking a little wild, or in the dirt wild, or even hit a batter in the back wild, I'm talking throw the ball over the backstop wild. Eventually the umpires told him to knock it off, but it was pretty darn effective while it lasted.

✍ Although recess seemed to be the most important part of school to us, we actually did do other things at school besides play on the playground. School lunch – in the 60's and 70's a school lunch probably meant whatever was leftover in the refrigerator or cupboards of your home thrown into a paper bag and just enough money for a school milk. I know that there were lunch ladies at the school, but they weren't cooking food for a lot of us, probably three/fourths of us brought our lunches, I know we sure in the heck couldn't afford the school lunch every day, (which was like 40¢.) A list of typical potential packed lunches would have been: peanut butter sandwich, maybe a peanut butter and jelly sandwich, an apple, maybe a banana, a bologna sandwich, maybe a Dutch loaf or pickled pimento loaf sandwich, maybe a couple peanut butter cookies, or if you were really lucky something from Kennedy's bakery, like a devil dog or filled cupcake. This all changed a little bit when I got my Superman lunchbox with the thermos because I took chicken noodle soup about every day after that. I believe that white milk was 4¢ and only on certain days of the week could you get chocolate milk and it was 6¢. Buying the chocolate milk when it was available was a no-brainer, but I always had to either charge the 2¢ or try to borrow it from one of my rich friends who were sent to school with a whole dime.

✍ Speaking of that Superman lunchbox; I once moved into a neighborhood that had a lot of kids in it that we will call less than future Good Samaritans. I got picked on and harassed and beat up by the same five or six kids every day for about two weeks; me and my mom hid it from the Old Man for a good while but eventually he found out, "I don't know what's goin' on with you getting' beat up but the next time it happens I'm gonna crack your ass til you can't sit down."

So after living my entire eight years on Earth as a pacifist I told myself over and over, "If they pick on me today, I'm fighting back with everything I've got."

And right on cue, here they come when I'm walking home from school. It took one push from them and I turned into a whirling dervish of Superman lunchbox destruction. I whacked one kid in the side of the head and he took off running and then I turned and drilled his brother right on top of the cranium and kept bopping him over and over once he was down. Finally some neighbor lady came out and pulled me off of him, "It's about time you stood up to those little bastards. You did good. Now go on home now."

I went home and was so worked up that I was crying because I had blood on the corner of my lunchbox and I thought I had killed the kid, (Superman lunchboxes were made of real U.S. steel). She calmed me down and when she told the story to my dad, he gave me a dollar. That seemed way better than getting the belt from him.

Must've been something about that neighborhood and cracked heads because that is where I cracked my head open jumping on my bed. Of course jumping on beds certainly isn't confined to kids from the 60's and 70's, they still do it today. (I'm pretty sure that I was 40 or so before I stopped jumping on the bed of every hotel room I ever stayed in.) I do know that I was way more afraid of the Old Man coming home than about the stitches they were going to sew into my scalp. But I will say that having that fear of discipline in the back of my mind probably kept me from doing a lot of crazy things (of course once you read more into the book you'll think that it didn't slow me down too much, but it did, it really did).

✍ Physical Education – Obviously as much as we loved recess, we enjoyed "gym" about just as much. We only had "gym" once or twice a week and sometimes it got cancelled for various reasons so we couldn't mentally prepare for "gym" the way that we could for recess. Plus, at recess we could plan our own activities and didn't have to play with girls. But our "gym" teacher did a great job of channeling our wildness and actually taught us a great deal about movement, and teamwork, and the rules of various sports. I do know that out on the playground we didn't have a parachute or scooters like we did in "gym." When we were in the lower elementary grades our eyes would light up when we walked in and saw the parachute laying in the middle of the floor. I think it lost a little bit of its luster as we got older, but as six and seven-year olds it was exhilarating to throw the parachute into the air and then crawl underneath it or run around it.

As soon as the scooters came out it was almost a 100% guarantee that our fingers were going to get run over, but when we saw them I think we had dreams and delusions of flying around the gym at Mach speed; it just never materialized the way we thought. Top speed while crab walking on a scooter was probably little more than two mph.

We didn't play it very often, but this was the infancy of our dodgeball careers. A few girls would hang in there and give it a good showing, but most of them made pretty quick exits, I suppose maybe on purpose. Most of the guys in our class had no problem drilling a girl in the face with a close range dodgeball throw, so it was definitely in their best interest to defend themselves.

It was kind of refreshing to have someone other than the alpha males officiating the games. We always had to laugh when one of them was called out by our "gym" teacher and as badly as they wanted to, they definitely weren't going to question his calls.

✍ Our classrooms – Our elementary teachers were true Renaissance ladies and gentlemen; they did a little bit of everything and honestly they were pretty good at all of them. They could teach Math, Science, Spelling, Reading, History, then they would switch hats and help us with our Art projects, (Lord knows there was never an empty bulletin board), they seemed like they were good singers, most of them were good cooks because they'd bring us cookies every once in a while, and most of them could throw a football around with you when no one else was around.

We all had our own cubby, now I don't know why it was called a "cubby", I suppose it meant cubby hole, which again, I really don't know what that means either. Why we didn't just have little lockers is beyond me; apparently we weren't ready for lockers until we were closer to being teenagers. Anyways, those cubbies held quite the assortment of items throughout the year: our lunches and lunch boxes, our coats, jackets, sweaters, and our extra big art shirt, and yes our rubber boots.

We also had our own little desks where we jammed all of our books and papers and erasers and homework and graded papers and time sensitive papers that were supposed be signed by our parents but never made it home on time and scissors and glue and candy and candy wrappers and sunflower seeds and a lot of stuff that just plain should have been thrown away but wasn't. Looking back, it really wouldn't have been that much of a stretch for a mouse to be living in our desks, nibbling on sunflower seeds and half-eaten candy bars.

The end of the year was then, and even still is today an amazing display of just how much junk one person (and in this case hundreds of little tiny people) can collect throughout a nine month span. We were the original *Hoarders*. We'd find papers that needed signed the first week of school, old M&M's that we'd pop into our mouth when no one was looking even though they had probably been sitting in filth for five or six months. Of course there was always a few Hall's or Luden's

Cough Drops leftover from the cold we had back in December. "Oh, that's where that Hot Wheel was", that you'd thought was lost forever. The walk home from the last day of school each year was like sifting through a forgotten treasure chest; of course the luster wore off as soon as we walked in the door of our homes and tossed our new found prizes into our toy boxes, probably never to be seen again for at least another year.

✍ Graduation- At the end of it all, we all had an elementary graduation. It was a celebration of surviving seven years of education, seven years of learning, seven years of cooperating, seven years of spending 184 days a year with the same 47 other students that shared the exact same experiences that you did. And I guess, when I look at the next step in our educational process, it was somewhat of a going away party, not unlike the party they should have given to those on *The Titanic's* maiden voyage; because the difference from elementary school to junior high school was... well, immeasurable. At sixth grade graduation the boys had to wear ties and the girls had to wear dresses; we practiced our stage entrance and exit several times, and rehearsed our songs for a week or two. I believe we sang *Tie a Yellow Ribbon* by Tony Orlando, and *Joy to the World* by Three Dog Night.

✍ The only other time we ever had to dress up was to go to Sunday School. My parents didn't go to church, but for some reason I was forced to go to Sunday School; I didn't have to go to the actual church service, but every Sunday I had to go to Sunday School. I have no idea how much religion was discussed, as I recall it was more socialization and coloring and trying to burn an hour with a room full of other kids that didn't want to be there either. I think I was given a dime or a quarter to give to some sort of offering. I don't think the church built any new wings based on my donations. I think my mom and dad just liked seeing me dressed up and I'm gonna guess that the idea of me going to church might have made my old man believe that it might be enough inspiration for me not to follow in many of his not so straight and narrow footsteps.

✍ So what did we do after school as elementary kids? Our worlds were much smaller as eight through twelve-year olds than it would become over the next few years. Basically we were limited to adventures that we could discover within a five or six-house radius of our own home. Potentially, your best friend could live across the street and you wouldn't be allowed to play with them because you weren't allowed to cross the street yet. You often saw little kids playing catch with a football or throwing a baseball back and forth across the street because of their asphalt boundaries. Inevitably, through some kind of Murphy's Law, the ball would somehow come to rest in the middle of the street, which would force someone to make a move to go out and retrieve the ball; and yes inevitably, that would be the exact instant when one of your parents would walk outside and see you out in the middle of the street.

"How many &^%$ times do I have to tell you to stay out of the $%^& street? Get your butt in the house."

Of course there were some kids that were allowed to cross the street, and there were still others that snuck across the street over and over again and never got caught and never got in trouble. That of course, wasn't me.

I know as real little kids, we were escorted hand-in-hand by our mothers across the street to go play with other kids. When you were five or six-years old you didn't mind so much, but when you got to be nine or ten and your mom still wanted to help you across the street, then it just got to be embarrassing. Thinking back on it now, I'm guessing that we would have just assumed get hit by a car than to have our mom's hold our hand across the street.

✍ All throughout our young lives, I think we were all subjected at some point to some form of embarrassment caused by our parents. God love 'em, they were trying their best to do the best for us, and just like all of us today who are parents, sometimes we cross the line. Most parents during the sixties and seventies weren't afraid to parent us in loud, abrasive, no question as to their meaning methods. We knew what was expected of us and we knew the consequences. We weren't given repeated threats over and over and over with no end result, whatever we were threatened with as far as punishment for not listening to the rules, we got. It didn't matter if we broke the rules in the confines of our home, or in the middle of a crowded supermarket; you were going to take a smacking if you screwed up. I look at today's parents and they try so hard to be friends with their kids and are so afraid of losing that friendship that they forget the toughness and discipline and respect factors that are needed to properly raise a child. Our parents gave us respect when we earned it and also gave us discipline when we deserved it.

✍   When we were kids we were extremely inventive and usually very easily amused. We didn't need much to keep us occupied. For the most part it cost nothing for us to be amused. I think of how I now feel like I'm an entertainment director sometimes; but our parents would just say, "Go play", and off we'd go. We needed no directions, we needed no specific toys, we didn't have to spend any money, we just played, and most of the time we didn't have any supervision either. Anything we could find, we could use to entertain ourselves:

Sticks- sticks could be whatever we wanted them to be; swords, clubs, bats, magic wands, whips, spears, drawing utensils, the beginnings of a fort. We used them to poke at and knock down hornet
s nests, we used them to poke at various dead animals that we were too afraid to pick up because we weren't sure if they were dead or not, we used them to make cane poles for fishing (especially fishing for crawdads down at the creek), we used them to get balls out of spoutings and gutters. And once *Star Wars* came out, well... you can imagine, yes we used them as lightsabers. If you can think of a way to use a stick, we used it for that. Sometimes we would get a really good stick; it was the right size, and shape, and weight, and basically it was perfect, so we would take special care and

hide the stick when we went inside for the night, hoping like heck that no one messed with our stick. (How stupid is that?)

Rocks- well I'm gonna go out on a limb and say that I never went one day of my childhood in which I didn't throw a rock or a snowball. Although we spent most of our time throwing the rocks, we also used them as hammers, when in a pinch you might try to use one as a wrench to loosen a bolt, we tried Boy Scout crap of clicking two rocks together to make a fire (which absolutely, positively never worked), we used them to put under boards to make ramps, and yes we even used them in catapults of varying success. But in the end, we threw them: we threw them at cats, we threw them at dogs, we threw them into sewer holes, we threw them at cans, we threw them at windows on old vacant houses, we threw them at the little glass electric insulators at the top of telephone poles, we threw them at each other, we skipped them across the water, and we tossed them randomly into the sky. Kids of our generation could throw a friggin' rock, I can tell you that.

Dirt- How about just plain playing in the dirt? Lifting it up and dropping it over and over and over and watching it fall back down to the ground in a cloudy little waterfall. We stacked dirt, we broke up dirt clods. We also threw dirt and made it explode against walls or the sidewalk. We had dirt clod and mudball fights. We dug in the dirt and we slid and dove into the dirt. A couple times I was given permission by my old man to dig in the dirt. I remember hearing so many stories about digging a hole to China; I think I gave it a pretty good run. I suppose I was about four feet into it before I figured that little China men weren't going to be popping out of this hole. My dad must've been laughing like crazy watching me dig a shovel full of dirt then look into the hole for someone to be coming out of the other side.

Trees- we looked for climbing trees, there had to be either a reachable first branch or an angle in the tree that would allow us to shimmy up far enough to grab onto that first branch. I ain't gonna lie, I was a pretty crappy tree climber, but I had buddies that were like *Planet of the Friggin' Apes*, they would get up in trees 30 or 40-feet high and move around on branches that didn't look like they could hold a good-sized squirrel, let alone a 100-pound kid. We also hid behind trees, used them for bases, and like I mentioned before, some trees were perfect for running up like a ramp and propelling yourself up as high as you could; basically it showed you what a 50-inch vertical jump would feel like. Having a good tree climber within your group of friends was actually pretty valuable because you never knew when a football or whiffleball or Frisbee was going to get stuck in a tree, or if you were a girl it wasn't out of the ordinary to have some mean boy throw your doll up into a tree. I can vividly remember seeing a three-pronged Frisbee boomerang-like thing stuck up in a tree for literally years; obviously that person didn't have a good tree climbing friend.

There were a handful of treehouses throughout town and I know there was at least one of them in our neighborhood. I know that I had a hard time even climbing up the tree in the first place, I wasn't crazy about the height, and if you've ever seen a treehouse that was built by a 12 or 13-year old kid you'd know that it is not going to make the front page of Architectural Digest. It was supposed to be a good make out spot; well good luck with that, it was a lot easier to break into Mr. Hamm's barn with some of the pretty neighborhood girls.

Other stuff- there is no way that I can list the things that we played with as little kids, we played with whatever was available; in today's society I'm sure that someone would complain and call the police and call people unfit parents, but we were having fun, and I don't think that we got hurt any more than today's kids get hurt. We played with old tires; we would roll them at each other or get inside and have someone roll us down a hill. We would jump on tires, or use them like a football team would use them for high knee drills.

We played with, on, and in, old junk cars; we drove hundreds of fantasy miles behind the wheel being chased by the police or being the police chasing down the bank robbers.

We played in tool sheds, we played in garages, we played in barns, we played in fields, we played along creeks, we played in the street, we played in the green grass, we played on sidewalks, we played in parking lots, we played on front porches, and back porches, we climbed tv antennas and telephone poles, and we played in the gravel alleys behind our houses. We didn't ask permission to do most of the things we did, we just did them. We didn't ask 5,000 questions about what we could do, and we sure in the heck didn't sit around whining to our parents that we were bored. We could make a game out of following shadows on the ground or spend time categorizing bugs into peanut butter jars, (which would always stink like crazy after about two days). We could wrestle in the grass or sit under the porch steps and look out through the latticework having a pretend clubhouse. It wasn't anything to lie in the middle of a backyard for half-an-hour or so and just look at the clouds and use our imagination to figure out what each cloud looked like. We played a game when we went out to the farm to lie in the middle of a field and try to see if you could stay motionless long enough for a turkey vulture to come down and peck at you, thankfully it never worked, but we gave it a pretty good try. Imagine that, a great big turkey vulture and somehow as ten-year olds we weren't afraid.

When we weren't alone we had plenty of options too, although we always loved to revert back to sports, I'm talking right now about ways that we kept ourselves busy without any purchased objects, just imagination: There was always tag; you had regular tag, freeze tag, flashlight tag, duck duck goose, TV tag, Pop tag, and a gazillion other tag games including chase and Kick-the-Can which was really more like Hide-and-Go Seek and we will definitely discuss those games later. I already talked about throwing rocks and dirt at each other, but we also threw fruit and vegetables; it was awesome to have tomato fights, but our green apple fights as we got older were legendary. Imagine fifteen/sixteen-year old boys who played sports nearly every waking hour of the day throwing baseball size, hard as a rock, green apples at each other from as far away as 100-feet to as close as five-feet away with absolutely no limitations or restrictions. With over 20-green apple fights under my belt, I never saw one that didn't end in loud screaming followed by uncontrollable crying then followed by a group of guys surrounding the victim saying, "Dude, I think you're gonna be all right, hang in there, I don't think it looks that bad. Maybe you better not go home right now I think the swelling will go down in a little bit." I can vouch for being on the crying end of that conversation at least half a dozen times. Getting hit with a green apple thrown at full speed from 15-feet away does amazing damage to one's face.

I'd say that 20-30% of my school pictures were basically ruined by some sort of black eye from an apple fight, ramping my bike accident, little kid fist fight, or a bad haircut the day before pictures.

The ice cream truck was always stressful as well. Things would be going fine, we would be knee deep in the middle of some kind of game or competition and then we would hear that enchanting, spellbinding melody that hypnotized us with visions of frozen treasures. We would drop everything that we were doing and make a beeline for that magical sound; but none of us, and I mean none of us ever had any money to buy anything. Every once in a while one of our mothers would walk down to the truck and buy treats for all of us. At that point you'd see a handful of eight-year olds with a 50-50 mix of chocolate ice cream and dirt covering their faces.

Chapter 2
Toys, Toys, Toys

Of course we also had toys; most of us had closets full of toys, but for the most part we didn't sit around playing with them very often, at least not until the weather was so crappy that we weren't allowed to go outside. We hated to be stuck inside, we would rather endure a little bit of torrential rain, or a little bit of golf ball size hail, or a little bit of frostbite, rather than to have to be stuck inside. A lot of toys weren't dragged out from under our beds or even taken out of their boxes until a friend came over to our house on one of those cold, rainy, miserable days.

All of us had a stack of games that we stored away as a last resort back-up plan for when friends came over and we were quarantined because of the weather. Unlike today's world where playing with a game (PlayStation, X-box, Wii, etc.) is the first and only idea of what kids can do when they get together; it was our absolute last resort. We hated dragging out those stupid games, but after the fifth or sixth time of listening to your mom and dad tell you that since you didn't have anything to do maybe you should get out one of your games, we would finally give in and sort through our variety of boxed entertainment options in such board games as: Cootie, Operation, Candyland, Chutes and Ladders, Stratego, Battleship, Risk, Monopoly, Life, Trouble, Parcheesi, Barrel of Monkeys, Chinese checkers, Mousetrap, Rook, Old Maid, checkers, chess, and probably a bunch of others that I can't exactly remember right now.

For some of these board games we would actually sit down and play from beginning to end, while others we would start, try them for a while, finagle the rules around until they suited us a little bit better, and then back into the box they would go until that same extreme wave of boredom and bad weather overtook us and we pulled them out again.

Personally, I actually liked playing Stratego and chess, but I couldn't con any of my friends into sitting in one place long enough to actually finish a game. It's funny, but I don't remember one time after I was five or six years old, that I ever played any of those games with my parents, yet I sat on the floor or at the dinner table and played a board game or a card game with my kids at least a couple times a month when they lived at home.

When we got older we tried to use the game of Twister as a license to bump up against and intertwine with members of the opposite sex. It was fun for giggles but it certainly didn't materialize into the forbidden fantasies that we boys dreamed up when we watched the Twister tv commercial.

Then there was our collection of random, miscellaneous toys that we had piled up in the corner of our room, or thrown onto a heap in the basement, or maybe they were crammed into a special toy closet that would rain toys down on our heads if we pulled out the wrong toy from the bottom of the stack, ala Flintstone-style.

I think we all had some sort of toy box. It may have been as fancy as a store-bought wooden box with a lid that actually had *Toy Box* painted on it, or it may have just been a big old cardboard box that our parents dug out of the trash from behind Bargain City; but regardless of how glamorous our storage units were, they all served the same purpose: those toy boxes of the sixties and seventies held an amazing collection of unique distractions that both entertained us and stimulated our imaginations.

Although they all started out as orderly, well-organized, containment units, that's not how they ended up. Every toy box I ever had, I ever saw, or I ever dove into all looked the same; miscellaneous broken crayons and hot-wheels with missing tires lined the bottom of the box. Throw in a few stray marbles, a few assorted baseball cards, a couple hot-wheel track connectors, a Lego or two, a few Lincoln Logs, and of course all of the missing puzzle pieces that you had been in search of for the last three or four years would serve as an excellent base for this concoction of toy box stew.

The rest of the toy box had bits and pieces from the following array of marvelous plastic, metal, wooden, and cardboard attractions.

Some of our toys were carryovers from our parent's generation, while others were distinctive toys invented in and specifically for the 60's and 70's. Many of our toys have lasted through the decades and when I see those toys in stores today, they re-charge my memory banks and remind me of the hours we spent crawling around on the floor entertaining ourselves as the rain and snow held us captive.

I think it may have been a State Law back in the 70's that all girls had to have a collection of Barbies and of course they also had to have the pink Barbie Corvette. I'd be lying if I said we didn't borrow that Corvette from time to time and load up some G.I. Joes in it and take them for a spin, which usually meant driving it off a cliff. Girls were far more delicate and careful with their toys than us boys; if a girl's toy was broken it was probably because their little brothers or boy cousins or one of the neighbor boys had gotten a hold of it, rough-housed around with it, and left it broken. We were famous for digging through our sister's or friend's sister's toy boxes and dragging out things that we thought we could use. Even though we couldn't find a use for an Easy Bake oven or the ever-popular kitchen set, we did think that jump ropes were extremely useful for 1000 things that had nothing to do with jumping rope and hula hoops came in handy for games like human ring toss, rolling them down huge hills towards moving cars, and they also made great bases for whiffleball or kickball games. Even though I was voted the best dancer in my class, and was as loose through the hips as anyone, I couldn't hula hoop more than two spins to save my life.

We rarely just played with one toy at a time, we were amazing at being able to use all of the resources that we had at our disposal and could mix and match nearly every toy that we had into some sort of crazy toy casserole, hardly ever using those particular toys in their intended manner. Most of the time our playtime ended with a crash, explosion, or loud thunderclap of metal vs metal, or metal vs plastic, or as the older we got plastic vs plastic. We practiced the laws of physics on a daily basis; laws of centrifugal force as we spun ourselves around or spun objects around and then whizzed them out of the arc with tremendous speed and deadly inaccuracy. We didn't know the formulas to calculate speed, or power, or force, but we knew that if we used our heaviest Hot Wheel and rolled it down 30 feet of track at a near free-fall incline, it had the power to knock the crap out of awaiting army men or maybe even a poor, unsuspecting, and extremely defenseless Mr. Potato Head.

It would have been hard to find a boy that didn't own at least a dozen Hot Wheels, and many boys owned and even collected hundreds of Hot Wheels.

Maybe I didn't have enough money in my family to be much of a collector of anything, but me and most of the guys I grew up with didn't buy toys to keep them securely and sanitarily stored inside plastic coated boxes. The toys we had were, well,... basically used until they were broken, and even then we continued to use them until we either lost them or our mothers threw them away when we weren't looking. I will say that as we got older we found new and really "explosive", "dynamic", and often "loud" ways to end the life of our once favorite toys. Firecrackers were easily attainable during the sixties and seventies and we certainly weren't going to waste them on lighting them and throwing them on the ground and making them go boom. We would strap them to Barbies or G.I. Joe's and watch the body parts fly off. We would stick them down ant colony holes and blow their little ant kingdoms to smithereens. Occasionally we'd miscalculate the time it took a firecracker to go off and many a boy in this time period either went home with fingers that didn't work properly for a few days or less fingers than they started with that morning. On one of those occasions we tried to make super firecrackers by letting them soak in gasoline overnight; well they were super all right, not only did we multiply their power to half a stick of dynamite, but we also multiplied how fast the wick burn. I hid powder burned fingers and wrote my school work with my left hand for a week before my right hand became functional again.

Even though there were a lot of optional accessories you could buy for your Hot Wheels like loop-the-loop, turbo boosters, and special carrying cases, most of us didn't have those luxuries, what we did have was about ten pieces of yellow-orange Hot Wheel track, ten red or purple track connectors, and if you were lucky and didn't break it the first day you owned it, one 180° banked turn. The turn never lasted because it was made of hard plastic while the track was made of very pliable plastic. As far as the ten connectors, I know that Mattel sold us enough to connect all of our track together, but ten connectors, turned into nine, then, eight, then pretty soon we were taking the lone remaining connecter that we had and using it as a pattern to draw on a piece of cardboard to cut out and make new connectors, which sounded like a wonderful plan but absolutely never worked.

Those connectors, along with marbles, army men, and everything else small enough to fit into the holes, always found their ways down the heating register vents. I don't know how many times I dropped stuff down the register, could actually see it down there, but just couldn't quite reach it. We were all pretty adept at yanking the register from the floor so we could reach down and collect a fortune full of miniature booty. I assume that some of that stuff would eventually make it all the way down to the actual furnace where it would meet some sort of fiery doom.

The Hot Wheel tracks always, without a doubt, turned into semi-lethal weapons. We would pummel each other with these two-foot long strips of plastic in wild swash-buckling sword fights, which invariably ended with someone getting hurt and crying. (Actually, most of our contests ended this way.) Even though we slapped each other across the face, arms, legs, and as many groin shots as possible with Hot Wheel tracks, they never brought the fear to us as they did when our parents would pick one up and threaten to beat our butt with them. I know a couple households I frequented where Hot Wheel track was the number one choice to deliver corporal punishment; it was so effective that a few of my friends would actually give me their extra track so that their mothers would have to find something a little less damaging to hit them with.

✍ Allow me to get off "track" for a second. Younger readers must think that our parents were absolute monsters; hitting us poor innocent kids with belts, and Hot Wheel tracks, and assorted backhand slaps, karate moves, rabbit punches and what-not. First off, we weren't innocent little angels; again we grew up in very tough and economically depressed times with about one tenth of the amount of supervision that kids have today. I can't lay claim to all of these vices, (I guess I can, all but the smoking and drinking) but as kids, even young elementary age kids, we lied, we stole, we broke into buildings, we caught stuff on fire, we blew stuff up, we threw rocks at everything that moved or didn't move, we knocked on doors and ran, we played in the sewers, we played in vacant houses, we fought, we cussed, we smoked, we drank, and in general, we did a bunch of crazy things that 11 and 12-year old kids probably shouldn't have been doing. We probably deserved a lot more beatings than we actually got. Secondly, it was a different world 40 years ago; our parents didn't have child psychologists and internet articles and volumes of books to refer to when they had a problem with their children. Justice was served swiftly, as often as needed, and usually in a loud and often physical manner. But you know what, we learned from it, even if sometimes all we really learned was how to not get caught doing that same thing again. But it was effective and it was how the world was operated at that time. Our parents weren't particularly interested in being our friends, they were far more interested in figuring out how to pay the bills and keep a roof over our heads, and food in our bellies, and when they heard about us screwing up, they got frustrated and beat our butts with whatever was near them at the time. Hearing that little Johnny hit the little neighbor girl in the head with a piece of spouting that he ripped off of the garage, probably deserved a smack. Hearing that little Johnny and his friends tied the neighborhood cat to Annie Rivers' German shepherd, probably deserved a smack. And call me crazy for thinking that stealing bowling balls from the bowling alley so they could be used to roll down Children's Home Hill and try to hit cars on the highway, probably deserved a good smack. It's amazing that more of us didn't end up in reform school. (One of those balls, traveling at...oh hell, I don't know 60 mph, went airborne, crossed Wheeling Avenue and went through the front door of what was luckily a vacant house. We were so brave and dumb and cock sure of ourselves that we walked down the hill later in the day, walked into the house (no doubt through the broken door caused by the cannonball we had created), and retrieved the ball so we could do it again.) I'm thinking we might not have gotten smacked enough!

✍ I'm a little surprised that most of us didn't grow up and join the military. We loved playing with army men and we loved shooting stuff. We enjoyed sleeping out in tents and half of us thought that we could live off of the land for months at a time if we had to. Maybe I missed the boat on my actual skill set. Anyways, playing with army men was about as straight forward as you could possibly get, you set up your guys, I set up mine, we can get fancy and hide them behind some sort of Lincoln Log, Lego, or Erector set fort, and then we take turns rolling marbles (steelies were the best) trying to knock down each other's men. Not sure how we spent hours doing that, but we did. I remember those stupid little plastic army men: you had the guy that held the gun over his head, he was the worst, he wouldn't stand up on his own and always had to be leaned against something. You had the guy who was kneeling on one knee shooting a rifle and he was the best, he had great balance and was pretty sturdy. And then you had 20 of the guys that lay down on their stomachs to shoot, and to this day, I have no idea how you were ever supposed to kill them, they were already lying on the ground.

✍   Like I said, we loved to shoot things, which meant we needed guns, we loved guns and we all had plenty of them when we were little kids. Every little boy in North America owned some sort of cowboy gun and holster set, which usually included a badge of some kind and of course a cowboy hat. The gun was solid pot iron covered with chrome with a white handle that shot caps. On paper, the design of the cap gun worked like a million dollars, but for five and six-year-olds to be able to put those little cap rolls into the gun and tether the cap paper through the tiny little opening was next to impossible. We almost always took the caps and popped them with a rock or sometimes even a hammer that we'd sneak out of the garage. We'd smash them on the sidewalk with the grand finale being trying to pop a full roll of caps at one time which absolutely never worked. Eventually we progressed up to snap 'n pops which were tiny little bags of gun powder that you threw on the ground to make small, popping explosions. Then obviously we progressed up to firecrackers and M-80s, (luckily we never proceeded to TNT).

Our world has definitely changed over the past 40 or 50 years, as 14/15-year-old kids, we would walk down the street with loaded shotguns or loaded 22 rifles. We shot them in town and no one ever said a word to us. Can you imagine in today's world, a group of three or four teenage boys walking down the street with loaded rifles and watch them walk into the back alley and start shooting at cans and bottles?

We did however start with BB guns of which you had two kinds to choose from: a typical western-looking, wooden stock, single cock Daisy or you had a new-age, military-looking, multi-pump, Crossman pellet gun. Personally, I didn't like the pellet guns; you seemed to stand there all day cranking this thing that supposedly could shoot BB's at three times the speed of a Daisy, but that never seemed to play out as advertised.

✍   I remember one summer I saw some sort of high-powered slingshot at Bargain City and told my dad it looked pretty cool; I never in a million years thought that I would get it, but for whatever reason he bought it for me the next day. Now this wasn't your average Y-shaped piece of wood with a couple of rubber bands attached to it. This thing was metal, with an attachment that hooked on your forearm for stability and increased power, and instead of a floppy rubber band this thing used surgical tubing as its powerful catalyst. We took turns shooting this thing for about three days and with a unanimous vote we put it away and never brought it back out. This thing without a doubt in the world could kill a horse, cow, human, whatever. Don't ask me why, it just sounded like a good idea at the time, but we shot a marble straight through the side of a semi's trailer, looked at each other, and put it away forever. Any kid in town could have gone out and bought one of these things, walked around town, and shot it at whatever or whomever they wanted. No one even blinked an eye at kids carrying weapons like this. But for the most part, we didn't abuse the responsibilities that went along with owning these weapons. I will admit to shooting my brother in the back of the neck with my BB gun and telling my mom, "I think he got stung by a bee." And I did shoot a window air conditioner's compressor one time with a 22 just to see what it would do, (it blew up violently, and the neighbor guy told my dad that his *&^%ing air conditioner was working so *&^%ing hard that it *&^%ing blew up the other night). He was pissed. Yet another time that the Old Man would've literally killed me if he had found out what I'd done.

✍ We weren't completely responsible though, we did have BB gun fights, which were pretty cool. We put on extra clothes and usually wore shielded motorcycle helmets or at least goggles and then we chased each other around the neighborhood blasting each other with BB guns. More than one +50 year-old man has to still be walking around with a BB or two still lodged under his skin somewhere. Could it have killed us? Probably not. Did it hurt like hell to take a BB to the inside of your thigh, or back of your hand, or to the side of your neck? You bet it did.

✍ I want to remind everybody that these were very normal things that kids in my neighborhood were doing, kids in other neighborhoods were doing, and I fully assume that they were also happening in other neighborhoods across the United States during the 60's and 70's. I'm not trying to tell my life story, I'm helping everyone either relive those years and experiences or shed some light to the poor and unfortunate souls that didn't get to grow up old school. If you had the privilege to have grown up old school, a child during the 60's, 70's, and maybe the early 80's, you grew up in what is without a doubt the greatest time period to have ever been a kid in America. A journey that can never be duplicated only cherished through memories and re-told as many times as we can tell it before we die.

✍ While the boys were busy shooting each other the girls of this era definitely had a doll fetish; although I mentioned Barbies, those weren't the only dolls that girls played with. Girls cut out paper dolls out of popular ladies magazines and Sunday papers, and paper doll books in which they could cut out accessories or even use crayons and design their own. Here's a list of dolls that young girls may have owned during the 60's and 70's: Ginny, Krissy, Baby First Step, Chatty Cathy, Thumbelina, Lolly Dolly, Troll dolls, Tressy, Baby Small Walk, Baby Small Talk, Betsy Wetsy, Ragedy Ann and Andy, Holly Hobbie, Rub-a-Dub Dolly, Shirley Temple, Flatsys, Mrs. Beasley, Pollyanna, Kewpie Dolls, and although Cabbage Patch Kids and Strawberry Shortcake actually came out in 1978 but they didn't become super-popular until the 80's.

Don't go thinking that girls had a monopoly on dolls, boys certainly had their share of "action figures", (but there was no way in hell we were gonna call them dolls). I'm positive that a lot of our fathers weren't real keen about the idea of their boys playing with dolls; I mean "action figures".

The way for Hasbro to double their sales opportunities was to get boys in on the doll market, this was simple, his name: G.I. Joe. Well actually his name wasn't G.I. Joe to start with, originally in '64, there was "Rocky" the Marine, "Skip" the

Sailor, and "Ace" the Pilot. Even though there is no way that you can distinguish accessorizing G.I. Joes as compared to Barbies, we boys would have adamantly disagreed that we were playing with dolls. But I can guarantee you that we boys fully got into changing these little guy's outfits and went out and bought little helmets and belts and an arsenal of firearms for them to use against our other G.I. Joes. We had G.I. Joe Jeeps, and G.I. Joe tanks, and G.I. Joe helicopters, and eventually even G.I. Joe cartoons. And yes, there was the famous G.I. Joe with the *Kung Fu* grip.

Boys also had dolls like: Gumby and Pokey, which were rubbery little guys that stayed somewhat in place because of the wire that was inside them that always broke through at some point and stabbed you whenever you picked them up. We also had Stretch Armstrong, (which was about the most useless superhero you could have, because once his arms got stretched they never went back to normal), and a whole variety of dolls originating from television shows: Grizzly Adams, The Bionic Man, Superman, Batman, the characters from Welcome Back Kotter, Man from U.N.C.L.E., Star Trek, Planet of the Apes, Davey Crockett, Starsky & Hutch, Chips, and even a Broadway Joe Namath doll.

I'll be real honest here, it really didn't matter which of these action figures that we played with, the script always went something like this: Action figure is propped up and run over by one of our various vehicles, or action figure is propped up and a large object falls from the sky and crushes said action figure, or action figure is launched through the sky and lands poorly, or action figure A is held in the left hand while action figure B is held in the right hand, there is a few seconds of bouncing the two figures around with some trash talking and then the action figures are slammed into each other followed by the victor standing over the defeated action figure.

Yes, at times we were destructive little terrors, but there were other times in which we were pretty inventive little engineers. I'm sure we all started out with plain old blocks; little wooden building blocks with letters and numbers on every side, painted in bright primary colors. We learned our colors with these blocks, we learned how to balance and stack, we learned our letters and numbers with these blocks, we learned how to spell by using these blocks, and yes we learned how to build and create structures with these little wooden cubes.

As we got older, we got more sophisticated with our materials and certainly got more sophisticated with our engineering marvels: houses, barns, forts, castles, catapults, buildings, cities, alien planets; there wasn't a lot that we didn't think of building. Lincoln Logs made excellent building material for forts and obviously anything dealing with the old west. They were moderately easy to use but always made the same boxy, boring log cabin with no windows and a roof that fell down in the first few minutes.

We had Tinker Toys, which were basically long toothpicks that we stuck into little wheel-like cogs. I don't think we actually could make anything with them, but we could spend hours fiddling around making Jetson-like buildings.

A lot of kids had Legos, they were a little bit too expensive for some families, but at some point I think all kids of our generation stuck those little blocks together and with enough of them could build some pretty creative things. I know that sometimes you would make something that you were so proud of that you wanted to keep it and then you had the conundrum of keeping this grand masterpiece or tearing it apart so you could build something else. We always eventually tore them apart with the idea that, "I can always re-build it just like before", but we couldn't, and we didn't, and we just moved on to building something else. I've done that many times throughout my life but as I have gotten older, I've learned to hold on to things a little longer and appreciate them a little more, because some things aren't always able to be duplicated or replaced or recovered.

And then there were Erector Sets. Erector Sets were the absolute pinnacle in the world of building. We had advanced from wood, to plastic, and now to steel; real metal that used nuts and bolts to hold everything together. It came with a little electric motor that if you knew what you were doing, could be used to build actual moving inventions such as cars, trucks, wenches, cranes, you name it. I'm not saying that I knew how to do that, but on the commercial those kids could make a fully automated Erector world.

✍ Ah, the 70's toy commercials; these companies went all out on their quest in addicting us to toys that couldn't be sold any other way than to bombard us with Stephen Spielberg-quality commercials that played over and over and over. I'm pretty sure that our parents knew that these darn things wouldn't work like they showed on tv, but we wouldn't shut up about our need to possess them; it was more potent than pumping heroin through the tv antenna. Ad men for these companies had worked overtime making these world class duds come out looking like the world's greatest toys. Let me give you a few examples:

Monday Night Electric Football. By the time you got done watching that commercial it made you feel un-American if you didn't own one. That is the only present that I ever peeked on in the closet before Christmas; I kept tearing back pieces of the wrapping paper until there was almost nothing left. When you plugged it in and turned it on, the daggone thing sounded like a 747 with the muffler falling off as it shook and vibrated and bounced the players onto the floor. You had to stick this little piece of cotton under the running back's arm and on tv he makes a mad sprint into the end zone; in real life he spun around in circles and invariably went the wrong way. There is no way we spent more than an hour playing with this semi-expensive toy.

Mousetrap. I don't think anyone ever actually played the game as it was intended; all we ever wanted to do was to try to set the thing up like it showed on the commercial and watch it go through all of its fancy actions and then wind up catching the mouse. You had about a 5% chance of it actually working. Yet another hour long lifespan purchase.

SSP Smash-up Derby. An SSP was a little plastic car in which you threaded this geared zipline through and then pulled real hard and the car went buzzing along the floor. All great in theory, but the zipline would invariably get hung up and cocked sideways which made it useless. Then add in the fact that you had two of these cars that were supposed to crash into each other and you had an extremely high failure rate. Trying to time the pulls and aim them so they would hit each other was virtually impossible, then throw in the fact that when they did hit something (usually a wall), the cars were built to explode into a hundred pieces, usually never to be found again. But I will say that on tv, they looked awesome.

Snow cone Maker and E-Z Bake Oven. To be fair I think the E-Z Bake oven did work, but it could only make a cupcake about as big as your thumbnail using its lightbulb powered heat source. But on tv, it showed a cake that looked like it could be served up for a birthday party of 20. The Snow cone Maker was about as mythical as Big Foot or the Loch Ness Monster, I know that we certainly spent a lot of time drooling over the idea of owning one of these summertime fantasy machines, but in my entire childhood I never knew anyone who ever owned one. They looked so good on the commercial; we thought about getting one and putting the Convenient Food Mart ICEE machine out of business. Didn't happen.

How about wood burning sets? Can you believe that they geared these things to be sold to kids? I didn't know this off of the top of my head so I looked it up; a wood burner could get up to 900° ! Nine friggin' hundred degrees! As ten-year olds it was basically a rite of passage that you got a scar from bumping up against the business end of a wood burner. Now mind you, on tv these little kids are shown making Rembrandt quality reproductions. At best we burnt our initials into a scrap piece of wood that would be thrown away by our mothers. Many a father's workbench also took on our initials.

We also had those machines where we poured boiling hot secret goo into molds and made everything from spiders and bugs to weird monsters. On the commercials, these kids are kicking out perfect bugs and monsters at an assembly line rate. In reality, you couldn't get the goo at the right consistency or temperature and you either overfilled the mold which created a giant ball of nothingness or they were underfilled and you ended up with a one eared, one legged Frankenstein or a three-legged spider.

I don't know if these things were ever put on a television ad, but I can verify that they were worthless; miniature pool tables. I'm not talking about a nine-foot table cut down to a six-foot table, I'm talking about a little plastic pool table that was a foot long that used plastic pool balls that were a little bigger than a marble and pool sticks that were nothing more than glorified chopsticks. I'm sitting here laughing at just how worthless these things were and how much we whined to our parents about owning one.

Here's one that I thought actually lived up to the hype: Rock 'em Sockem Robots. They didn't have a particularly long life expectancy, but while they lasted they were pretty cool. Those little guys would go at it like crazy and sure enough if you landed that perfect uppercut, the other robot's head would lift up a good two or three inches right off of his shoulders. We would get so wound up playing it, that we'd break it within the first hour or so, usually only one of the robots would be broken and the head would never re-attach and the other robot would be fine.

Here's a couple doozie toys that albeit were designed just for fun, but they were misleading to us kids. Ouija boards and the Magic Eight-Ball. Ouija boards were only brought out when there was a big group of kids gathered together, like a birthday party or some kind of boy/girl kissing get together.

"Do you like Robin?"

"Do you want to kiss Mike?"

"How many kids will Jenny have?"

These were the type of questions that we just had to have answered. By putting your hands on top of the pointer, through some sort of voo-doo black magic, it would drift toward the answer to your question. What is even funnier is that as dumb as this was there are still people today that actually believe in this stuff. So you are telling me that there is some kind of know-all, tell-all spirit that exists in a piece of plastic that has been pressed through an assembly line in China. Really?

The Magic Eight-Ball was a little different in that we didn't play with a Ouija board very often but we all had access to a Magic Eight-Ball; most of us had one, we grabbed one every time we went into someone's house, and we grabbed one every time we walked into Bargain City. Here was how to officially use this visionary device: shake up the Eight-Ball and say "Magic Eight-Ball (insert question here), and then one of about twenty answers would appear through the blue dye. *Yes-definitely, outlook good, signs point to yes, ask again later, don't count on it, my reply is no, very doubtful.* If the answer was good, it was gospel and got our hopes up pretty high, if the answer was bad we went on about how dumb the Eight-Ball was, yet we'd always pick one up and try again the next time.

✍ Here's a random list of other toys that we played with, some I wouldn't mind playing with again if I could find them:

Paddleball – Yet another toy that turned into a weapon for our parents to use on us. When the paddleball worked, it was fun to see just how many hits in a row you could muster before you missed. Unfortunately, the rubber band always broke, which was usually due to us hitting it too hard, many times trying to whack someone in the head with the little rubber ball from long distance. The most memorable part of paddleball for me wasn't hitting triple digits for consecutive hits, it was watching one of the paddles splinter into half a dozen pieces on one of my friends butt, due to their parents rage. Funny now, funny then too actually, just glad it wasn't my butt that it was used on. My old man was a hands-on kind of guy; hot wheel tracks, tree branches, or paddles just weren't his thing, (although, I can remember hearing the jangle of his belt as he took it off right before I got pummeled a couple times).

Clackers – Maybe just giving us a set of steak knives would have been a little bit safer. Two plastic balls about the size and density of a cue ball were connected by a string with the goal being to make them bang against each other over and over, ricocheting and banging against each other. This concerto would continue until they mashed your fingers or other body parts, hit against something (which usually broke whatever you hit), or the string broke and these super-compact plastic projectiles would go flying off and invariably nail someone in the face or find a plate glass window. Some have called it one of the most dangerous toys ever produced, but it didn't stop us from wanting one.

Lite Brite – Lite Brite was fun to play with, but the pictures never turned out quite as cool as what you thought they would. You were always a few bulbs short of what you needed and then it didn't help when those little bulbs fell down into the floor register vents or where ever else miniature pieces of toys evaporated to. As far as a sit-in-the-house-by yourself-because-you-were-grounded toy went, it was pretty good.

Spirograph - Spirograph was a great way to get full usage out of your Bic four-color pen. If you didn't have a Bic four-color pen, you wanted one; we always used up the red and green ink in the first couple days. Heck at 50+ years old, I still like the Bic four-color pen, (ain't gonna lie, I wrote this book with one). Although there was no particular rhyme or reason to Spirograph pictures, they were fun to draw and were put on many a refrigerator throughout the years. Maybe I was the only one, but I would always get 99% around the circle and my cog would slip and then draw a line across what would have been a perfect... whatever it was.

Etch-a-Sketch – Everyone owned an Etch-a-Sketch, they were cheap, they were pretty durable, and they held our attention, especially on car trips. We could draw the crap out of boxy, straight line objects but as soon as we had to draw a

45° angle or heaven forbid a circle, we were screwed. We all tried like the dickens to make pictures of people and star shapes but they looked like someone was drawing a picture while riding on a Conestoga wagon ride. Nowadays, there are Etch-a-Sketch artists that draw perfect Mona Lisa's and The Last Supper. I tried the other day; I still can't draw a triangle.

View Master – You talk about the poor man's movie projector, wow. I remember sliding in those circular discs and pulling down the handle to view the next 3-D picture. We all liked View Masters and would sit and look at those goofy pictures for hours. Every once in a while you would run across someone who had 15 or 20 different discs, and you knew that they were rich. Remember, kids didn't have their own tvs, we could only watch cartoons on Saturday mornings on the only tv that was in the house, and 3-D wasn't something that we were totally familiar with; so when we had the chance to look at 12 different zoo animals, or 12 pictures of Scooby-Doo, or 12 pictures of the Flintstones, we took full advantage of that.

I want all of the people who grew up in the 80's or 90's or later than that who may be reading this book to understand something. We had one tv in the house, maybe by the late 70's there were occasional households that had two television sets, but by and large the only television set in the house sat right in the middle of the living room. It was a gigantic wooden console monstrosity that probably weighed a couple hundred pounds and had a 24-inch screen. It was probably a Zenith or a Magnavox, and forget about remote control, you were the remote control. I have no idea how my dad turned the channel when I wasn't home, well I guess I do; Mom.

Mr. Potato Head – A lot of kids had a Mr. Potato Head, but looking back on it, I'm not sure why. The parts were small and easily lost and there were only so many real options you had in making a new face; the best part of the whole thing was to put body parts in the wrong holes. In the end you always had a Mr. Potato Head with an ear for an eye, and an arm coming out of where his mouth should've been. I don't know how much fun that could've been but they did sell a bunch of them over the years.

Springy Horse – Here's another one that I think every boy in America had; the Springy Horse. We all sat on those crazy plastic horses with the four springs in the corners. I guess as real little, 30-pound kids, they were just about the right strength but as we got older and heavier and we demanded more and more excitement; the Springy Horse became just another impending disaster. We would rock that stupid thing until the nose and tail took turns touching the ground. We would fall off, get bucked off, flipped off, or slide down into the springs and get our skin caught, (daggone that sounds painful). At some point one of the springs was going to break and if the four-springed horse was dangerous, the three-springed horse was just plain ridiculous to try and ride; it was like 8 seconds on Diablo the Killer Bull.

Squirt guns, yellow BB guns, and flying disc guns – We all had squirt guns of varying strengths and holding capacities. As we got older the squirt guns turned into gigantic long-range monsters, but as smaller kids they were Derringer-sized and could be easily hidden in a sock or a pocket. Whenever the word squirt gun was used, it was usually used within a negative sentence in which there was some kind of ornery behavior involved. I think every boy had a story of, (I know this is going to sound sick, but....) peeing in their squirt gun and trying to con a buddy into drinking out of it. At some point during the last few days of school, we all tried to sneak a squirt gun into school. We always got caught, usually when three or four of us boys would return from the restroom and one or all of us looked like we had fallen into the commode.

The BB gun that shot little yellow rubber BB's was pretty fun. We bought them specifically just to shoot each other. They couldn't shoot very far, maybe only 15 feet or so. Those battles were usually indoor affairs and you'd be finding those little yellow BB's in the house for the next year and a half. They didn't particularly hurt and I remember the gun would plug up and misfire like crazy.

The flying disc guns were really something, they would send those plastic discs flying at a pretty good rate. Again, they were primarily used for indoor battles, and again they couldn't particularly hurt you. As adults, (I use that word pretty tongue and cheek) we bought a set of those guns a few years ago and pummeled each other for about half-an-hour before the guns finally just broke in half. So try to imagine, two successful +forty-year old men hiding behind couches shooting each other with yellow BB's and flying discs.

Marbles – I think everyone I knew had a bag of marbles lying around. We really didn't know what to do with them, so we used them for a little bit of everything; we used them to knock over our army men, we used them to roll around our Hot Wheel tracks, we used them to shoot out of slingshots (even though they were amazingly devastating), and we even attempted to play the game of marbles with them. I figure the generation before us actually played the game and probably knew the rules, but we made them up best we could. I do remember we had special marbles called Cat's Eyes, Shooters, and Steelies.

Playdoh – Playdoh sure seemed like a good idea on paper, but in reality it never formed the amazing projects that we thought they would and as soon as the different colors touched each other, they could never be separated again. Playdoh was another substance that could always be found under couches and ground into the carpets. Playdoh was like buying a boat, the two most awesome days of Playdoh ownership was the day you bought it, and the day your mother threw it away. The chances of us putting the cap on tightly enough so that the Playdoh didn't dry out was about the same as seeing a shooting star in the daytime.

Silly Putty – Everyone from our generation remembers Silly Putty (and Leggs pantyhose) being packaged in an egg. Once you dumped out your Silly Putty you had several options; you could stretch it and form objects similar to what you may do with Playdoh, you could ball it up and bounce it like a superball, and our favorite was to mash it down onto a comic book or newspaper and the image would transfer onto the Silly Putty. I don't think Silly Putty would work on today's high quality paper and ink, but in our era of newspapers in which the ink would dirty your hands before you got to the Sports section, it worked great.

Remember, we didn't have USA Today, we didn't have Google and Yahoo news updates. We had to read the newspaper to know what was going on in the world, and everyone had it delivered to their house Monday through Friday, then your dad would go to the newsstand and pick up the Sunday paper every week. It was chuck full of coupons that our mothers would cut out and most importantly it had its own comic section that was in color. We actually looked forward to swiping that Sunday Comic section and reading some of our favorites: Peanuts, Dennis the Menace, Dagwood and Blondie, The Phantom, Popeye, Andy Capp, Alley Oop, Family Circus, Marmaduke, and Beetle Bailey.

Superballs – Superballs came in a full assortment of colors and sizes. We mainly used Superballs to throw against walls and steps to play catch with, which I will discuss later. A real Superball was made of a very grippy super dense half plastic, half rubber compound that would bounce in alternate directions because of its tremendous traction. Real Superballs would start to break and splinter after a while and then usually in some dramatic fashion they would completely split into two or three pieces. We eventually started playing with purely rubber balls, and finally we thought we found the Cadillac of bouncy balls when we discovered the Super Pinky, which was about as indestructible as any toy we ever owned. Park School, (my elementary school) sat on top of a hill, I've seen a Superball bounce off of a wall at recess, hop a three-feet high fence and bounce its way completely out of site, probably something close to a quarter mile, while we all stood against the fence watching as it ricocheted off of cars, semis, and downtown store fronts.

Jacks – I can't believe that this was a game that could keep us occupied for hours, but at times it did. You dropped the ball and picked up the jacks, (which looked like little four-way tire tools). That was basically all there was; it didn't take much to amuse us. The main thing jacks did was to find their way under our bare feet. They hurt like crazy. You always had to be careful if you stayed overnight at someone's house who had a sister, because you could wake up in the middle of the night to go to the bathroom, step on a couple jacks, and almost kill yourself as you hopped around on one foot.

Musical Instruments – We were all given an assortment of musical instruments throughout the years. I don't know if our parents wanted to try to make us well-rounded or if we got those instruments from a relative that wanted to punish our parents. I don't think that the junk instruments we received from our parents pushed us towards Carnegie Hall. There were plastic guitars, various ultra-crappy plastic horns, tinkly-sounding pianos, organs (which were all pretty good, it is apparently hard to screw up an electric organ), most of us had a xylophone of which we used the sticks to bop everything except the xylophone, the occasional drum set or at least a tom tom, and the instrument that everyone had, was a harmonica. Sometimes we would carry those stupid harmonicas around in our pockets, pull them out and blow out some little bluesy ditty; I think the lure of being a hobo was too much for us sometimes. Riding around on the back of trains, eating beans out of a can, staying up as long as we wanted, and no baths; what could be a greater way to live for a ten-year old boy.

Puzzles and Coloring Books – I don't think that any boy actually ever asked for a puzzle, but hey, if someone went to the trouble of buying it for us, we may as well try to put it together. Puzzles came in a variety of sizes, difficulty levels, and of course number of pieces. If you could find a 1000 piece puzzle with more than 950 pieces in it, then you weren't looking in the same toy boxes that I was looking in. Some people actually glued the puzzle together when they finished it, which I thought was dumb, but looking back it made sense, because we were never gonna play with that puzzle again anyways, and it was the last time all the pieces would be in one place. I will readily admit to being somewhat puzzle-retarded; all I could ever figure out were the edges, or I got too bored and just had to walk away from it. Looking back, it had to be a focus issue because on IQ tests I usually score really high in spatial relations.

Coloring books were found in every home in the United States. They were stored in grandma's house so the kids would have something to do when they came over, they were found at the Beauty Salon so you wouldn't bother your mom when she was getting her hair done, they were found at the doctor's office to take our minds off of the shot we were going to get, we could find them at the Laundromat when we went with our mothers to do laundry, let's face it, coloring books were everywhere. And like salt and pepper, or thunder and lightning, coloring books had to have a partner: crayons. You had two brands of crayons; Crayola or Rose Art, Crayola were the Cadillac of crayons and Rose Art were the Chevettes of crayons, yet they cost the same price, so it was frustrating as hell when your mom bought the stupid Rose Art crayons. Rose Art crayons were about as effective as taking a dandelion and rubbing it on your coloring book page. Meanwhile, Crayola crayons were awesome, they worked every time, they were easy to sharpen, and eventually they had a ton of colors; but in the beginning we were limited to eight colors: black, blue, red, green, brown, orange, yellow, and violet, but as the years went on, so did the number of potential colors. The crayons would break, primarily from either getting stepped on or our lack of touch when we colored and cracked them beneath the power of our stroke. Many times we would color half of our pictures with only two or three colors. When they threw in the automatic crayon sharpener in the bottom of the box, we were in hog heaven, because we weren't at the mercy of our moms to use the "Perry Knife" to sharpen the crayons for us. Sometimes we would sneak the "Perry Knife" into our rooms and sharpen our own crayons. I never knew what to do with the shavings, so I always threw them down the register; I threw a lot of stuff down the register throughout the years that I'm sure I wasn't supposed to.

By the way, I now know that it is called a "paring knife", but growing up in Cambridge, in the Heart of Appalachia, I can guarantee you that it was never at any point pronounced anything but "Perry Knife." I always assumed it was named after a guy named Perry, kind of like a "Bowie Knife."

Models – I don't know if this would be put in the puzzle category or transportation category so I will stick in here between both. Model cars were a big deal to a lot of boys, they took extreme care to paint every part, assemble the engine, transmission, interior, and a lot of them were able to be assembled with some moving parts. It could take these guys weeks to properly assemble their 1/16 scale model cars, they were true works of art when they were finished. Whereas, I could put a model together in about 20 minutes; if the hood was closed you'd never know there wasn't an engine in it, moving parts? What Moving parts? Glue it all. "Dad, you got any paint leftover from the house you painted on 7th street?" Boom. Done. Masterpiece.

Wow did we like playing with different modes of transportation and imaginary modes of transportation. There were certainly days that we spent the entire day playing with these toys. Here's a sampling of those mobile machines: First off, here are some of our imaginary modes of transportation, these were toys that actually couldn't transport us anywhere, but we used our imagination and they took us all over the world and throughout the universe.

Metal car and trucks – In our youngest years, before plastic was a viable material, we all had metal cars, trucks, dump trucks, and fire trucks. If I could go back in time and salvage some toys, these would be some of the ones I would save and store away and just marvel at their high quality craftsmanship. They were highly durable, had a lot of moving parts, and cluttered yards all over town. There wasn't a street anywhere in the country where you couldn't see a yellow Tonka dump truck, turned upside down, lying under the front shrubs. Being that they were metal, it would have been a tremendous idea for us to store them indoors, but alas they had to endure the elements and always, always rusted and got ruined.

Plastic cars – Unfortunately, plastic entered our lives and started taking over as the primary material of our toys. The plastic car was the worst, you could buy them for 99¢, and while they looked great in the store, they only had about a 30-minute life expectancy in the real world. We tried like heck to drive our G.I. Joes and Barbies around in them, but you could always count on one of the tires bending the wrong way which left you with a three wheeled car, (and nobody wants a three wheeled car.)

Slot cars – AFX slot cars sets were ways that we could burn up four or five hours pretty easily. The tracks were connected by snapping them together (taking them apart sometimes was a little bit more challenging), you either had the choice of a straight piece or a quarter turn piece; and in the end you had to make sure that the pieces all connected together with no gaps. Little electric strips covered the track and the cars buzzed around the track, being controlled by a gun-looking controller; too fast and your car would flip on the turns, too slow and they would stall out in the middle of the track. The cars were somewhat expensive, which was probably why I didn't have one and had to play with a friend's AFX cars. I can still remember the whirring sound of those fast little cars. (Call me crazy, but I think I'm gonna look for a set on EBay.)

Train sets – Ah, yes the famous Lionel Train. At some point in a young boy's life this was number one on the Christmas Wish List. It didn't necessarily mean that we got one, but we sure wanted one. Like most things we owned, it worked really well the first time we played with it, but eventually the track pieces got lost or broken and the train's engine would often burn out, (gee, I wonder why, when we tried to have the train carry weights, or five-pound bags of potatoes, or the cat, or other things that a seven ounce plastic train shouldn't be expected to haul).

✍ I mentioned our Christmas Wish List, well here's how that worked: our mothers would go down to J.C. Penney's and Sears in September and pick up a Christmas catalog. These things were real deal pieces of work, about half as thick as a New York City phonebook. The day she brought them home we zoomed right to the toy section and basically memorized the articles on all of the toy pages. I will admit that when we got to be teenagers we would all sneak peeks at the bikini and bra sections.

The books always had some high-end pages loaded with expensive stuff that we knew darn well we had no chance of ever affording but we stared at those super dream pages and wondered what it would be like to own a pool table, or electric dart board, or motorized remote control planes or boats. Our parents would eventually give us a few pages that we had to pick from and those high-end pages were never included in the list of possible choices.

✍ Our Orbital World was somewhat limited, yes they did sell radio controlled gas powered airplanes, but even if our parents could afford them, they sure weren't going to buy them for us to crash a $200 toy into the ground and break into a 1000 pieces. So with the $200 airplane out of the question, we had to settle for something a little bit lower down the economic scale; here were our choices:

Water Rockets – These were plastic rockets that were filled halfway up with water, then we would pump air into them, hit a button, and off this thing would go. Of course unless it landed into a creek or a cushion of raked leaves, the plastic had little chance of surviving a head on collision with the pavement from 75 feet in the air. Another, it was fun while it lasted toy.

Balsa Wood Planes – You could find balsa wood planes close to the checkout of nearly any store in town. They were so inexpensive that we'd buy them four or five times a year (which demonstrates their durability.) If you don't know what balsa wood is, it is the world's lightest wood, and depending upon the air current, they could really fly. A good balsa plane trip could get into the 75-80 yard range; of course a plane made of the world's lightest material probably wasn't going to last very long, and they didn't.

Parachute Soldier – Wow! Why can't I invent something like this? Here was a plastic army man with four strings tied to his back, which were then tied to an extra flimsy piece of plastic shaped like a parachute. Wouldn't you figure that a toy had to work at least half of the time? It didn't. I'd say if you were lucky, 98% of the time, it may have slowed the parachutist down one or two percent, and then maybe two percent of the time it actually made what could have appeared to have been a semi-survivable landing. The parachute itself ripped, re-ripped, and then became absolutely useless. Of course, I'm not sure that this toy was supposed to have been dropped from the heights that we dropped it from; we found the absolute highest peak we could safely get to, then tossed the parachutist into the air, hoping beyond hope that the chute was going to open and the little man was going to gently make his way down to Earth.

Finally there were <u>paper airplanes</u>. They cost nothing more than a scrap piece of paper from our notebooks. We didn't care about the life expectancy, when they went down in flames it just gave us an excuse to make another one. The precision of the folds would determine the success of the flight. I once saw a paper airplane thrown from the top seats of the Schottenstein Center at the Ohio State High School Basketball Tournament, make three nearly complete spiraling loops around the arena; 10,000 people watched and finally applauded. But most of our airplanes only made it from the back of the classroom to the front.

✍ Let's talk about the various modes of transportation that consumed a huge chunk of our time.

Turn the clock back ten million years so we can take a look at one of our earliest modes of transportation, The <u>Flinstonemobile</u> - There was a Flintstonemobile on every street, they were usually sitting unattended, often found half in the street, sometimes laying on their sides, and occasionally even upside down. The yellow tops and red frame of these giant pieces of indestructible plastic could be seen from a block away. I don't even know if they had a steering wheel, which wouldn't have mattered anyways, there was no axle or steering column; the front wheels turned when and where they wanted. Little kids would get in these pre-historic autos and move them around with their feet ala Fred Flintstone; they couldn't move fast enough to hurt anyone. Flinstonemobiles usually met their untimely death when older kids would try to get in them and roll down some huge hill, ending in a dramatic and invariably painful crash.

Some of us had tricycles, some of us had Big Wheels, and a few of us had both. It had to have been funny for parents to look out of their windows and see eight or nine Big Wheel and tricyclists pedaling down the sidewalks like some mini-Hell's Angels. We took riding those machines very seriously; we would pedal our little legs off from the time we woke up until the time our mothers stood on the front porch yelling for us to come home. Those three-wheeled chariots were well constructed and had the capability to hold up for years, we however continued to ride them long after we were 60 pounds too heavy to be on them and started to ramp them off of homemade ramps. The Big Wheel usually met its maker when as 14 or 15-year olds we stood on them with one foot and pushed off and launched ourselves down the street with the other foot and then suddenly our weight would break the Big Wheel in half.

Of course there was always the joy of riding Big Wheels down the biggest hills we could find, putting our feet up on the handlebars so the pedals could fly around uninterrupted; we could reach some pretty harrowing speeds. The only way to stop one of these out-of-control plastic missiles was to turn the handle as quickly and as far as possible and let it slide to a *Dukes of Hazzard-style* stop.

It's no wonder we all grew up and bought Corvettes, Camaros, Mustangs, GTOs, Trans-Ams, Chevelles, and every other muscle car that could throw us back into our seat, squeal its tires, and give us the thrills that we had grown accustomed to as little kids.

Our bicycles. Man, did we love riding our bikes. We quickly progressed from the days of wobbling around on training wheels to eventual daredevil near-death experiences.

"I'm going to go ride my bike", was one of our favorite sayings. We'd jump on our bikes at 8:00 in the morning and come riding home at 9:00 that night. If we couldn't find someone to go goof off with, we would just ride around town for hours at a time by ourselves; no real agenda, no exercise routine, just pedaling down the streets and through the back alleys looking for everything, looking for nothing. I would guess that we rode our bikes 25-30 miles on a normal do-nothing day.

Of course there were times that riding our bikes for transportation just wasn't good enough, we had to go faster, we had to ramp higher, and basically, we had to escalate the danger factor. And without any doubt, our main hero and role model for half of the dangerous things that we ever dreamed up concerning bicycles or motorcycles when we were kids was none other than Robert Craig Knievel, we knew him better as Evel Knievel. From the ramps, to the wheelies, and even right down to the capes, we did our best to emulate Evel Knievel; unfortunately that also meant imitating his actions right down to the number of broken bones and also the mangled pieces of machinery that often lay on the ground after one of our gravity-defying displays of bravery and stupidity.

Our ramps started out as six-inch blocks of wood under a stray board that we would find in an empty lot or in the back of our dad's garage. We'd ride along at 10 to 15-miles per hour, and then with any kind of luck we'd be able to get both tires off of the ground at the same time and land safely. Through the years the ramps got higher and higher, our speeds got faster and faster and the distances that we covered in the air certainly got further and further. At some point, (based on the accomplishments of Mr. Knievel) we felt the need to try to jump over THINGS: gullies, streams, sidewalks, little trees, rocks, and I can recall a couple times some of us being brave enough to actually lay on the ground and allow a bicycle to jump over top of us. Oh yeah, we definitely landed on each other. I can recall several times walking around with tire tread marks on my arm or stomach.

Here's how one of the big jumps would play out: a lot of times we would leave the house after watching ABC Wide World of Sports and they would have had this dramatic build-up of a world-record attempt by Evel Knievel, and if he made it safely across or not really made no difference, we were gonna try to duplicate it the best we could. We all had certain jobs; there was the engineer/mechanic, he was the guy that could get the tools and set up the actual ramp. There was the materials supplier, he was the guy that either had some lumber lying around his house or knew where he could steal as much lumber as we needed, (I don't feel the need to sugarcoat subjects in this book; if we needed something we stole it. I'm not proud of it now, but honestly back then we didn't think twice about just grabbing something that we needed. We never got in trouble for it and maybe people were glad that we took some of this junk off of their hands). Then there was the guy who was going to be the first one to go off of the new ramp. If he was successful, we were all going to try it, (at least until our luck ran out and one of us got seriously hurt, the ramp broke, the bike broke, or our parents caught us).

After the ramp was built, we would situate it where we could build up a tremendous amount of speed, hit the ramp, and fly through the air. If we didn't pull back on the handlebars a little bit, we'd land on our front wheel first and then flip over the handlebars; never a pretty landing, (honestly, kind of a worst-case scenario which happened about half the time). If we pulled back too far on the handlebars, we'd possibly land on our back tire and then scrape our back and the back of our head along the ground for 15 to 20 feet. I can guarantee you that I am three or four-inches shorter because of a landing that crammed my head into the ground. I have no idea how me and all of my buddies aren't cruising around in souped-up wheelchairs right now. There was one other possible landing and it was probably the least appetizing to all of us; the bike would land perfectly even with both tires hitting the ground at the same time, our feet would slip off of the pedals, and we would slam our very private parts down onto the middle bar of the bike. There was no controlling the bike at that point, and it would wobble and wiggle and throw us to the ground. With any luck we would regain our composure possibly sometime within the next day or so.

Many times, especially when we were real young Evels, we would ride around on our bikes with a bed sheet or beach towel tied around our necks. Jeez, we must've really looked like we were straight out of the nuthouse; riding around with bed sheets flowing in the breeze, wearing a pair of our mother's sunglasses or sister's chemistry goggles, and a pair of gardening gloves flying down the street trying to pop wheelies over every sidewalk crack around the block.

Those Schwinns and Huffys filled our dreams at night and filled our hours during the day. For those of you who have heard about kids from our generation taking baseball cards and clipping them onto our bikes with a clothespin so that the cards would make a flapping sound as we rode down the street, those stories are all very true. We didn't know, care, or believe that a Johnny Bench rookie card would be worth $475 in today's world; all we knew was that we had 30 Johnny Bench rookie cards and it made a real cool sound as we rode down the street.

We would tie squirrel tails on our sissy bars and we had streamers coming out of the handlebars, (I kind of glazed over that whole squirrel tail thing didn't I? Well, if someone from our family or a neighbor guy went squirrel hunting they would save us the tails. And then there was always the good fortune of finding a dead squirrel or raccoon along the side of the road, Voila bike ornaments). We would do so many wheelies during a day that we would actually pull the gooseneck out of our bikes and have our handlebars in our hands unconnected to our bicycles. I knew a few guys that could ride wheelies for blocks at a time; if I could get 30 pedals out of a wheelie I was pretty happy.

We eventually graduated up to 5-speeds and then to 10-speeds, it didn't stop us from doing wheelies, but it did tend to curb our desire to build three-feet high ramps. The 5-speed Schwinns were amazing; they had big banana seats with a sissy bar on the back, the front tire was real little and the back tire was a big racing slick. The shifter was like a car shifter that was right in the middle of the bike frame. It was light years ahead of its time and every boy in America wanted one. They were given cool names based on their color: Cotton Picker (white), Grey Ghost (gray), Lemon Peeler (yellow), Orange Krate (orange), you get the picture. These vintage bicycles can now be found on the internet to the tune of about $1500, but back then we threw them down without using the kickstand, just like we did every other bike we ever had. I will say that I took pretty good care of my stuff, based on the fact that if my dad ever saw me throw down my bike without using the kickstand, I'd probably got thrown down equally as hard.

✍   Like I said, we were all little hoodlums and thieves, so if you owned a bike, you had better owned a chain lock for it. No lock, probably meant no bike by the end of the day. Everyone would wrap that little plastic coated chain combination lock around the bar right underneath the seat, but unless we were planning on leaving the bike for more than a couple hours, we'd never chain up our bikes. Of course if our bike got stolen we were sobbing and crying and explaining to our parents that we had no idea how someone could've stolen our bike with it locked safely to the bike rack. I guess I should throw in liars onto our list of corrupted behaviors.

I suppose we all lie. If we didn't lie, at least a little bit, the world would become extremely uncomfortable at times. Use your imagination, there are certainly things that you still lie about today: Santa, really? Tooth Fairy, really? What were you and mommy doing? Wrestling, really? Well as kids we lied all of the time, usually to cover our tracks from crimes well worse than lying. Sometimes it saved us from a well-deserved beating, and sometimes the lies would actually contribute to the well-deserved beatings. It surprises me now, how naturally we lied about things that we probably didn't even need to lie about. I don't think our parents investigated too deeply into our stories or they could have cut our defenses into Swiss cheese. As parents, they loved us, and wanted to believe us; so for the most part what we told them they believed. I guess as a parent now, I would rather deal with the truth than have my kids lie to me, so they get into far worse trouble for lying than telling me the truth about something dumb they may have done; my system seems to work, (but I know they still throw out a few white lies here and there.)

Here's a situation about telling the truth: In junior high our Social Studies teacher stepped out of the room for a minute or two, that doesn't seem too long, but in junior high time that is a very long time to sit still and not do something stupid. A few of us boys took that time to go to a window from our third floor classroom and drop gum out and or spit onto some of the teacher's cars below. The Social Studies teacher apparently had been watching most of our nutty behavior and made a loud noise in the hallway before re-entering the room. Of course we all scurried back to our seats like a bunch of little mice being chased by the cat.

"Does anyone want to tell me what was going on when I was out in the hallway?" he gruffly asked.

No one said a word, but those of us who were doing the gum dropping were certainly feeling the heat.

"I'm gonna ask one more time, was anyone doing something they shouldn't have been doing, when I was out in the hallway."

I stood up and told on myself, "I dropped my gum out of the window." I mumbled, hardly audible, except for the pin-drop silent room.

"Well, Mr. LaFollette, congratulations for standing up and being a man. By the way, I could see all of you boys from around the corner, so I know what all of you did. Mr. LaFollette, you get a reprieve this time, you other three boys, and we know who you are; stick around after class so we can work out your punishment." He said all of this as he was slapping his paddle across the palm of his hand.

Wow, talk about dodging a bullet. I changed the way I approached things from that point on; I'm sure I still lied, but for the most part I didn't mind telling the truth and telling on myself when I had done mild, mischievous acts. You've got to figure that everyone was a kid once and chances are that they also had done some goofy things when they were growing up, I was hoping that they thought my little acts of mischief would be a bit humorous. At least I wasn't going to get in trouble for doing the act and then in trouble again for lying about it. I'm going to admit that over the last 40 years or so, I've gotten into a lot less trouble for admitting my mistakes than the times I've tried to lie my way out of it.

Chapter 3
Junior High School

🖎 I'm gonna tell you right now, anything that I put into print over these next few pages will not be able to accurately describe the terrorizing ambience of Junior High School.

In life, we all go through various struggles; some are real, some are imagined, some are physical, some are mental, but whatever those struggles are, they are scary, painful, and real to us at that time and we all have to find our own ways of dealing with them. As twelve to fifteen-year olds (you probably shouldn't be fifteen in junior high and I know darn well you shouldn't be sixteen and still be in the eighth grade, but we had plenty of guys in that age group and a few that even drove to school in jr. high) we really weren't equipped to handle the barrage of psychological hazards that awaited us at nearly every turn.

Here was the physical lay of the land: we had seven elementary schools that converged into one seventh and eighth grade junior high school building; something in the neighborhood of 550-600 students walked our hallways. The seven elementary schools all had their own separate personality, type of kid, and distinct pros and cons that they brought to the table. Strictly country kids came from one of the schools, impoverished city kids came from another, still another brought well-to-do kids into the fold, and the list goes on. Maybe we had all been thrown together to become future Bobcats, but there was a real anxiety and apprehension between us, we were too young to understand that if we had banded together we could have overcame any obstacle; so instead, we all fought our own battles, not letting on to anyone that we ever had any issues. It was funny years later to hear nearly identical tales of survival and perseverance from dozens of grown men who had somehow gotten through IT, whatever IT was.

Even the building itself was intimidating; a three-story brick behemoth that sat right in the middle of town, it looked more like the county jail than an inviting institute of learning. I'm positive that there were sunny days during the two years that I went there, but the gloom and darkness and overall feeling of helplessness and doom never seemed to dissipate, it was always there. I could feel the despair even as a grown-up when I drove by, right up until the day they tore it down. Good riddens.

There were hallways and staircases in that building that seemingly went nowhere, there were stairways that led to forbidden areas of the school, some forbidden by administration and some forbidden because if you got caught down there by older kids there was no telling what would happen. There was a cafeteria/study hall area that was half as big as a football field, there were locker rooms in the gym, there were lockers in the hallway, there was a woodshop down in the basement (I guess the junior high had four floors with the basement included), there were lab rooms, there was a band room, and there were rooms that we didn't have any idea what they were and for the most part there seemed to be little if any supervision in any area of the school. All of these physical surroundings were new to us and they were intimidating, frustrating, confusing, and really hard to get a handle on.

We had spent the last seven years walking into school and staying in the same room with the same teacher all day long; that teacher knew us, they had talked to our mothers, they would call our homes if we weren't there and check up on us, they would give us lunch money if we forgot ours, they would give us birthday parties; to say that our elementary teachers watched over us would be a huge understatement.

Well, all of that was gone. We now had an eight period schedule with eight different teachers. We now had a homeroom, which was a place where we all met in the mornings so the teachers could take attendance, pass out pertinent paperwork, listen to the morning announcements, and we'd spend a lot of time copying each other's homework and get a good start of the day by goofing off and being as juvenile as our homeroom teacher would allow.

We had forty-minute periods and two minutes in between them to navigate our way to the next class; which could be next door or could be up two floors and completely on the other side of the building. The teachers weren't overly understanding concerning tardiness so it was in our best interest to make it to their class on time with all of the appropriate books, notebooks, binders, pencils, etc.

Even if you knew how to get from class to class in a timely manner there were various pitfalls, distractions, and diversions that could put your chances of being on time in serious jeopardy:

1. You could get frogged. Well chances were pretty good that you were going to get frogged at some point of the day. Getting frogged meant that someone would stick their middle knuckle out and hit you in the tricep (back of your arm) as hard as they could, the result would be that you would get a very immediate one to two-inch lump at the area of impact and your arm would go completely numb. About half of the time you would drop your books, and often they would go spilling to the floor and just as often they would be kicked halfway down the hallway by some of our eighth grade hellions.

2. You could get rodeoed, in which someone would leap frog on top of your shoulders, wrap their legs around your head, and take you down to the ground head first; again, usually resulting in your books hitting the ground and getting kicked halfway to China.

3. As seventh graders you learned to walk on the opposite side of the restrooms, eighth graders would lay in wait and pull in unsuspecting newcomers into the land of torture and ridicule. On my first day of junior high school, I walked into a restroom, much like a normal person would do if they had to use the bathroom, inside were five or six kids smoking cigarettes, another kid standing at the door as a lookout, and

three or four other boys who as far as I could figure were trying to drown one of my Park School buddies in the toilet. I broke free, bolted down the hallway, and never went to any of the junior high restrooms again for the rest of that year. Now imagine going to school for 184 days, six and half-hours a day, and never being able to go the restroom no matter how badly you had to go. Welcome to junior high.

4. And of course you could always have locker issues, locker issues could range from waiting patiently for a pretty girl to get out of your way so you could open your locker to combinations not working, or even worse, someone closing your locker after you spent time opening it, and making you start the whole process over again.

5. You could also get rousted for money right in the middle of the hallway, for the most part you were pretty safe if you walked down the main hallways, but if you had to go down any of the less used hallways you were free game to some of the future professional criminals. Sometimes they would come up with some kind of excuse as to why they needed money: "Hey, I ain't got enough lunch money, can I have a quarter?"

"You got a quarter? I've got to buy a notebook."

But eventually the excuses stopped and they just threatened you or punched you in the chest, "Give me a quarter or I'm gonna beat your ass." The latter seemed way more effective and made you cough up the money without near as much debate.

6. Flinches – A lot of the guys liked to play Flinch, which wasn't much of a game as far as I was concerned. They would draw back and act like they were going to hit you, and if you flinched (which to me seems like good reflexes) they punched you. Stupid.

✎   The junior high staff was certainly unique as well; having taught elementary, junior high, and senior high students I can testify to the distinct qualities needed to be successful at those various levels. Our junior high school teachers were loud and abrasive; many of the men were large, hulking figures that demanded your immediate attention just through their mere size. The men that weren't N.F.L. linebacker size were aggressive, rabid badgers that had no problem going for the jugular. The lady teachers were worldly, self-confident matriarchs that tolerated absolutely none of our juvenile foolishness. These were certainly not the nice little ladies that were our motherly substitutes during elementary school.

Our elementary teachers would throw out occasional hugs or pats on the back but those weren't particularly being doled out by the junior high teachers; but that didn't mean that there wasn't a physical presence attached to the staff members. These were different times than they are today; it was quite normal for a teacher to grab a kid by the arm or scruff of the neck. If there happened to be a fight in the hallway, you could almost count on at least one of the fisticuffers to be vaulted into the lockers by the first teacher that showed up at the crime scene. Boys who leaned back on their chairs would sometimes have them flipped by the teachers, resulting in a loud crash and then followed by the class erupting into guffawed, semi-subdued laughter. Students who bravely but unwisely slept in class were often arisen from their calm serenity with a smack to the back of the head or a hard slap on their desk right next to their head; it was funny to watch the teacher walk up to the sleeping subject because we all knew what was coming next. At least one teacher seemed to drive great joy and satisfaction to walking up behind unsuspecting ruffians and horseplayers and give them what we affectionately called, "The Freeze Squeeze". We didn't know if he stole it from Spock on *Star Trek* or if he just knew about human physiology because he was a science teacher, but when he grabbed your trapezium muscle (in between your shoulder and your neck), it would not only freeze you, but it would make you slide straight down to the floor. Funny to watch, not real funny to receive.

Regardless of any of the other physical actions that teachers used to keep us in line, the main detractor and attention-getter was definitely the paddle. In the 60's and 70's

I can verify that corporal punishment was very much alive and well. I don't think I can recall even one teacher in our junior high school that didn't prominently display their paddle: long paddles, short paddles, thin paddles, wide paddles, paddles with holes drilled in them (to generate more speed and make a more intimidating whistle, right before it pelted you). Some paddles had writing on them, signatures on them, notches carved into them, many of them had their own names such as *The Board of Education,* or *Old Hickory,* or *Ole Betsy.* It was almost a guarantee that at some point in the week, the paddle was going to come into action or come into conversation in nearly every class. We were threatened or should I say, reminded of the possibility of that board being slammed against our behinds almost daily.

As a teacher, I had the opportunity three or four times early in my career to "heat a kid up", (paddle them). It was tough to restrain my temporary anger and disdain for the culprit and not turn it into some sort of megaforce swing of destruction, but luckily I was able to contain my emotions and deliver a meaningful and well-aimed blow. I thought I would like it more than I did; after the first few attempts at delivering corporal punishment I outsourced the beatings to some of the more experienced teachers who seemed to have no problem swinging the lumber.

Apparently there was some sort of legal limit as to exactly how many beatings the school could actually give the students within a typical school day. I guess if the students hit the saturation point of whacks, the kids were automatically suspended out of school. We had two very mischievous hellions in junior high that had an on-going competition to see who could get the most whacks during the school year. I had the opportunity to witness both of these characters and they had the undeniable ability to get under a teacher's skin. When given the choice of suspension, detentions, or whacks these two always choose the whacks; it wasn't anything for them to get ten to fifteen whacks in a week. I don't think they cared for it, as a matter-of-fact I saw them come back into class with tears in their eyes after taking a couple swats, so you know they didn't have some sort of Teflon butt cheeks or anything. But these two boys worked every single day to crank up their whack count which had to be well over 100 before the end of the year. On the last day of school the boy that was losing the competition walked up to one of our hardest hitting teachers and asked to be whacked, even though for a change he hadn't actually done anything wrong. Without blinking an eye, the old teacher said, "Sure come on out in the hallway, how many do you need?"

We sat there in study hall and listened to this teacher rip through four of the loudest hits we had ever heard. Halfway through, we heard the student yell, "Goddamn" and saw him run down the hallway rubbing his butt, but he came back to get the rest of his requested whacks.

I had the misfortune of collected about ten whacks throughout my junior high and high school career; none of them felt very darn good, it wasn't exactly something that you could get used to. But I vividly remember my first ones: as I was leaving study hall I got hit with a big ball of paper, I picked it up, tried to hit the person who had thrown it at me and instead I hit one of our meanest teachers right in the face. It was one of those moments where you just knew instantly that you were in deep crap. I was taken into the office and had to sit there and wait to see the principal. There seemed to be a lot going on in that office; it was loud, it was very hectic, there were a lot of people going in and out, there were a lot of..., we'll call them troubled youths, that I didn't see on a normal day, going in and out of the office and sitting in seats next to me. I knew I didn't particularly belong in there but I couldn't exactly take back that misfortunate throw. I was asked to come into the principal's office and I took a seat as he shut the door. "What's your name? I don't think I've ever seen you in here before."

"Tab LaFollette, and no I've never been here before'"

"Well, I don't want to see you in here again, ok?"

"No problem, I'm sorry sir." I said as I got up and started for the door.

"Well go ahead and take everything out of your back pockets." He said as he pulled the paddle off of his desk.

I can't adequately describe how I felt at that particular second. My heart stopped and then started again, beating at triple speed. I had given myself the illusion that I had dodged the bullet but nah, it wasn't gonna play out like that. I was now a criminal, I was going to be beaten with a piece of wood, and there was no getting around it. I thought about crying and begging for forgiveness, I had seen some other students do this but it seemed like they got hit harder than usual for their cowardice. Anyways, the principal seemed pretty matter-of-fact about what needed done.

"Go ahead and put your hands on the desk. Hey, uh, you said your name was LaFollette, are you related to Bob LaFollette the senator of Wisconsin?"

"No." Was all I could muster. Maybe a good story about how ole *Fighting Bob LaFollette* was my favorite uncle would have gotten me out of that office without a piece of pine cracked against my behind but alas my mind wasn't exactly thinking that quickly.

I couldn't believe how hard he swung that paddle on the first hit. It was a combination of knocking the breath out of me and paralyzing and numbing all of my nerve endings. I had a hard time believing that this was legal, but I didn't exactly have a lot of time to debate the legality of the whole corporal punishment process because the second swat was already on its way. That one really buckled my legs; luckily my crime only constituted two whacks, I don't know if I could have taken a third one. I walked back to class and stood outside the door for a couple seconds making sure that the tears were completely out of my eyes before I made my entrance; I don't think I actually cried, I think that water was pushed through my body and out of my eyes. I was a new member of a fraternity that I wasn't sure I wanted to belong to, but it was a done deal now. I got a lot of thumbs up and the boys whispered questions as to how was it? I wasn't in any position to start bragging about how well I took it; fact of the matter was I could hardly sit down.

✍ When you think of a typical Physical Education teacher, you probably envision a big, thundering specimen who was probably short on words and heavy on action; ours was no different. I made sure I followed every one of his rules to the letter and so did most of my meek and mild friends, there didn't seem to be much of a future in angering this bear of a man. One of our fellow classmates, a special education student we will call, Jimmy, who probably didn't weigh 90 pounds soaking wet with a rock in his pocket either didn't understand the rules of the class or didn't think that this teacher would follow through on the rules, but he had reached the limit of times that he didn't dress for gym and that equaled a swat. Personally, I would have stolen, borrowed, rented, or sewn together a new set of gym clothes to avoid that swat, but Jimmy didn't understand the depth of the situation. The teacher motioned for the student to come to him, but Jimmy just shook his head no. The teacher walked a step closer and called for the boy to come to him, again Jimmy, refused, "Uh, uh, you ain't hitting me." He said as he shook his head back and forth.

27 of us sat there watching to see what was going to happen next, we all kind of sat there with our heads down, but kept glancing up to see what was going to happen next. As the teacher stepped toward him, Jimmy bolted out of the bleachers and started running around the gym. If nothing else he did have a speed advantage over the built-for-power gym teacher. The whole thing was absolute over-the-top excitement, after about four or five seconds (which probably seemed like an hour) of watching this rhino chase this little field mouse. Two of our more physically mature football-type athletes stepped onto the floor and helped corral this little completely petrified student. The gym teacher snatched the student up by the back of the shirt like he was carrying a gallon of milk, and whisked him away into his office.

"Hold still Jimmy and this will be over real quick." We could hear him say in a very annoyed voice; the same voice we use as adults on our little kids when they won't sit still for a shot, or a haircut, or taking out a splinter.

Then we heard what sounded like a tornado tearing through a building with a variety of books and papers and phys. ed. equipment hitting the floor followed by a huge thunderclap, which was that piece of wood finding ole' Jimmy's butt. Then little Jimmy crashed through the Phys. Ed. office door, screaming at the gym teacher, "You ain't F-ing hitting me no more" as he sprinted out the back door of the school. We all sat there thanking God it wasn't us that forgot our gym clothes.

Although, that wasn't a typical day for junior high, it wasn't exactly an A-typical day either. I guess that's why I don't get overly excited when I see a fight or some other altercation at the school I work in; chances are I saw a heck of a lot worse just in junior high school.

Sometimes teachers would light up a student right there in the classroom. There is no way that this would happen in today's media driven society, but back then if a kid got cute in class or forgot their homework or threw something at the teacher while they were turned around writing at the board, there was definitely a chance of a public flogging. I probably saw five or six of these events and heard of ten or twelve other ones. The teacher would call the kid up to the desk and everyone knew that there was going to be some kind of fireworks, the teacher would say something like, "Well Mr. Gibson, it looks like you're going to have to serve a week's detention for being late (pick a crime here), unless you'd like to take a whack right here in class."

So when the teacher hit that word unless…. we were sitting on pins and needles awaiting the next move. There were two potential scenarios:

1. The kid was going to agree to the whack and we were going to sit there and watch a grown man hit one of our wild heathens with a piece of wood, or....

2. The kid was going to go bonkers, throw some sort of raging fit, maybe sweep books off of the teacher's desk or slam the door on the way out of the room and probably out of the building. As you can see there was no losing scenario. We were going to get out of a few minutes of lecture and get a free show to boot. It was also going to be the topic of discussion at lunch and every class after that for the rest of the day.

There were also times when there was a mass whacking, in which several kids were taken into the hallway and beaten one right after another. This might have been the result of accumulative demerits or some act of group mischief, but when it happened it created a silence within the classroom that could not be matched. We would sit there quieter than any living object could be and listen for that crack. No matter what group of kids received the whacks there was always at least one that was a screamer and a crier. Ten toughest kids in school, didn't matter, I'm telling you that one of them was going to let loose with a scream. I'm going to guess that the anxiety of hearing and watching four or five of your cronies getting lit up played havoc on your ability to stay calm. It's a wonder that kids from our generation aren't completely mentally screwed up, but I think we are way more adjusted than the generations of kids that followed us.

✍ I once got caught making bird calls in study hall. Now before you can understand the whole jest of this crime, you have to know a little bit about study hall. Our study hall also served as our cafeteria, it was huge. I would guess the measurements to be close to 100-feet by 80-feet with a stage on one end and a set of in-and-out kitchen doors at the other. Study halls were run differently by different teachers, some of them allowed students to talk and walk around and arm wrestle and play bloody knuckles and paper football, and obviously it was a tremendous waste of time academically, but an easy way for those teachers to kill 40 minutes or so. The other type of study hall was the one where you had to sit there in dead silence and you had to have a book open, no one was allowed to put their heads down, talk to one another, or move around for any reason. Throughout the years everybody found their way into both types of these study halls and they were equally stressful for different reasons.

In the wild study hall you could get hit, stabbed, jabbed, frogged, headlocked, gum put in your hair, books thrown to the floor, seat pulled out from under you, basically there was no knowing what was going to happen next. Sometimes a substitute teacher would be in charge and then you could multiply the insanity by ten.

Like I said, we were all mean and nasty little Godless heathens. We had a deaf student in our class who wore a box amplifier on his chest which connected wires to his ears. He fell asleep in study hall one time and I crawled underneath the table and gave the volume dial a big crank, which gave an amazingly loud high pitched buzz through the earplugs. The deaf boy jumped up screaming cuss words, (only as a deaf person could) trying to dial down the amplifier, while I crawled back to my seat. It was glorious!

In the same study hall I remember putting a tack into the eraser of a pencil. It was something we all did, for a couple weeks anyways. What you would do was, rub the tack across your notebook as fast as you could for about twenty seconds, and this would generate 100+ degree temperatures to the head of the tack and then you would push these into someone's arm. It was fairly harmless and didn't leave lifetime scars, but it certainly got your attention. A student bravely fell completely asleep in this wild study hall, the kind of sleep where you are drooling and wake up and have no idea where you are at. While he was in his deepest REM sleep and with about fifteen of my cronies watching and egging me on, I started the rapid-fire motion for my tack friction gun, I really revved it up and got it hotter than I'd ever dared before. When I put it on the back of his neck (wow, just think about that for a second, ouch) this boy let out a war hoop, bloodcurdling scream that brought absolute full attention to not only our table, but specifically to me as I sat there with this stupid pencil friction machine in my hand, just inches above this kids head. There was no getting around that one and I got the board for my little prank.

In the quiet, studious study hall, time seemed to stand still. A forty minute period seemed to last a day and a half, and it certainly didn't help to sit there and watch the clock move one tick at a time. I guess if we had actually used that time to open a book and read the words inside it, the period may have went a little faster, but alas 95% of us had absolutely no intention of doing that. Even though the teachers that monitored these quiet study halls were very good at their craft, allowing very few shenanigans to go on under their supervision, there was always someone brave enough to break up the monotony. Some days there were paper airplanes that were secretly sent flying, or maybe on some other days, paper footballs or pennies would go flashing across the room. One day a series of animal sounds started echoing around the room, now try to imagine two men trying to watch 100-150 kids all at the same time in this massive 8,000-square foot assemblage, it is tough, (I can tell you from experience). Moo's, meow's, dogs barking, wolves howling, you could tell that the teachers were getting mad, but again when there are that many kids throwing a wrench into the system it is hard to catch them. It was difficult to fight the peer pressure and not get caught up in the mob mentality, so I let loose with my best bird call, it was a dandy too, except for the fact that one of the teachers was standing right behind me. He reached down and grabbed the back of my neck and told me to come with him. Out into the hallway we went and his teammate tag-team teacher was right behind him.

"I caught a little bird." He said as he winked to his buddy.

"Well, I guess we'll just have to make an example out of him." He said back to my captor.

"I'm gonna give him an option since he's really never given us any problems before. Since you like to whistle so much, you can go up on the stage and whistle *Dixie*, for all of your little buddies or you can take two whacks, which do you want?"

This was a no-brainer for me, I'm sure that a lot of kids would have had some sort of stage fright in front of 150 of their peers, but these two teachers, one of whom was about 6'4", and had a nasty reputation of really being able to swing the paddle. So, I stood on that study hall stage sweating like crazy, and my stomach twisting in knots, and I whistled *Dixie* to the best of my ability. I am positive that those two teachers retold that story for quite a long time.

✍ Maybe this next little tale shows our age as a sign of our times. I mentioned this huge cafeteria/study hall. It had 25-feet high ceilings with a window perch so that anyone on the second floor could look down and see everything that was going on. One of the main people that looked down from that perch was our assistant principal; he was small in stature but cast a huge shadow. He had spent his entire life as a disciplinarian administrator and made his bones by being fearless and taking on the toughest nuts that walked the Cambridge hallways. His voice was as recognizable as most people's faces and when you heard it he immediately had the upper hand. Your heart raced, your nerves were fried, the hair stood up on the back of your neck, and you felt an overwhelming sense of paranoia. He could be telling you that he was proud of your latest academic or sports achievement, or just be saying "Good morning" to you, but you would instantly get an upset stomach just from hearing his voice.

It must have been winter because all us boys had handkerchiefs, which meant half of us had colds and used the handkerchiefs (hankies) to blow our nose into, (I don't think that Kleenex tissues were up and running at this point). It was mashed potato and hamburger gravy day, how would I know that, because we were given butter pats for bread and butter, extra ones if we wanted on those days. (I know that you are probably thinking where in the heck is this going? Just hold on, it will become clear in a minute.) We must've gotten done eating early and it was obvious that a couple guys were up to something because a small crowd of boys were grouping together at one of the tables. Two of our biggest students had their hankies out, they took a butter pat and laid it in the middle of the hankie, at this point I still had no idea what they were doing, I figured they were going to smear it on a chair or in someone's face or something. Then with a quick snap, they shot the butter pat straight into the air. Upon further review, it was obvious they had been at it for a while because there were about 50 butter pats stuck on the ceiling 30 feet above our heads. I had never seen anything so hilarious. Of course I had a hankie in my pocket, as did fifteen other guys and we all started firing butter pats up to the ceiling like Vietnam mortar fire. As I was admiring one of my shots, I took a quick glance up toward the perch window and... Holy crap, the assistant principal was watching; I evaporated back to my seat like smoke in the wind. It took the little drill sergeant assistant principal about two seconds to leave his perch and get down to the cafeteria.

"Alright, I've seen enough. All of you sit down and shut up." Oh man, I can still hear his distinctively shrill and raspy voice as it carried halfway through the school. I don't know how a voice could be so powerful on such a little man, but it was. I don't think any of us could have moved a muscle if we tried, we were paralyzed with fear.

I don't know if he actually saw our biggest student leading the charge or if his plan was to take out the biggest threat and then the rest would fall like dominoes, but he put his nose right into the middle of this student's chest and started a verbal tirade that none of us had ever seen or heard before, well at least not at school we'd all got plenty of this kind of punishment at home. But the student, good gosh, I'll give him credit, he hung in there and stood his ground and even started to give a little back. Now up to this point the diminutive administrator didn't really know what we were up to, he just knew that a crowd of boys laughing and carrying on always meant they were up to something; so he really didn't know what we were up to until... the butter started to melt! It started slowly, plop, nine or ten second pause, plop, five or six second pause, plop, plop, plop. It was landing on tables, in people's hair, on their clothes, on the floor, and oh yeah the melting butter landed on these two main characters. The little administrator, using *The Force* I suppose, darn near lifted this 200+ pound student off the ground with one hand and led him out of the cafeteria to a silent roar of muffled guffaws as we all watched the precipitation of butter falling from the ceiling. The janitors and cafeteria ladies must've been ready to kill us, what a mess. We had thrown food before: raisins, peas, grapes and the like, but this butter thing was higher level mischief than the school personnel could have ever foreseen. Butter pats were handed out very sparsely after that day.

✍ I remember arriving to school the first day, there was a string of allies that was pretty much a straight shot from my house to the back doors of the school, so I thought that would be a good way to go to school. As I got to within a block away from the school, I soon discovered that I wasn't the only one who knew about this back alley; fifteen to twenty "students" (man am I using that term loosely), were scattered on either side of the alley, some between garages, some behind bushes, and still others half noticeable behind cars. These "students" were involved in everything from morning make-out sessions, to smoking cigarettes, to drinking alcohol of some kind, I know that I sure in the heck didn't know what it was and I wasn't exactly standing around to find out. I ignored the calls,

"Hey, come here."

"What the *&^% you looking at?"

"Come here for a second, I wanna talk to you."

I just kept on walking, not staring but definitely watching them out of the corner of my eye, looking at the ground so I didn't make eye contact, but using my peripheral vision still keeping track of what was going on. That was something I had to learn living in Cambridge (pick any city here), there were a million great things in that town, but there were a thousand things that you'd better be aware of and not be naïve about or you could very quickly have a really bad day. Looking a violent troublemaker in the eye was definitely considered a threat, but you still had to make sure you saw everything around you.

I was now a couple hundred feet from the school and I was going to make it there without too much grief and then as I took one more quick glance to the left I saw two intertwined bodies. Now mind you, I was twelve-years old at the time, I was one of the youngest kids in my class, and I had certainly never seen two people having sex before, and definitely not behind a garage fifteen minutes before school was ready to start. But now I think maybe I had. What kind of place was I being sent to? I liked elementary school; there I had no bigger concern than who would be on my team at recess. Did my parents know what kind of stuff was going on down here? Did the school know what was going on just outside its doors? Who should I report this stuff to? Should I report it at all? Is this place for real? No way is this place for real!

When we walked in that first day we had to find our names on a list posted on the wall and then find the corresponding homeroom. 275 seventh graders wandering around like so many lost sheep, none of us really having a clue where to go, all of us scared and intimidated, and all of us at the mercy of the all-powerful, all-knowing, all mean as snakes eighth graders who stalked us like packs of wolves.

I guess we were all assuming that once we got inside the doors of the school, it would be a safe haven, just like elementary school; well, we quickly figured out that we weren't in Kansas anymore. There were no big helpful signs that explained where we should go, instead there were notebook sized sheets of paper on the wall with our name hidden somewhere on them like the Vietnam Veterans Memorial Wall, written in about size eight font with a room number listed on them that told us absolutely nothing; how in the heck were we supposed to know where room 104 was or room 236? There were no teachers standing in the hallways lovingly making sure that we got to our intended destination, there were however mean, grouchy, loud, over-bearing prison guards popping out into the hallway every once in a while only to yell at us and commanding us to hurry up and get out of "their" hallway.

✍ So after finally making it to our homerooms we quickly gravitated to our old elementary chums. It was somewhat comforting to see a few of our old classmates, at least our male classmates; our female classmates were as foreign to us as the rest of the school. They had left sixth grade as... well, buddies of ours, they had had no problem sitting beside us in class, talking to us for no particular reason, they would give us puddings or chocolate milks that they didn't want, they would play catch with us if there were no boys to play with. Heck, most of these girls had been to our birthday parties or us at theirs for the last ten years. But now, wow! Who in the heck were these girls? They were dressed in completely different clothes than they wore in elementary school (painter's pants, bell-bottoms, bib overalls, and clogs), they had different haircuts (feathered, feathered, feathered), and they all smelled the same (Love's Baby Soft). Apparently at some point during the summer every sixth grade girl from all seven elementary schools had gotten together and read *The Complete Guide to Junior High Fashion and Other Important Things*, of which boys were not privy to this information.

How did the girls know all of this stuff and we boys knew absolutely nothing; we came into this penal colony with the assumption that it was just an extension of elementary school, heck the whole thing was completely different. 180 different!

✍ I will say that after whining to my mom for the first nine weeks of school about how stupid I looked compared to everybody else, that she somehow talked the Old Man into buying me some "cool clothes". I remember wearing a Cleveland Browns football jersey and a pair of carpenter pants at least twice a week for two consecutive years. Throw in a pair of white with a red swoosh Nike Cortez shoes and I was officially caught up with 90% of my class. There were still a

10% of upper-echelon guys who were wearing puka shell necklaces and a bunch of other stuff that I had no interest in trying to keep up with. I just didn't want to continue to take a daily beating for wearing a pair of Bargain City Specials. I listened to the Old Man complain about the cost of those Nikes for two years, I can still hear him,

"Jesus *&^% ! 20 dollars ! 20 *&^%ing dollars for a pair of %$#@ing tennis shoes ! Those sumbitches better last for 10 &^%ing years !"

Now mind you, it was ok for the Old Man to drink away all of his paycheck, or spend money on three packs of cigarettes a day, or buy an electric guitar that he couldn't play, or a motorcycle that he couldn't ride, or a racehorse that never won a race, but $20 for a pair of shoes so his kid didn't look like a friggin' mook was out of line.

He certainly wasn't the only dad like this, in fact for this era he was probably the norm. You saw very, very few dads out in the yard playing catch with their sons and you certainly didn't see them doing much with their daughters. Not everything during the 60's and 70's was good and this was definitely an area of deficit. I'm positive that he did the best he could; he just didn't know any better.

✍ The seventh grade girls were now prized possessions being chased and sought after by the bigger, stronger, and higher on the socio-evolutionary rung eighth grade boys. Maybe if we had known that the girls had so much sexual potential we would have pursued them more rigorously in elementary school. Nah, that wouldn't have happened; fact of the matter was, we didn't care if our female classmates were being pursued by these mean and hateful eighth grade boys, we just didn't understand why they didn't even seem to recognize us any longer. The girls somehow bonded with girls from other schools and spent their time with them talking about the eighth grade boys and a few of the more physically mature seventh grade boys from other schools and completely ignored the boys that they had been in school with since kindergarten. All of this seemed like a lot for us boys to have to figure out.

I don't know how the girls kept up with their class work, of which they always seemed way more competent at than the boys. The girls wrote and passed notes back and forth like it was their full-time jobs. Most of us boys had no idea what were in these notes, at times we were used as go-betweens if notes had to be passed across the room, but for the most part the contents of these daily mini-newspapers were as mysterious to us boys as the goings on at Area 51. About the only time we found out what were in the *Girl Notes* was when a teacher would intercept one and read it out loud to the class. I will definitely admit to doing this as a teacher myself and I can tell you that it all but eliminates the distribution of said notes. By the way, there is nothing of value in them; new haircuts, Johnny is cute, I like your shoes, etc. all written in big fluffy girl writing, yet another thing put in the *Girl's Guide* that us boys never figured out.

✍ In elementary school we all were just students of that school, whatever happened at school happened to all of us. We didn't see color differences, we didn't see economic differences, and we didn't pay attention to what someone was wearing, or how they talked, or where they lived. We may have made fun of someone for their inability to catch a ball or make a shot in basketball, but it was a good old fashioned ribbing, it wasn't anything that we would disown someone for. But now, everything was different, everything was worse; all of the good moral lessons we had learned and believed in from elementary school were of no value and at least temporarily abandoned. This junior high world brought out the absolute worst in all of us. When you combined unbelievable fear, uncertainty at every step, peer pressure that we'd never faced before, and physiological chemical changes in our bodies and brains it was bound to have some kind of negative effect, and it did.

We all, 95% of us anyways, sold our souls so as not to be eaten by the mob. One-on-one nearly every kid in the school was at least tolerable, but when grouped together they changed; they became spiteful, they became aggressive, and they went into a self-preservation mode and became very dangerous. The rule was very simple: if they picked on someone, they weren't the ones being picked on. There was always someone lower on the evolutionary ladder than them, someone who had a slight difference, someone who wasn't exactly like them, and to save themselves from the mob they quickly threw this different person under the bus. It didn't even matter if the difference made the person better than them; maybe they picked on someone for having nice clothes, or a nice haircut, or their dad drove a nice car, anything and everything was fair game.

So what were these huge differences that were so bad that they prompted beatings and constant harassment and unrelenting mental anguish? How about pants that were shorter than other classmates, or a haircut that differed from the elite members of the mob, or maybe it was where you lived, or the pencils that you used, or the socks that you wore, or the way you ate your lunch, or answering too many questions in class, or walking down the wrong side of the hallway, or getting a drink out of a water fountain that they didn't think you should drink from, or the bike you rode wasn't cool enough, or something your family did, or the kind of dog you had, or... as you can see just about anything! You talk about a group of kids that had no self-confidence, no self-esteem. Even though there were certainly bigger, stronger, more mature kids in the school that could do serious bodily harm, in general these weren't the guys who were causing the problems, oh sure they were standing around and didn't mind joining into the fray once it got started, but by and large it was the little weasels that quite frankly none of us were afraid of individually who were causing all of the problems. I could sit here and rattle off each one of their names and at one point in my life I had vowed to get revenge on all of them, but I'm sure that time has evened the score. If I wasn't sitting here writing this section of the book, I wouldn't have even remembered them; most of them did nothing productive in their lives. You know, no one had a rougher home life than I did, and I knew that didn't give me or anyone else a license to be a jerk; who knows why some people do the things they do?

I can remember a couple of occasions when these little instigators chose the wrong guy to pick on and got their clocks cleaned and when that happened it was absolutely glorious. Eventually we all stood up for ourselves and the bullies and bad seeds and village idiots became smaller and smaller problems until THEY turned into the joke and all we could do was laugh at how these puny-minded creatures could have brought so much terror into our lives. But the fear was certainly real and the prospect of having six or seven guys jump you after school, or in the restroom, or in one of the numerous forbidden nooks and crannies that went unsupervised in that cavernous structure they called Junior High was a daily reminder to watch your back. Even though it was called "initiation", it went well beyond a humorous and well-spirited ribbing. Pushing pennies with your nose or carrying someone's books for them were quickly eclipsed by slaps, punches, kicks, and outright assaults. An initiation has a beginning and an end; it doesn't last for years at a time.

✍ Almost all of us naturally fell into some sort of clique, while others tried desperately to change everything about themselves to join a specific clique. There were cliques for druggies, cliques for jocks, cliques for bandsies, cliques for general hoodlums, cliques for good kids, cliques for brainiacs, cliques based on your neighborhood, cliques for nerds, cliques for just about any type of kid you could think of, and of course there was the ultimate clique that half of the school was trying to get into which was the clique of all of the cool kids. These kids had money, or at least acted like it, they were the first ones to drink alcohol, they were the first ones to have sex, they were the first ones to wear the top fashions, and they were the first ones to make me and my buddies tired, it got nauseating watching these kids spend every waking hour working on being cool. These types of people still make me tired today. They weren't any better than anybody else but they certainly tried their hardest to make you feel like you were the biggest turd in the pond. They were just as bad as the hooligans, at least you could come up with excuses as to why the hooligans acted the way they did, what excuses did these elite students have to be absolute jerks? None that I can think of.

But I would like to thank that super cool clique for helping me become the person that I am today. A lot of the things I've accomplished in my life (two degrees, a Master's degree, a successful collegiate sports career, 25+ great years of service as a teacher, State Coach of the Year awards, multiple published books, and two of the greatest kids anyone could ever have) are at least a little bit the result of trying to show those elite, country club, good ole boy, look down their noses at people kids who had all of the advantages, that I was and am just as good as them. This world is hard enough for all of us, no matter how much or how little money someone has we all have to pay our bills, we all experience illness, we all experience pain, we all live a little bit, then we all die, we all suffer. If we believe in God we are all the exact same in His eyes, and if we don't believe in God we all turn into the same amount of dust when we die. Tell me now which clique is the best. Silence.

✍ The classes were harder and we had a lot of different types of teachers that we had to try to adjust to. Some teachers were really funny, they seemed to tell jokes the whole period and gave very easy tests that everyone passed with no problems, some teachers were dictators that were trying to disseminate college information to thirteen-year olds, some classes made you take notes and keep perfect binders, and some classes didn't seem to have any homework and very few tests. There was certainly a wide variety as far as teachers and teaching styles were concerned. Unlike today's schools which have to teach from the State of Ohio playbook, we had very few standardized tests and nothing that counted towards a State Report Card. I suppose the only thing the State kept track of in those days was the dropout rate, and I'm not sure we didn't have a couple of those in junior high.

✍ I remember that we had a pencil and notebook vending machine in junior high. I'm gonna say that pencils were a nickel and notebooks were a quarter. The notebooks had the Cambridge Bobcat logo on the front and said, Cambridge Junior High. I suppose Walmart and Target have all but eliminated the need for such an item in schools any more. There was always someone in the hallway dumping money into those machines in between every period, and then you heard that notebook chunk, chunk, chunking its way down through the machine. It doesn't take much for me to still hear that today in my mind.

✍ Every worksheet, quiz, test, diagram, or any other paper we ever received from our teachers were printed from a ditto. Every younger reader is sitting there saying, "What is a ditto?"

A ditto machine was an old crank up printing press which kicked out copies one copy per crank. It was loaded with some sort of blue dye or blue chalk stuff that was spread very unevenly across the page. There were often big sections of homework papers that were so thick with ink they could not be read or so thin with ink they could not be seen. Each page definitely had a unique smell as well, one of which any 50-year old person would recognize immediately. I recall as a first year teacher having to use the ditto machine for a week when our copier was on its dying days; my hands were blue and I ruined three or four shirts and a pair of pants. Now I can find worksheets from a website, click print from my desk, the copies will print in the office, and an office aide will deliver them to me. Wow, have things changed.

Many of our teachers, especially Math teachers, spent a lot of their time standing at the chalkboard click, click, clicking that chalk against that big ole chalkboard that often circled completely around the room. You could almost spot a Math teacher by the amount of chalk that covered their pants. It was always quite stressful, at least for me, to be called up to the board to work out a Math problem. Holding that chalk in your hand seemed to freeze the synapses from your brain to your hand. They could have asked me what 2 + 2 was and I would have had at least a ten-second delay.

The English teachers and Music teachers also had a unique little devise which held four pieces of chalk at the same time and they could make straight lines across the chalkboard; helpful for writing sentences and notes for music class.

✍ Other teaching tools used by our teachers were film strips and double reel film projectors. These items sound absolutely prehistoric now, but back in the day they were top of the line technology and something that we kind of looked forward to. They broke the monotony of lectures, for us and the teachers as well I suppose. Our History class was sent a weekly filmstrip from our Daily Newspaper that we watched every Friday that covered current events that had been in the paper that week. I suppose our "give it to me immediately or sooner" society of today would laugh at those weekly current event filmstrips but honestly they helped keep us up-to-speed on local, national, and international events. News wasn't the immediate, watch it exactly when it happens like it is today; you had 6:00 pm and 11:00 pm television news, you had a newspaper you could buy everyday, and you had radio which may have had news on it once an hour for five minutes at a time, that was pretty much it.

Now the reel-to-reel projectors, (they may have been 8mm but I honestly don't have any idea) were big events. When the teachers pulled these bad boys out we knew that class was shut down for the day. In college we actually had to take an audio video class to help us figure out how to run these beasts, and I can tell you that it was a frustrating and laborious process trying to thread the film through and over and around all of the little cogs and wheels and spindles. The film would periodically break and the bulbs had a very short life span. Teachers must've really wanted to get out of teaching to drag out these monstrosities. Then when you added in the whirring noise and clack, clack, clacking of the film being pulled through the projector you had quite day.

We had students that would fall asleep as soon as the lights went out; how they could fall asleep through the noise of the projector and the high volume of the film I have no idea, but there were always one or two boys that would have to be shaken to wake up to go to their next class. We thought it was pretty hilarious when the teacher had the entire class quietly exit and allowed these kids to sleep long after the tardy bell for the next class. I can only imagine how disoriented they must've been, wondering where in the heck everyone went.

And of course anytime the audio video equipment was used the teachers always had to pull down the projector screen. We also had maps in the History rooms and planets or periodic element charts on rolled up screens in the Science rooms. The screens could never be pulled down the first time, it took five or six pulls, sometimes they wouldn't pull down at all, and then other times they wouldn't catch and would bounce right back up. It was always funniest when these spring loaded screens would go flying back up during a movie or right after a teacher sat down that had been trying to get it to catch for the last five minutes.

✍ We spent an inordinate amount of time doing dumb stuff that had nothing to do with school. I talked about the girls writing and passing notes and they also had this origami thing that they made in which they put their fingers in and moved the four parts around then unfurled it to answer some question, (usually as to what boy liked them).

We boys had no problem finding useless things to keep us busy:

1. Paper football – we would fold a piece of paper into a little triangle and skid them across our desks, if the triangle hung over the edge it was a touchdown and then you got to kick an extra point. It was that darn extra point that got us into trouble; you held the triangle with one finger and flicked it through the uprights which were our buddies holding their thumbs together and pointing their index fingers toward the

sky. Invariably the triangle football would fly twenty feet further than expected and bring the attention of the teacher.

2. Coin hockey – using three coins, we placed them into a triangle and flicked one coin splitting the other two, then you had to continually pass another coin through the gap of the other two until you were ready to try a scoring shot into the hockey goal. The hockey goal consisted of the other player holding their index and little finger spread apart at the edge of the desk or table.

3. Flipping coins – two players would simultaneously flip a coin and then cover it with their other hand. One of the players would say "match" or "no match"; obviously two heads or two tails were a match, heads and tails was a no match. The winner took both coins. I didn't like that game, not sure I ever actually won and there was a pretty good chance I was being cheated.

4. Rubber band weapons – We snapped each other with up-close sneak attacks, we could shoot a rubber band 20 feet with a good bit of accuracy, and we could shoot a paper bullet out of the rubber band like a slingshot about 40-feet. No wonder our teachers didn't like us having rubber bands. Every once in a while we would use a paper clip as ammunition and that was a real deadly and painful projectile. It's actually a wonder more of us don't have glass eyes.

5. Dots – This wasn't the most exciting game, but it was one that we could play with the girls and usually didn't get us in trouble like the other games we played. The strategy was pretty simple, someone sat there for five minutes and drew little tiny dots on a piece of paper in numerous well-organized rows. Then each person took turns connecting the dots, if you could use one line and complete a box, you wrote your initial in it. The game was slow but picked up speed at the end. At the end of the game the person with the most boxes won.

6. Yo-yo's – there was probably a five or six-week life span, (similar to a scourge of 17-year locust), in which yo-yo's temporarily took over our junior high school. It seemed like every kid in school had a yo-yo. I would have liked to have

owned Duncan Yo-Yo stock at that time because it had to be worth more than Microsoft. Regular yo-yo's, glow in the dark yo-yo's, butterfly yo-yo's, Duncan Imperial, whatever yo-yo they made, we bought. We all walked around with them in our pockets and every spare second we could find we pulled them out and started yo-yo'ing. We made this slipknot sort of contraption that we put our finger in and there were several guys, including myself that slammed the yo-yo down real hard (to get maximum spin time and make the yo-yo sleep, or spin without bouncing right back up) and the string would tighten like the world's tightest tourniquet around our finger. It wouldn't surprise me at all to hear that kids across the country cut off their own fingers with those crazy yo-yo slipknots.

The yo-yo's which originally started out as Aboriginal weapons had returned as weapons to our junior high hallways. The yo-yo's didn't always sleep when they were thrown down, and would bounce back up and hit the yo-yoer in the face. They would be spun around in orbital flight patterns and conk classmates on the head. Often times the string would break and the yo-yo would go flying out of the thrower's hand and crash into who knows what. I'll go out on a limb and say that a teacher or administrator got hit with a stray yo-yo and that is what ended the Great Yo-Yo Fad of 1973.

✍ Another popular item of our junior high years were Charms lollipops, not the Blo-Pops, but just the regular cherry suckers. There were a few weeks that went by in which every store in town were sold out of these sweet hard-tack treats. When that happened, it triggered a black market frenzy that jacked up the price from 2 for 25¢ to $1 apiece; and apparently kids were so addicted that they actually coughed up the money.

There were plenty of little mom and pop stores in all of our neighborhoods but the main place to load up on our junior high vices was at a little newsstand that stood about a block away from the school and it was open in the mornings (like newsstands tend to be). I always enjoyed wandering through the narrow aisles; the place had a certain smell to it, a tobacco, candy, freshly printed magazine smell. It was neat to glance through the car magazines, comic books, and mad magazines, while trying to get a glimpse of one of the *Playboy's*.

The first time I walked into this newsstand in the morning before school it seemed like there was an inordinate amount of cream-of-the-crop derelicts hanging out in the alley around the corner. Then once inside, the place was crowded with kids and the poor cashier seemed to have her hands full twisting back and forth trying to watch all of the "customers". As soon as the cashier would turn their head, these young "customers" would stuff candy, cigarettes, cigars, bottles of pop, magazines, lighters, whatever they could get into their pockets, or duffle bags, or inside of their coats. Some of these thieves worked in teams, one distracted the clerk while the other loaded up, yet others were lone wolves. No clue how this place was able to stay in business, the daily losses had to be amazing. Once outside, the thieves would meet up with awaiting customers or brethren cronies in the back alley and they would divvy up the goods. All I wanted to do was buy a *Three Musketeers*.

There were so many back alleys, and basement stairwells, and open garages near the junior high and they all served as shady, shadowy little hideouts for any number of criminal and less than proper activities. The amount of junior high kids that felt pressured to smoke cigarettes was really high; kids you'd never expect to see in these back alleys were getting a quick smoke, while others were drinking everything from *Little Kings* to *Boone's Farm*.   It was in your best interest to stay on the well-beaten path when going to and from school. I lived about a mile and a half from school and could make it from the front doors of the school to the front door of my house in just under ten minutes, yes I went on to have a pretty successful track career; maybe I should thank some of those Junior High hooligans I was trying to avoid for those fast legs.

✍ Apparently kids could smoke if they weren't on school property because they would stand directly across the street from the school and smoke right in plain sight of the teachers, parents driving by, the police who often parked by the school, or whomever. They lit up as soon as they walked out of school. It doesn't seem like it would have been too hard to catch these kids in school with cigarettes but I guess the principals had bigger problems than tobacco to deal with.

If we can look back honestly, smoking was certainly not encouraged, but adults weren't going out of their way to discourage it either. Almost every household had at least one parent who smoked and in a lot of cases both parents smoked. Coming home with cigarette smell on your clothes wasn't going to raise any red flags,

A) how would they even be able to tell; there was so much smoke in your own house, and

B) every house that you visited had smoking adults in it so actually if you didn't come home with your clothes smelling like smoke it would have been more concerning.

There were times when you had groups of adults together and the nicotine fog that enveloped the room was like something from a Cheech and Chong scene. Thanksgiving, Christmas, birthdays, really any social event that landed inside your house would create that toxic cloud. Every house had multiple ashtrays lying around, and there were often some spares hidden in drawers or in the junk cabinet; when the ashtrays got full, it was ok to put the butts out in a beer bottle or pop bottle. As bad as the smoke was inside the house, it was magnified exponentially on car rides. At least in the house you could escape to your room, or the basement, or some other bastion of solitude; but when you were stuck in the car the toxicity made it really hard to breathe. You could forget about rolling down the window too, that was just something that you didn't do; there was no touching of the stuff in your dad's car. Don't touch the radio! Don't be messing with the windows! Leave those vents alone, they're right where I want 'em! Quit playing with the ashtrays! (I will admit to sitting in the back seat, pushing in the cigarette lighter and to test how hot it was I touched it with my thumb, which left a lighter pattern for several weeks). Basically you had to sit still, look out the window, watch for people who might pull in front of you (because with no seatbelts, any sudden stops sent you reeling into the dashboard), and try to extrapolate as much oxygen from the oxygen/nicotine environment that you could. Although I've never held a cigarette in my hand and smoked it, I've probably smoked 45,000 of them through second-hand smoke.

    ✍   When we walked out of school there was a church parking lot that also served as a downtown pay parking lot that was about 100 feet from the school. I remember taking a parking ticket off a guy's car one time and ripping it up, I can only assume that the guy got nailed with some sort of additional fines for not paying this ticket that he honestly never knew about. We thought it was hilarious then, but if that happened to me now, I'd be fuming.

"I never had a ticket on my car."

"Sure buddy. Just admit to it and pay your bill."

But the main thing this particular lot was known for was that is where most of our after-school fights were staged. If two kids had some sort of confrontation during school that didn't erupt into instant fireworks the two combatants would meet up in this parking lot. It was perfect because it was far enough away from the school that teachers couldn't see what was going on, but close enough so someone could actually run around and get a teacher if someone was close to getting killed. Eventually a teacher was assigned there every day after school, but for a while you could count on a fight there once or twice a week. Unfortunately, I was involved in one of these little fisticuffs; at least I was scheduled to be in one. A teacher was slow to get back to her class after lunch and one of the biggest kids in our class thought it would be funny to pick on one of the smallest kids in the class, normally at this time in my life I wasn't exactly the hero type but for some reason this whole scenario just seemed wrong, wrong enough that I was going to do something about it. I walked up in between the two and kind of pushed the little kid into his seat and told the big kid to leave him alone.

"What are you going to do about it?" He snarled as he pushed me in the chest.

Instinctively like a cat (and with about as much effect) I swung at his nose and connected with a grazing blow. I know it didn't hurt him, but it did start to bleed a little bit. Two seconds after my ineffectively annoying swing, the teacher walked in and started her lecture without paying any attention to us whatsoever. The whole class period this kid who was sitting one seat back and one seat over from me was continuously going through the multiple ways in which he was going to kill me.

"You wait until I get you in the parking lot tonight, you just wait." He kept whispering.

After half-an-hour of listening to this never ending chorus I snapped back in a brisk whisper. "Fine, whatever, just shut up." I responded, still full of adrenaline apparently.

All day long I kept thinking about that Godforsaken parking lot. I'd been in fights before, but they were quick little three swings and it was over with, kind of heat of the moment deals. My stomach was churning; there wasn't two seconds that went by that I didn't think about this stupid fight. The longer the day went, the bigger that kid seemed to get. Here I was 5'5" 130 pounds and this kid was every bit of 6'0", maybe 175 pounds; for crying out loud, I was gonna get killed. I knew if I didn't go to the parking lot, I was just going to delay the inevitable and take the chance of maybe getting sucker punched out of the clear blue or ganged up on by him and his friends, so when that last bell rang I took a deep breath, walked out the front doors, and stood at the edge of the parking lot and got ready for round two with this guy, which I knew darn well wasn't going to go as well as round one had. I waited, and waited, and then I thought well maybe he isn't going to show, I was starting to feel pretty good about things, and then here he comes, jogging out the front door. He glanced over toward the parking lot, gave me a head nod, and then ran onto an awaiting bus... his bus apparently. Whew! He never again said a word to me about the incident, maybe I tricked him into thinking I was tough or something, or maybe he just forgot, he was so big maybe a full supply of oxygen didn't reach his brain on a regular basis. I had no idea why we didn't square off that day but was grateful nonetheless.

Science class was still Science class, Math class was still Math class, all of the classes were basically the same but completely different. They were so much more difficult than they were in elementary school and they went at a pace that you either kept up with or you didn't, the teachers didn't slow down for you, you had to speed up. There were a lot of kids that weren't interested in even trying to keep up, they slept in class, never turned in homework, skipped classes; I have no idea how they ever got out of junior high, they certainly couldn't have been passing these classes. I suppose the teachers didn't want to have these hooligans in class for another year, so they moved them through.

Even though most of our classes still had the same names that they did in grade school, we had several classes now that didn't exist before: French, Spanish, Industrial Arts, Home Economics, Band, and Physical Education (this was by no stretch of the imagination the same as our elementary gym class).

Foreign language classes were not taken by bullies or any of the cool boys, so I guess it was a forty-minute safe haven for me. I didn't know anything about French class before I took it, I just knew that everyone told me my name was French, so.... it seemed like a good idea to take the class. We were all in the same boat because absolutely none of us knew anything about speaking a different language. I think forty-years later I can still count to eight in French; maybe that isn't a glowing recommendation for the class.

Although there were very few students actually taking a foreign language in junior high there was one new language that we were all starting to speak and that was the language of cussing. Try to imagine a group of young teenage boys (and a fair share of teenage girls) talking to each other trying to fit in as many cuss words into a sentence as many times as they possibly could. The sentences didn't even make sense by the time they got done talking. I suppose it was the peer pressure, or hormones, or wanting to show off, or attempts to seem grown up. I'm sure I threw out a few zingers when I was in junior high, but it wasn't a big priority for me; I had grown up in a house with a professional cusser and he could put these young bucks to shame; so I knew when it came time for me to lay down a gauntlet of four-letter words I'd be just fine. Plus my old man would still put a knot on my head if he heard me cussing, so it really wasn't worth it for me. In elementary school if you let a bad word slip your mom would grab you by the scruff of the neck and drag you into the bathroom and give you the option of washing your own mouth out with soap or having her do it. It was way easier to do it yourself, when they did it they weren't overly gentle.

✍ Industrial Arts was a class that only boys could enroll; try to envision that in today's society. To get to the "wood shop" you had to go down one of the forbidden staircases that led to the inner bowels of the school. You never knew who, (or what kind of animal) was going to be lurking down in that stairwell so you always tried to time it up so you entered the stairwell with a couple of buddies. Why take a chance, right? Although I couldn't personally hammer a nail into a piece of wood without bending it, there were plenty of guys in my class that lived on farms or were just naturally gifted carpenters. It was somewhat unbelievable that we were allowed and encouraged to use power tools that could easily chop off any number of useful body parts. Many of us had never used, touched, or even seen most of these electrically charged monsters: belt sanders, table saws, jigsaws, drill presses, the list goes on; I know that I was seriously scared of all of them and still ain't particularly interested in getting around a table saw. When I buy wood I make up some excuse for the guy at Lowe's to cut it for me.

All of us had projects that we needed to accomplish in order to get our grade, I'm pretty sure we had to make candle holders. I traded one of our best young carpenters my shop clean up skills for him doing my candle holder project. Call me crazy but the alternative would've been for me to walk around the rest of my life with eight or nine fingers.

✍ A few kids were introduced to band in grade school, but it became a full-fledged class once they got into junior high. The band kids then, as they still do now, developed their own subculture, which was ironic in the fact that they got teased for being in the band but they also were shielded from some of these problems because they were off in their own little universe which was sheltered from the rest of the school. I would've given anything to have known how to play the piano or electric guitar at that age or even now, but the stigma of being associated with the band was too much to even consider; plus all they seemed to be offering was trumpet, and clarinet, and trombone instruction, and what cool band had those kinds of crappy instruments?

✍ Although we had Physical Education in grade school and for most of us it was far-and-away our most beloved class, junior high Physical Education was a completely different animal.

1. First of all we had to go into the locker room and change into school issued phys. ed. uniforms of which you didn't have the option of not dressing; no dress/no grade. Everyone who ever went to Cambridge Junior High owned the same white t-shirt with a blue ringer collar with a bobcat head on the left chest with blue gym shorts and the same bobcat logo. Individuality was not encouraged whatsoever.

2. We were told that we also had to purchase a jockstrap. What the heck was a jockstrap? I remember going down to the sporting goods store with my mom to buy this thing that the school told me I had to get, I wasn't exactly sure what it was and my mom had no idea what it was, when we found out together,.... well that was embarrassing. We boys had

played sports for over a decade and our man-packages had managed to stay intact. Those two years of junior high were the first and last time any of us ever wore those stupid things.

3. We were told that we needed to bring deodorant and use it before or after class; apparently we hadn't stunk until junior high. The smell of Right Guard was so thick in the air you could actually taste it, yuck!

4. But the absolute worst part about junior high gym class was the fact that we had to take showers. It was absolutely the most mentally stressful two minutes of my day; try to understand the whole logistics of it: you had some twelve year-old boys who were at least a year and a half away from even starting puberty and you had some fifteen year-old boys who were already having regular sex with real girls. You had boys with absolutely no pubic hair and others with full afros down there; guess which one I was. (I know that there is no correlation to having sex and having a hairy pubic region, but I'm just making a point here.) The showers had an entrance that you walked through and thirty-feet later you came out another exit. The big ole grizzly bear gym teacher sat there with a clipboard checking your name off as you came out of the shower. You know darn well that the guy didn't like this part of his job but one of his bosses said that taking showers was mandatory so what was he supposed to do? The key was to wrap the towel around your body, toss it towards where you would exit, and run through the shower, and then quickly wrap up in the towel again when you exited. You didn't particularly even have to get wet; you could zig-zag through and barely get your feet wet if you knew what you were doing. Luckily the teacher didn't make us do this every day but it was stressful because you never knew when he was going to bring that stupid clipboard into the locker room. I used to closely watch the clock during class and would sigh in relief when we didn't have enough time to go through the whole shower rigmarole.

5. This was also the first time that the boys didn't have gym class with the girls. I'm positive that this made it better for both groups; the girls could do their own thing without fear

of being teased by the boys or getting rough housed by the boys. And the boys could go wild and be ultra-competitive without fear of hurting a girl and getting in trouble for it.

The competitiveness was really ratcheted up, not only because the boys and girls were separated but because you had seven elementary schools combining into one junior high gym class which meant you had alpha males all over the place and also new up-and-coming athletes who were trying to make a name for themselves as well. There wasn't one thing we ever did in that class that wasn't unbelievably competitive. We played a lot of dodgeball, basketball, and whiffleball; we also spent a couple weeks wrestling and used a full-sized trampoline. The trampoline was awesome, except for when one of the students got off-center and instead of his spotters catching him; he landed on the gym floor with a compound fractured arm. It makes for an awesome story, but it had to hurt like crazy. We also had those crazy ropes that went from floor to ceiling that we had to climb for a grade; call me crazy but the idea of sending young kids up a 30-foot rope and dangle for dear life over top of a 2-inch thick mat seems a little gung-ho, even for me.

During our eighth-grade year the teachers went on strike, it was one of the oddest days of our educational career. We arrived at school to find most of our teachers outside the school carrying signs, picketing the school, better wages or benefits I would guess. So all 500 of us, or at least the ones that didn't just take off when they saw the teachers outside, were corralled into the gymnasium. Five or six teachers who either didn't believe in striking or were chosen by the other teachers to monitor us awaited our arrival into the gym. I don't think that they had spent much time planning all of this out. It didn't take long before our volume began to rise, and we began to get fidgety and started pushing and punching each other. We weren't designed to sit in a small confined space for that long without something to do. After 45 minutes or so, the teachers brought out some basketballs, so several hundred kids hit the floor and bounced and crashed around. It was basically a disaster, full court shots smashing into unsuspecting kid's faces, hooligans climbing up the net and hanging on the rim, just basically a complete clusterbang.

After another 45 minutes or so, a rack of volleyballs were rolled out and we were instructed to split into two even teams as we were going to have a huge dodgeball game with the entire student body. Now that was a good idea! With over 200 players on each side, it was hard to find a place to feel comfortable let alone feel safe. Then try to factor in the dozen or so fully pumped up volleyballs that were coming in at all angles and the 200 quickly became 100 and just as quickly became 50 then 20 and then finally just two. The two remaining gladiators were anything but heroes on a normal day, but every dog has his day and today was theirs. One combatant was a long-limbed, gangly country boy who wasn't particularly known for his quick wit, while the other boy was anything but a Rhodes Scholar himself, with his biggest claim to fame before this was walking around school with a pocket full of pennies and jingling them around acting like he was rich. The stands were full of hooting and hollering teenagers choosing their champion. A normal ending to a 500-person dodgeball game just wouldn't do. The city kid with the pocket full of coins casually walked up to half court with two dodgeballs, his demeanor was one of someone who was tired and defeated and ready to give up. With an underhanded swoop, he tossed up a ball that neared the rafters, the country bumpkin ran up wildly to catch the ball, his arms were wide open, and his eyes never veered from the prize. He knew that as soon as he caught this ball, he would be the ultimate dodgeball champion, 500 of us sat there ready to crown this unlikely hero. Then like a chameleon the coin king switched his colors and went on the attack, and with one amazingly accurate throw, he unloaded his second ball and hit the gonna-be, would've been hero right in the face and dropped him like a sack of potatoes. Not one of us saw it coming, and none of us really believed that this kid was crafty enough to have pulled this off, but legends are made in a lot of different ways. I still use that move today on unsuspecting kids in the gym classes that I teach.

✍   We also began our dancing careers in junior high; we had a school dance about once every six-weeks back then which would then ramp up to twice a week (Friday and Saturday nights) when we got older, (I will just talk about junior high dances at this point, but we will certainly cover the high school dances). For a certain number of us the dances were big events that we really looked forward to, I think a lot of us had visions of passionate grandeur, (which never materialized at least not for me or any of my buddies at this age).

About half of the junior high dances had some kind of theme: Halloween, Valentine's Day, May Day, 50's, etc. As seventh graders all we did was bounce around punching each other and then spent time watching eighth grade boys slow dance with not only the eighth grade girls but most of the seventh grade girls as well. Wasn't a whole heck of a lot we could do about it except wait until they graduated to high school I suppose. I think the themed dances helped give us a little bit more courage; when you were wearing a mask for the Halloween Dance, or dressed up like Fonzie for the 50's dance you gained just enough confidence being incognito to maybe, just maybe, go ask a girl to dance. I don't know how many times I stood around wanting to go ask a girl to dance, waiting for some kind of perfect storm series of events to occur, that almost never came to fruition. You would tell yourself, "Next slow song, definitely the next slow song I'm gonna ask her." But inevitably something would happen that ruined the opportunity: her friends were standing around (nobody but the absolute bravest of souls asked a girl to dance unless she was standing there all alone), she went to the restroom, she went to get her coat to leave, or the absolute worst was when some other joker walked over and sealed the deal that you had been planning out all night; funny now, but certainly demoralizing back then.

I remember my first slow dance, (I only mention slow dances because boys didn't "fast dance" until high school, don't ask why, we just either couldn't or didn't), anyways, I must've looked extremely pitiful and of course it was the last song of the night, I was just about ready to go get my coat and go home when a neighbor girl walked up to me, grabbed my hand and said, "Come on", as she led me 15 feet further out onto the gym floor. A slow dance only consisted of the girl putting her arms around the boy's neck and the boy settling his hands near the small of the girl's back and you walked around in slow six-inch circles, but gosh darn was I nervous, and excited, and wow, I was holding a girl, and she was kind of holding me, and she really smelled good, and I was finding it hard to breathe, but I was really trying to be cool about the whole thing. The kicker was that she was an eighth grader, a popular eighth grader at that, and I know it was just some sort of a mercy dance, but at that point I just plain didn't care.

When I hear songs like, *Beach Baby, Kung Fu Fighting, Taking Care of Business*, or Olivia Newton John's *I Honestly Love You*, or how about a little *Smoke on the Water*, I can drift off to one of those junior high dances pretty quickly. Our generation was extremely blessed with some of the greatest recording artists of all-time and that definitely included my junior high school years; Elton John, Stevie Wonder, Eagles, Lynard Skynard, Doobie Brothers, Jackson 5, Jim Croce, Rolling Stones, Patti LaBelle, give me a break I'm just scratching the surface. You will see later that music was a big part of our young lives.

Those dances were part of a natural courtship learning curve that started the day we walked through those junior high school doors. We all progressed through sexuality at our own speed or maybe we just gave into temptation and urges at different times in our lives, but when our hormones kicked in, the chemical endorphins that surged through our bodies created a constant state of libido and confusion. Who knows why our urges turn into actions, I suppose there are a variety of factors that contribute to crossing that line: onset of puberty, physical maturity, religion, morality of the home, supervision or lack thereof, peer pressure, confidence or lack thereof, but we all know it's never just one thing.

For most of us boys there was absolutely no chance that a girl would look in our direction in the first place; we were barely 100-pounds soaking wet, we had the maturity of a seven or eight-year old, and we had absolutely no "game" whatsoever. We certainly enjoyed looking at and fantasizing about all of the girls, I don't know why this sudden change occurred because honestly we couldn't have given a hoot about girls in elementary school, but times were a changin' and they certainly had our full attention now. If you really think about it, most of the things we have done, both male and female from those junior high school years on, have revolved around attaining or retaining the attention of the opposite sex.

Our infatuations made for a lot of uncomfortable moments when put into situations with the opposite sex: sitting next to a girl in class, walking by girls in the hallway, having a girl next to your locker, needing to ask a girl for a pencil or piece of paper, or heaven forbid when a boy and girl got matched up for those daggone group projects in class.

In reality, the whole boyfriend/girlfriend thing kind of made us sick to our stomachs: holding hands out in public, spending every waking hour together, passing useless notes back and forth, completely ignoring your old friends, talking on the phone for hours at a time, give me a break. If that was what having a girlfriend meant count me out, all of that stuff seemed stupid to me and to most of the guys that I knew. Then you had all of that other stuff, that...sex stuff, ...that kissing stuff, ...and other stuff. We weren't really sure about any of it, we'd heard a lot of hearsay and we'd made some guesses as to what some of this stuff was but we really didn't know exactly what this stuff was. First base, second base, third base, what was all of that crap? I knew everything there was to know about sports and I knew that girls never fit into the equation before, so what did they know about baseball or what did baseball have to do with them? Kissing, and making out, and French kissing, were those things the same or different? What was a French kiss anyways? And sucker bites; I know I didn't want to walk around with one of those things on my neck, and I'm gonna say that my parents would've been upset to see their son disfigured like that. How did you do that anyways and better yet, why? Bras, those things looked pretty personal to me, but we heard guys talking about taking them off; didn't the girl get mad about that? It just didn't seem proper, and plus I wasn't overly sure how those things worked, they looked pretty complicated; hooks and straps and cups and lacy stuff, I'm gonna pass. There were about twenty other terms that guys threw around and most of us had no idea what they meant and I don't think that most of us were in any hurry to find out either. All of that stuff could wait, (and did) as far as I was concerned, at this point just looking at girls and an occasional slow dance with one of them every couple months was plenty, heck one slow dance kept my mind occupied for a couple months anyways. There were however a pretty large percentage of our junior high population who were having some sort of romantic relations including going all the way, which sounded about as scary as a runaway rollercoaster full of rabid zombies flying through a fiery tornado. I have no idea how I ever agreed to do that the first time!

✍ As isolated and homebound as we had been in elementary school, we were suddenly free to roam the mean streets of the entire town of Cambridge. We seemingly had no boundaries. I guess the idea of their babies now being in junior high made our parents giddy with the belief that we were growing up now and that we were safe to leave the nest; or maybe they did understand how unbelievably dangerous the Junior High was and figured that if we could find ways to survive that concrete jungle, running around town was no biggie. We walked or rode our bikes all over town; we would go to some of the different elementary schools and join in basketball games or football games, we would go downtown to the courthouse and play on the cannons, we would go out to the city park and find any number of interesting things to get into, we would walk down to the creek and find all kinds of dangerous things to stay occupied, or we would just wander around aimlessly doing nothing, looking for anything. I'm going to admit to this in print, which will probably mortify my mom; me and my friends were asked one Saturday morning by an older neighborhood buddy if we wanted to go to a Pittsburgh Pirates baseball game, Pittsburgh was probably about 80 miles away, I asked the guy when we would be home, he spit out a number that fell within my curfew so I jumped in the car and went to Pittsburgh, now mind you I was thirteen-years old, crossed the state line, and stayed away from the house for about eight or nine hours and no one cared, looked for me, or even knew I was gone. The game was good by the way, (Willie Stargell, Dave Parker, Kent Tekulve, Manny Sanguillen give me a break, those were real ballplayers.)

✍ Sometimes if we happened to be home, which wasn't very often, our parents would send us to the store, and again there were local markets in nearly every neighborhood. Compared to now, it was really nice that the checkout lady knew your name and might ask about how your mom was doing or how you were doing in school; now you get checked out by some 18-year old with purple hair, a nose ring, 14 earrings, and some ridiculous tattoo that all you can think about is how idiotic that thing is going to look when they are 40 because it already looks amazingly idiotic right now. Whew! Breathe! Anyways, we would be sent to the market with a note from our parents to pick up a pack or maybe even a case of cigarettes. I suppose it could've worked for a case of beer, I don't know, my old man did all of his drinking outside the house. We were usually allowed to spend whatever was left over, don't get too excited though it was usually 15 or 20 cents, and occasionally the prices would go up and there we were standing at the checkout without enough money to buy whatever we were sent for. You didn't want to come home empty handed, that would get you yelled at and called an idiot. Sometimes the checkout lady would tell you to bring the money in the next time you were in; either way you were going to get yelled at, I don't know how it was my fault that the price of my dad's cigarettes went up but me and my mom would get yelled at about it for a week. All I wanted was enough money left over to buy a Suzy-Q or a Yoo-Hoo.

We also had to pick up lunch meat which was cut fresh from the deli of all of these markets. Spice loaf, old fashioned loaf, and pickled pimento loaf were always pretty popular at my house, but I'd have to say that the king of all lunch meats in every household in Cambridge during this time was bologna and that will be the last time I write it out like that, let's call it what we called it, "baloney." Dad would come home with a big five or six-pound block of this stuff and mom would cut it up into half-inch slabs and fry it in the pan with bacon grease. Every house I ever visited back then had a cup of bacon grease that had been drained from the skillet when our mothers fried bacon, (which was probably a couple times a week). There wasn't much in the house that wasn't cooked in that bacon grease. Today we spend half of our lives worrying about stuffing our faces with fruits and vegetables to try to eliminate anything with fat, yet our grandparents lived to be 80 and 90 by frying everything in bacon grease and never putting on a pair of running shoes in their lives.

✍ If you lived during these years you probably at one point or another had some of these foods as well: liver and onions (absolutely demoralizing when you smelled it being cooked), Chef Boyardee boxed spaghetti, lima beans, pinto beans, ham and soup beans, fried green tomatoes (not the movie), tv dinners, chicken pot pies, pan fried (in Crisco or bacon grease) chicken (of which we would fight for the wishbone), hamburgers, Hamburger Helper, sloppy joes, chili, fried Spam, or grilled cheese. There were a lot of times we didn't have meat included in our meal, just couldn't afford it; lima beans and bread and butter along with Kool-Aid was a meal. Mom used to talk about eating Karo (which was like liquid sugar) sandwiches when she was a kid. Peanut butter and jelly (maybe not even jelly) was a potential meal. Truth was, once I got to be junior high school age I didn't particularly worry about what was for supper, I tried not to even be there, I ate a lot of meals at other people's houses or out of gardens that we passed by on our daily walks around town. If you got thirsty away from your home you had a lot of options as well: if you saw a garden hose on someone's house you had a free drink, if you were by a stream or creek you scooped up some water and drank it, and if you wanted some pop you could usually reach up into the pop machine and pull out a bottle without too much risk of getting your arm caught, or walk into the backroom of George Bliss' gas station and just grab a bottle, he knew darn well we were stealing them but never said a word to us. He'd stand there and have a conversation with you while you were holding three or four bottles of pop in your coat hoping they didn't rattle together when you walked.

✍ I remember for breakfast every morning before school during my junior high career I dipped toast into a small cup of hot chocolate as I sat there and watched *Popeye*. That routine never varied; I never ate anything different, I never watched another show, I never worked on homework or studied for a test, I just watched *Popeye* and ate my toast and hot chocolate. I honestly don't think I ever did homework or had homework or ever had any type of school project that needed to be brought home. Amazingly without computers or internet and our only reference material being something as ancient as books including volumes and volumes of encyclopedias we were able to be the most advanced country in the world, now where are we? The books that were given to me at school, stayed at school; I don't know when all of this excessive, three-hours' worth of homework per night thing started but it certainly wasn't during our era. You probably think I was some kind of slacker academic moron, but I actually earned A's and B's with a very occasional C thrown in there; we just weren't given any homework. Because we didn't have tons of homework we carried our books by hand to and from each class stopping at our lockers three or four times a day, if anyone during my time period would have come to school with a book bag or backpack, I can all but guarantee you that they would have been stuffed inside it and rolled down the back stairwell.

As traumatic and nerve-wracking as seventh grade was, eighth grade was actually pretty relaxing and enjoyable, as enjoyable as school could be I guess. We had an excellent lay of the land, we knew what potential landmines were out there, we knew who we could trust and who we should avoid; in general we thought we had things pretty well figured out. Most of the real dangerous, spiteful hoodlums had been advanced on to the high school and for the most part our fellow eighth graders were all tolerable to each other, we had endured a whole year of hell together so in some aspect we were joined by a common bond of survival.

Finally I could go to the restroom and not worry about getting kidnapped, assaulted, threatened, robbed, or drowned; I'm not going to say that crazy, illegal, immoral, and scary things weren't still going on in there, I'm just saying that I wasn't subject to anything harmful so I could now take a pee in peace and not hold have to hold it for six or seven hours.

The overall freedom of not always looking over our shoulders allowed us to see things in a much more beautiful light; the teachers were cooler, lunch was tastier, homework was easier, we seemed to be treated more like adults and less like POW's. But the main thing that seemed to be showing in a more beautiful light were the girls,

A) we weren't terrified of the girls in our grade any longer, there were some of them that still wanted to treat us like a dog turd stuck on the bottom of their shoe, but who friggin' cared, most of the eighth grade girls had no problem speaking to us or even goofing around with us now and

B) those seventh grade girls sure were pretty! It was way, way, way easier to talk to those poor little, unsure of themselves seventh grade girls than it was to try and have a conversation with some of our worldly eighth grade ladies. Of course every other eighth grade boy had the same idea as well, so the seventh grade girls were, let's say, "Well-cared for". I figure this was one of the reasons why the eighth grade girls showed us a little bit more attention, they were a touch jealous and most of the older guys they had hung around with last year were now in the high school, so we eighth grade boys prospered on both fronts. We were the new kings of the castle, and even though we knew it wouldn't last, we tried not to think about that too much, it's better to have been a king for a year than to have never been a king at all.

It's amazing what people can do when they are liberated and don't feel intimidated. As eighth grade students we felt freer to show our true colors, we didn't have to hide (quite as much anyways) from who we truly were. As a teacher in a small country school I see kids who have the luxury to be themselves all the way throughout their school careers, most of the time when we were kids we were too scrutinized and too chicken to just be ourselves. I always tell my students, and athletes, and my own kids to do whatever they want because the knuckleheads who are going to have some smartaleck comment about it aren't the ones who are going to be paying your bills five or six years from now, so who cares what they think. "Those who mind don't matter, and those who matter don't mind."

✍ We only had eight or nine channels at this point, but through the years of our childhood we definitely had a lot of good tv shows and a ton of great cartoons. Here are a few of the tv shows (over a ten-year period) that sometimes we wanted to watch and sometimes we had to suffer through with our parents: *All in the Family* (Archie Bunker yelling at Meathead was pretty funny), *M.A.S.H.* (extremely popular, never liked it), *Flip Wilson* (loved Geraldine), *I Love Lucy, Truth or Consequences* (Bob Barker before the *Price is Right,* or *Happy Gilmore* for you real youngsters), *Hawaii Five-O, Bonanza, Gunsmoke* (always liked Festus), *Ironside, Mannix, Sanford and Son* (must've watched every episode 50 times each), *Walton's* (hated that friggin' show), *Cannon, Rockford Files* (reason I liked Camaros and Firebirds), *Kojak, Sonny and Cher, Adam 12, CHiPs, Six Million Dollar Man* (we loved that show! We would make that stupid wa wa wa wa wa sound every time we'd run fast), *Good Times* (Dy-No-Mite), *Happy*

Days (we all liked Fonzie, but were probably way closer to being Richie Cunningham).

On Sunday nights you could always count on sitting down with the family and watching *Wonderful World of Disney*, there was also *Gentle Ben, The Andy Griffith Show* (always a moral lesson learned, I always thought Andy looked like my dad), *Ed Sullivan, Red Skelton, Carol Burnett* (loved it when Tim Conway and Harvey Korman would get the giggles), *Flipper, Leave it to Beaver* (loved me some Eddie Haskell), *Brady Bunch, Laverne and Shirley, Twilight Zone, My Three Sons, Hee Haw, Laugh In, Mod Squad, Partridge Family, Starsky and Hutch, Welcome Back Kotter* (Vinnie Barbarino made being dumb really cool), Alfred Hitchcock, Lassie, The Honeymooners, Beverly Hillbillies (Ellie May was hot), *Candid Camera, Gomer Pyle, Munsters* (Herman was awesome), *Addams Family* (pretty dark and creepy for a kids show), *Bewitched, Get Smart, Batman* (POW, BAM!), *Gilligan's Island, Daniel Boone*, and *The Smother's Brothers* (loved Tommy).

But I think it was cartoons and shows designed specifically for kids where I think we had a huge television advantage over today's kids. Here are some of the kid friendly shows that we got to enjoy as we grew up: *Captain Kangaroo* (wow, Mr. Green Jeans, Mr. Moose, and those crazy ping pong balls), *Romper Room* (I can see Jeffy and Kevin and Debbie... be a Do-Bee), *Lancelot Link Secret Chimp* (younger readers should *You Tube* this to really appreciate it), *Tennessee Tuxedo, Rocky and Bullwinkle, The Three Stooges* (our all-time favorite show, Curley please No Shemp, or Curley Joe), *Little Rascals* (Alfalfa, Spanky, Buckwheat, Butch, and Darla), *The Flintstones* (probably the best cartoon of all time, every sitcom plot since 1970 can be rooted back to a Flinstones episode), *Tom and Jerry*, of course all of the Disney cartoons (Mickey, Donald, Pluto, and the gang). *Popeye, The Banana Splits* (again, youngsters should *You Tube*), *Bugs Bunny, Roadrunner, Tweetie, Taz, Scooby-Doo* (everyone needs to understand that this was one of the few shows on tv that we would give up play time for), *Hong Kong Phooey, Jetsons, Magilla Gorilla, Grape Ape, Space Ghost* (liked that one), *Jonny*

Quest (one of our favorites, Race Banner was really cool and Bandit), *Atom Ant, Secret Squirrel and Morocco Mole* (I still do a good Morocco Mole imitation), *Underdog* (There's no need to fear), *Heckle and Jeckle, Speed Racer, Pixie and Dixie, Chip and Dale, Snagglepuss, Pink Panther, Yogi Bear, Speedy Gonzales, Quick Draw McGraw, Mighty Mouse, Alvin and the Chipmunks, Wally Gator, Shari Lewis and Lambchop*, and *The Mickey Mouse Club*. (We seemed to have had a lot of talking animal cartoons, maybe that's why I still talk to my pets like they are going to talk back to me.) Even our commercials were cool and educational to boot; *School House Rock* were three-minute educational infomercials that taught us such things as Grammar (*Conjunction Junction* what's that function?, *Lolly, Lolly, Lolly Get Your Adverbs Here*), Multiplication (12 videos giving songs to help us multiply, *My Hero Zero, Three is a Magic Number*), Science (*Do the Circulation Dance, The Victim of Gravity*), and I am proud that I know the Preamble to the Constitution, but I am somewhat embarrassed that I have to sing it as I learned it from *School House Rock*.

Growing up, probably starting in junior high and lasting throughout high school, we had a local tv legend that we absolutely lived for on Saturday nights: The Ghoul, (I'm sure most communities had some sort of late night creepy movie personality). The Ghoul, (Ron Sweed) on Cleveland's WKBF hosted a wacky, juvenile, slightly dark, and definitely late night show that featured scary movies, monster movies, whatever you want to call them. No one really cared about watching the movies; they were B movies at best, what we were waiting for was the intermission breaks where The Ghoul and his side kick Froggy (a rubber frog) would fully commit to an array of ludicrous adolescent stunts, usually revolving around blowing something up with firecrackers. An urban legend floated around about The Ghoul actually blowing up a real frog on live tv; I think most of us waited around for that to happen again, but I'm guessing it probably never really happened the first time. We were often allowed to heat up some Jiffypop on the stove and have a bottle of pop; we would be fully jazzed up when we were allowed to stay up and watch The Ghoul, however I don't think we ever made it more than an hour into the show before we were conked out on the floor. So many nights I would lay there on the floor in front of the tv, and have my mom wake me up and tell me to go to bed, every time I would fight with her, telling her that I was awake, or the classic, "I was just resting my eyes." Then the Old Man would chime in, "Get your ass to bed." Amazingly, I was fully coherent after that.

✍ Although we didn't see it happen very often,

A) because we weren't addicted to television like we are now, and

B) because we weren't allowed to stay up that late, but when we were growing up the television actually turned off; WHAT? I mean it turned off. It ran out of shows. The channels shut down for a few hours. If you remember this, I can almost tell you exactly how old you are. Somewhere between midnight and three in the morning, the channel would say something like, "This is WABC signing off the air", followed by a picture of an American flag fluttering in the wind to the tune of the National Anthem. When the music stopped there were a couple things that could possibly happen, either some sort of test pattern would appear on the screen, often with the channel number and call letters in it, or there would just be a snowy, buzzing screen that I can swear to you I have sat and stared at for at least 45 minutes (why I have no idea, probably too tired to move.)

✍ Remember, the 60's and 70's were very different times in our country than they are now; there was no such thing as political correctness, people didn't try to run your life for you, no one was giving out parenting advise unless they wanted punched in the mouth and that very well could've been by your mom if some busy body started telling her how she could be a better mother. Our dads often did stupid things and our moms tried to hold the household together with a shoestring budget; at least that's how it was at my house and all of the houses in my neighborhood. Our fathers would take us out every once in a while to just spend time with us I suppose, and there were a lot of times where if you judged those bonding experiences with bonding experiences of today you'd just shake your head, but they were ordinary things for dads to do with their boys at that time:

Bars - I can tell you that I'd been in 15-20 bars, (beer joints as they were called then) by the time I'd hit junior high school. My dad used to tell stories of how he'd taken me to his favorite beer joint when I was about two and he'd have me smoke a cigar. (Jesus Chriminently! Really!) And it wasn't like anyone was complaining about it, or telling him it might have been a bad idea, or calling the police on him for some sort of child abuse, hell I was a big hit, these other drunks looked forward to seeing a big fat baby sitting on the bar smoking a cigar. I'd have some of these guys come up to me when I was in my mid-twenties and relive that dumb story; like I was going to remember something from when I was two.

What I can remember though is my mom driving around from beer joint to beer joint looking for my old man, sometimes I would get sent in to find him and if I did I was supposed to tell him to come home (like that was going to work); probably before he drank up all of the rent money. You're probably figuring out that I didn't live the lifestyle of the rich and famous, but I'm telling you that these beer joints were filled wall-to-wall with other kids' dads and I'm sure they can attest to similar stories.

I ain't gonna lie, I liked going into the bars with my dad. He always emptied his pockets and threw out some quarters for me to go play pool or that shuffleboard bowling game. I remember I wasn't allowed to break, probably because he was worried about me tearing the felt on the pool table, and even though it probably took me twenty minutes to finally get all of the balls into the pockets, it was exciting for me to walk around with that pool stick and act like I was some kind of pool shark. You usually were allowed to order something from the menu: French fries, cheeseburger, hot dog, and always a

Coke. Eating out wasn't like it is today where we probably eat six of our potential twenty-one meals a week out at a restaurant, getting to eat food away from your house was a big deal back then.

Spot sheets - More than half of you have no idea what I'm talking about but a handful of you probably do. Every week during football season my dad would drive down to... well I shouldn't really tell you who's house it was or down to the bowling alley and pick up a spot sheet; a spot sheet was a gambling ticket that listed college games and pro games and gave the spot or point spread on them, (Example: Ohio State Home vs Michigan +10.) If you could pick five correct games you might get double your money back or seven picks might be triple your money. These sheets were printed and distributed by the Youngstown mafia; it was a real-deal criminal enterprise. Dad would sit there and cuss the tv every Saturday and Sunday because Ohio State screwed him again, or that damn Notre Dame knew what the spot was and made sure they didn't cover it, and those "F*&^ing Cleveland Browns !" More than once he drew back and was going to throw an ashtray or lamp through the tv, but luckily never followed through on it. At around eighth grade he started asking me if I wanted a sheet, what the heck why not. I don't think I ever won but it did raise my interest level in football and I suppose it gave me some common ground with the Old Man for at least a few hours a week.

Country drives - I would think that almost every kid during this era had some sort of impromptu driving lesson while on a back road country drive. Your dad would be driving and then all of the sudden he would pull off the road and call you over, now if you were really young, like six or seven you would sit on his lap and would steer as he pushed on the gas and brake pedals. It sounds sort of stupid now but it was pretty exciting back then; grabbing that wheel and steering the car made you feel like quite a bigshot. It usually ended in some dramatic life-saving tug on the wheel and you being basically tossed back to the passenger seat. There weren't any seat belts, (or if there were, they were jammed in-between the seat) so there was a lot of sliding around on those old leather bench seats. If you were a little bit older, twelve or thirteen I suppose, your dad would put the car in park, get out, and tell you to get behind the wheel. Whew, this was really nerve wracking because now you had control of not only the steering wheel, but the gas and brake as well. Your dad would still grab the wheel if you got into a pickle and every one of these escapades always seemed to end up in a near-death experience, but it was the beginning of our driving careers. If you had a good outing, on the next trip you always sat in the back hoping that once the car reached the spot where it stopped the last time he would stop again and let you have another go at it, sometimes it would happen sometimes it wouldn't. If there was a law against it (and I'm sure there was, obviously ten-year old kids couldn't drive cars even out on the country roads), that didn't seem to scare any of our parents, we would pass a Sheriff and the Old Man would wave and tell you to keep your eyes on *&^%ing the road. There was no way that the Sheriff could've thought a kid who could barely see over the steering wheel was old enough to drive. The 60's and 70's were just a different and much simpler time to live in our country.

Hunting and Fishing - A lot of our fathers would take their son's (probably not their daughters as much as would be the case in today's world) hunting and fishing. Personally, my dad would take me squirrel hunting and catfishing. Squirrel hunting and catfishing were basically the exact same thing except one used a gun and the other used a pole; you would walk seemingly forever until you found a spot which your dad deemed perfect, then you would just sit there for hours and hours being as silent as humanly possible. If you rustled the leaves, you would scare the squirrels, if you moved your gun too fast you would scare the squirrels, if you coughed, or sneezed, or whispered a question, you would scare the squirrels. If you saw a squirrel you aimed your 12-guage or 20-gauge shotgun, held it against your shoulder and pulled the trigger. There was always that moment of apprehension that you had right before you pulled that trigger because you knew that the shotgun was going to darn near rip your shoulder off. Then you had to scour the area where you thought the squirrel might have landed and sift through leaves and branches trying to find him. When you did find the squirrel, there was always that tentative moment of not being completely sure if he was dead or was just playing possum; I taught myself to poke his eye with a stick (this was the standard Death Test for all non-moving animals), we figured no animal could withstand a poke in the eye with a good sturdy stick. The prize for shooting a squirrel was his coveted tail of which we cut off and tied onto our bike's sissybar. On any given day you could see five or six neighborhood boys riding down the street with rodent tails streaming behind them in the wind.

Catfishing was a whole other animal; at least it was with my old man. After a two-mile walk through the woods carrying all of his fishing gear which included countless poles, tackle boxes, bait, a bag with sandwiches and pop, a couple Y-sticks (sticks dad had collected through the years that were perfectly shaped like a Y and you could rest your poles on, no decent fisherman would go searching for Y sticks at the fishing site, you had to take them with you), and his fishing chairs, we would finally get to the spot. We used chicken liver as bait, if you can imagine the grossest, stinkiest, slimiest, most putrid stuff to try to attach to a hook multiply that by ten and you had chicken liver. Remember, we brought sandwiches with us too, so you had to try to eat this sandwich with this amazingly stinky chicken liver smell on your hands and under your fingernails. You tried to put a huge chunk of this stuff on your hook but it had the molecular consistency of slightly stiff pudding and the longer you sat out in the sun, the soupier and stinkier it got. You then cast it out into the middle of the creek, many times you saw it fly off of the hook, but you had to just sit there and wait until your dad reeled in his pole because reeling in too much would scare the fish. So you sat there for maybe an hour and half staring at your line knowing full friggin' well that you didn't even have bait on the daggone hook. Then there was the backlash. Backlash was when you cast your pole and instead of the string going straight out, it rolled out of the side of the reel in what looked like a high-speed construction of a giant spider's web caught in a tornado. This is probably where I learned to connect multiple cusswords together into a sentence without a real noun or verb even included in the sentence. When that pole would backlash, the Old Man would let loose with a tirade of cuss words that froze every animal in the forest. I'm sitting here laughing now, but back then, it was one of the things that I least looked forward to; I know a couple times he just tossed the whole damn thing right into the creek. Then there was the actual catching of the fish; we weren't trying for little fish, so if we caught one it was usually a doozie. I will tell you right now, I was kind of scared of trying to grab a 40-pound catfish. Often the pole would bend in half and occasionally break right in half, just before it went flying into the creek; the Old Man made some pretty acrobat dives to catch his pole over the years. As the catfish pulled and dove and swayed back and forth through the water, my job was to reel the other poles in before they got tangled; more often than not dad would get pulled close to the muddy bank, often slipping into the water and me trying not laugh (like I am now), knowing that a soliloquy of cuss words was about to follow.

One time we took a big 20-pound catfish home with us and I put it into a washtub full of water, the water got all muddy from the dirty catfish, and my friends and I played a game of who could catch the catfish with their bare hands the fastest. I'm pretty sure that the game ended when the catfish barb punctured through the webbing of my hand.

I absolutely hated going fishing with my dad; I take my kids bluegill and bass fishing now so they can throw stuff into the water and laugh and be as loud as they want to and it doesn't affect the fishing one bit. But dad didn't think bass fisherman to be too manly. If the fish couldn't kill you it wasn't worth catching.

One of the sea creatures that occasionally jumped on our hooks even repulsed the Old Man. We'd go fishing at large, fast-moving rivers sometimes and you never really knew what might take your bait. The most disgusting, scary, slimy, evil-looking thing that could attach itself to your hook was without a doubt...a waterdog. A waterdog was also called a mudpuppy, hellbender, or devil dog. It was basically a giant salamander with these creepy little T-Rex arms and legs coming out of the sides of its body. Its mouth stretched twice the length of a normal mouth of any other species and they made these God-awful bellowing screeches like it was possessed or something. Dad would cut the line immediately if he saw that he had snagged one, but sometimes when we were night fishing and only had the light from a crummy lantern it was hard to tell what kind of sea beast you had on the line until you already had it on shore. A mudpuppy movie would be twice as scary as *Jaws*, that's all I can tell you.

✍ Of course there were times that we spent time with our mothers too, but most of them weren't exactly things that we were just dying to do. For example: Every couple weeks we had to go with our mothers to the Beauty Shop; I used to beg to be left alone at home and promised I wouldn't go anywhere or catch anything on fire while she was gone but I'd still get dragged off to this den of estrogen anyways. I can still smell the hairspray and perm solution, and I'm sitting here gagging, thinking about that smell stuck in the back of my throat. Occasionally there would be another boy your own age who had also been kidnapped and forced to go on one of these God-forsaken trips. I remember sitting there for about two hours looking at women's magazines trying to find some kind of article that at least semi-interested me and trying to not get caught glancing at the bra ads. Then there was always the question, "So how does my hair look?" Oh my goodness, I hated that question, I've hated that question from every woman who has ever asked it. "Ok, I guess", was my standard answer. It seemed to keep mom somewhat happy and me out of trouble.

Another great trip (sarcasm) with our mothers was the weekly visit to the Laundromat. The Laundromat was a little more kid-friendly because at least we had the freedom to get out of our seats and run around, even though we were quarantined for a couple hours within the cornucopia of washers and dryers. I remember being allowed to bring Hot Wheels and I'd roll them across the floor, occasionally rolling them over some stray ladies foot. There were tables to crawl under and vending machines to bug your mother about because you knew she had plenty of spare change. I used to be in charge of carrying a couple of the laundry baskets; I'm sure I was more of a nuisance than any real help. There were plenty of magazines to scan through and it's funny that I remember a Kid's Bible; sad to say that I probably learned most of my religion from glancing through those pages, plenty of colored pictures especially in the Noah's Ark section. The smell of the Laundromat was unique; bleach, fabric softener, detergent, and a dryer smell that could not be duplicated, it wasn't bad; it just reminded you where you were. The sounds were also unmistakable from the bill changing machine kicking out quarters, to the varying stages of the washing machine, filling up with water, chug, chug, chugging back and forth, then finally whirring around in the rinse cycle, then there were the dryers and their constant buzzing, and of course the rhythmical clanking of metal buttons hitting the dryer or the thud of someone's shoe that was put into the dryer. You would catch yourself watching the hypnotic dance of a pair of jeans and a white t-shirt as they were rolled to the top of the dryer and fell gracefully to the bottom and then began their dance once more.

I know that my mom didn't always have the luxury of going to the Laundromat; I can remember her down in the basement messing around with an old wringer washtub. Even after spending hours hand-washing the clothes and cranking them through the wringer, she still had to go out to the clothesline and hand up all of the clothes with wooden clothespins, the whole time hoping it didn't rain. (I guess I don't know what the heck we did in the winter as far as hanging up clothes.)

Anyways, mom would always come home from the Laundromat and spend a couple more hours ironing all of our clothes; I know that I have an iron in the house somewhere, although I'm not real positive where it is and I know for sure that I don't know how to properly use it. I don't know if fabrics have changed over the years and there is no need to iron clothes anymore or if I'm just a slob, but I do know that my mom and most of the other mothers of this time period took great pride in keeping our clothes clean and pressed and neatly folded.

I went with mom to the grocery store a good bit too. We didn't go to the grocery store and buy a week's worth of food, our family more or less bought stuff on a day-to-day basis. Of course everything was put into paper bags and they were famous for ripping out. One of the bonuses back in those days were the S & H Green Stamps (Sperry & Hutchinson) that were given out at some of the grocery stores and also at some of the gas stations. You earned Green Stamps according to the amount of groceries or gas that you purchased; once you collected enough stamps you could earn prizes (Icee cups had the same format as well). I suppose some of the top prizes were unbelievable, but very few people could ever collect that amount of stamps. I know I liked to glance through the S & H catalog, even though I probably wasn't getting anything. God love her, my mom could make more meals out of less money than anyone I've ever seen.

Chapter 4
High School

As we get older and think back to our childhood, we seem to spend a lot more time lost in our high school years than our other years of schooling. I don't know if it is because it is the most recent of our childhood memories, the most exciting of our childhood memories, or if it was just a special time in our lives when we started to become adults and started to mold ourselves into the people that we are today. Good memories or bad, those four years of our education were some of our last bastions of being children and proved to be some of our first steps into an adult world.

We would enter Cambridge High School as 14 and 15-year old pups, wet behind the ears, more or less scared of our own shadows but we would leave 48 months later ready to take on the world in our own ways, most of us full of fire and vinegar, ready to explore and accept the challenges of adulthood. Most of the childhood innocence that we possessed as we walked through those doors as freshmen were lost by the time that diploma hit our hands.

As old farts in our 40's and 50's we talk to kids about how fast those high school years went by. We try like the dickens to impart our wisdom, assuming that since we've been through it that certainly those young bucks will listen to us. Yet we didn't listen, we just shook our heads and smiled and probably didn't even believe that the person talking to us was ever young, was ever in high school, was ever in our shoes; how could this old fart be like me? He doesn't know what the heck he is talking about. But Daggone, fast doesn't accurately describe the blinding speed in which high school passes by. Blink. It's gone. Just plain gone and on to the next phase of your life, a phase that certainly has more responsibility, a phase that probably isn't near as much fun, certainly not as care-free, certainly not as innocent, certainly not as energetic and full of life and full of potential. Just plain, Blink! Smarter people than me have described it in the exact same way. Blink, then it's gone!

✎   I am 55-years old and still in school (I'm a teacher), trust me, I love my summers just like I did when we were kids. It is depressing when I buy a gallon of milk and the expiration date is after the opening day of school. Our signals that school was right around the corner was the County Fair (demolition derby was the final sendoff), cross country practices through the park, the band practicing at Pine Field, cheerleaders practicing out in front of the school, and football double sessions. We didn't need to look at the calendar to know that we'd be getting in the car to go school shopping once we began to notice those series of events.

Although we knew we would be leaving our top rung of the junior high evolutionary ladder, it didn't seem nearly as intimidating as our entry into junior high. We thought that we had a pretty good idea of the potential pitfalls and landmines that lay ahead of us because of our experiences of navigating through the relentless hell of our seventh grade year. I suppose that argument held water to a degree but there were still plenty of unknown, unexpected, and unforeseen obstacles that would be thrown at our feet.

First off was the overall size of the school and the size of the student body: The Junior High School was basically a three-story tall box which stood at the edge of the Downtown Business section. St. Benedict's Church and Elementary School stood thirty yards behind the Junior High, two more churches were on either side of the Junior High building, and Steubenville Avenue, a major thoroughfare ran in front of the school.

Now the High School was also a three-story building, but it was spread out over three or four times the area of the Junior High. It also had its own campus area: staff parking, student parking, football stadium, two practice football fields, a front courtyard, and Pine Field across the street which served as the bus garage and marching band practice field. The High School was located out near the City Park amidst some of the best properties Cambridge had to offer. The physical differences between the two were like going from a school in The Bronx to one in Beverly Hills.

Just the school itself was different, better I guess I should say. There was now light; the old, dark, dungeon-like Junior High held a permanent cloud over that building that would not allow sunlight to penetrate its windows. But the High School was open, and free, and promoted light and air to rush in and brighten nearly every room.

The High School hallways were gigantic; you could easily drive a car through them, (of which we may or may not have driven a four-wheeler through). You could also map out numerous ways to get to your classes that would either keep you away from specific people you didn't want to see or allow you access to specific people you did want to see. The whole thing was glorious; it reduced the amount of anxiety between classes by at least half. Teachers were visible and the chances of being abducted and beaten in broad daylight seemed far less probable.

Of course if you did the math; we were leaving a building that housed just two grades and were trading that in for a building that now housed four grades and nearly twice as many teachers. Well over 1000 students attended Cambridge High School while I was in school. Obviously there are much bigger high schools out there, but 1000 students still created plenty of logistical problems.

Could it be possible that the guys who were a grade above us were now meaner? I'm gonna guess that they had survived a year of being picked on as freshmen and now that they were sophomores (well at least in their second year of high school) they were now going to take it out on us again. But you know what, there were a heck of a lot of us freshmen that had vowed to stand up for ourselves this time and we were, "Mad as hell and we weren't going to take it anymore."

I remember walking in to the High School on that first day and looking for my name on the homeroom rosters. There we were, hundreds of us standing out in the main foyer rummaging around, half scared, half excited, and I was approached by one of the loud but not particularly dangerous sophomores who pushed me and told me to get out of his hallway. Bing, bang, boom. I had swung without even really thinking about it, it knocked his glasses to the floor and as he raised himself to one knee I will be darned if another freshman buddy of mine didn't punch him too. I wasn't looking for any help, but I liked the idea of camaraderie amongst the ranks. All he said to me was, "That shit ain't starting again like in junior high."

So here we were thinking that we had our potential enemies pretty well scouted out, and lo and behold we are hit with two more grades worth of testosterone fueled psychopaths. Lovely. The difference now was that these guys were like full-grown men. A lot of these guys I couldn't tell if they were students or staff members. They were 6'0", 6'2", maybe some even 6'6", and big strapping lads 180, 200, 250 pounds in some cases. They had full beards, long flowing hair, they had girls hanging on them, and more than once I saw them carrying girls over their shoulders and walk down the hallway with them like they were friggin' cavemen. The teachers seemed to be on a first name basis with them, more like co-workers than teacher to student relationships. I would only had given my dad a 50/50 chance against some of these beasts and he was considered one of the toughest guys in town; Holy Crap!

The good news was that 90% of the juniors and seniors were so wrapped up in their own world that they didn't even know we existed. The most they would say to us would be, "Get the hell out of here" or, "Damn freshmen, looks like a bunch of little kids."

That was fine with me; it was a big part of my plan from the beginning of the year to stay off of their radar.

These guys were driving to school and always seemed to have a car full of heathens and misfits and hoodlums with them. They would fly into the parking lot and heaven forbid if there was snow because they spun out more doughnuts than Kennedy's Bakery. I stayed completely away from the parking lot. All I could ever picture was me getting kidnapped and dragged into one of these crime spree vehicles, getting knocked in the head, and tossed out of the window like a bag of unwanted kittens as the car was flying around a turn.

Across from the parking lot was *The Row*. It's hard to imagine that this was ever legal or ever even a good idea, and the concept of this today... well, all you can do is shake your head, but *The Row* was a six-feet by thirty-feet strip (row if you will) of grass where kids were allowed to smoke on school property. Yep, you heard that right, it was a place where kids could go out and smoke, right on school property. I will say that to my knowledge there were never any problems out at *The Row*, there were never any fights, or any fires, or any other craziness. They would stand out there, smoke a little bit, talk a little bit, then the bell would ring and they'd put out their cigarettes and walk into school. Every once in a while you'd see someone out there who was wearing a letter jacket, I don't think it got you kicked off the team, it wasn't like these guys were trying to hide it. Anyone in the school: coaches, teachers, kids, parents, whoever, could look out and see who was out there smoking. This was just one of those very unique to the time period sort of things that is hard to comprehend in today's world.

The Row was another locale that I avoided like The Plague. I can't think of one reason why I'd ever even wander near it. I think it was mandatory that you spent most of your time there if you were in the O.W.E. class (Occupational Work Experience); I wanna say that is where they took their class picture. That O.W.E. bunch was a pretty salty crew, probably pretty good with a wrench but not a bunch of guys you wanted to introduce to your sister.

Compared to the Junior High building, the High School had much fewer isolated areas that you had to pass by on a daily basis of which you could potentially get dragged into and get robbed, stabbed, punched, frogged, Dutch rubbed, Indian burned, spit on, or otherwise accosted. Don't get me wrong, if you were looking for a place to hide and do something criminal, the High School afforded numerous locales but you had to actively search for them; by and large you could walk from class to class without a lot of concern. Now this still wasn't some tropical paradise; I sure in the heck didn't go to the restroom very many times as a freshman, that seemed to be just asking for trouble, if I had to go I usually either pee'd in an alley or between some houses on the way to school or at lunchtime. Apparently we learned amazing bowel control during these days.

✍ There were some places in the school that were not freshman friendly whatsoever: Varsity locker rooms were off limits to most underclassmen, especially non-lettermen. The varsity athletes (and I'm talking males here) were awfully daggone territorial when it came to anything involving athletics; you could potentially get slapped in the back of the head just for looking into the locker room. The three trade shops: Wood Shop, Print Shop, and Metal Shop were run like a mafia cartel; unfortunately all freshman boys had to take these three classes so we could not avoid the criminal element that thrived in these areas. The teachers were at the top of the pecking order and gave orders to the seniors, many of whom had racked up half of their graduation credits in these trade shops. Woodshop was a pretty open area and our Wood Shop teacher didn't put up with a lot of crap so it was the safest of all of the shop classes, (other than the fact that I still couldn't run power machinery which meant I had to again offer my cleaning services to get my project built). I do remember a bunch of us idiotic freshmen boys gathering around during wood shop when we were done cleaning up and we played a game where someone would take ten really fast breaths (hyperventilating themselves), and blow out their tenth breath, and then a guy would grab them from behind and put them in a bear hug. Well, I can tell you the result is to pass out. I can further tell you that if the person squeezing you, just up and lets go, gravity takes over and you bounce your head a couple times on the floor. Yep, knot's still there.

Metal Shop was different in the fact that the machines were unlike the traditional woodworking tools that we were used to; we had to weld and use a metal lathe and there always seemed to be a lot of upperclassmen hanging around, usually making fun of our inabilities to operate most of the machinery. They had a way of intimidating us into cleaning up their messes and the Metal Shop teacher was always a little too busy to watch over us very closely. I do remember not being able to weld worth a darn; you had to lightly touch the arc thing to the metal which created a spark which was the only light that you used to see with and complete the weld, if you held it on too long (which turned out to be anything longer than a hundredth of a second) it stuck and the whole thing was ruined and you had no light to work with. I would have had an easier time learning Mandarin Chinese.

Print Shop was the coolest class, and potentially the most dangerous. Print Shop was a class in which you learned how to set print type, in other words, put tiny metal letters in a tray, backwards as I recall, then cover it with ink, then make newspapers or flyers or whatever (before ink jet printers obviously). There was a side room in which ink and cleaners were stored and you tried not to go in there for any reason; the seniors not only sniffed the cleaners and ink, but had enough alcohol hidden in the cabinets to stock a medium-sized wedding reception.

There were times also in which you didn't particularly want to get caught in the gym. There was a lot of unsupervised times, mainly during lunch and in the mornings and the gym was where a lot of us hung out. The gym had a folding partitioned wall, if the wall was open, things were usually pretty safe, and if things happened to get crazy you could sprint out of six or seven different doors to safety, but if the wall was closed you never really knew what was happening on the other side of the wall. A little five-foot high door allowed entry to the other side. Now here is a plan that sounds good now; if the partitioned wall is closed, DON"T GO IN ! But for some reason we weren't smart enough to figure that one out.

In the mornings, if you got to school early the gym was open to shoot around and play basketball. The games were pretty intense and often ended up in some sort of scuffle or at least a few cuss words exchanged and a ball thrown at someone's head. It must've been marvelous for all of the girls to have to sit next to us underclassmen guys who were sweating like pigs for the first two periods of the day. Oh well, we liked to play basketball, what can I say.

Anyways, the morning was pretty safe but lunchtime was a different story. There were days that we had intramurals and those were conducted at lunch. Intramurals were organized sports competitions between homerooms and we took those things pretty seriously. You might have intramural ping pong, or basketball, or speedball, or who knows what. The problem was that if the wall was closed, we didn't know if our team was playing on the other side or not, so we'd open the door and check it out. 90% of the time there was never a problem, it was always the same athletic-type kids (not all good, but they at least enjoyed athletics) banging around for 45 minutes or so, but 10% of the time there would upperclassmen, usually sophomores who would be on the other side of that wall. I don't know why they were there, maybe they ran out of beer money, or smoked all of their dope in the morning, or didn't have gas money to drive around during lunch and get high, or maybe they just decided that it was time to be jerks and dole out some punishment, but for whatever reason once we opened that tiny little partition door, there they were. We were bigger now, we were stronger now, we were more organized now, we were more resilient to their threats and bullcrap, and one-on-one few of them worried us very much, but a dozen or so of these cretin warmongers grouped together and that was going to be too much for us to handle.

A few of us walked through that little five-foot tall door, (I remember it had an odd door handle and you had to duck down to get in), and we were dragged in through the portal like we had been sucked into some sort of demented black hole. We gave a brief struggle to get back out through the door but it was blocked, the only other exit was the back stairway and it was a long way away and blocked as well. We weren't the only freshmen stuck in here, a few of our other buddies were dancing around the half gym trying to avoid getting pummeled by an assortment of dodgeballs from close range, coming in at an various angles. It was pretty easy to figure out that this wasn't part of intramurals and that there wasn't a teacher around for miles, because trust me if Mr. Cox the P.E. teacher would've been around, these turkeys wouldn't have been. The best you could do was to hide your face and man areas and turn your back and withstand the dodgeball (pumped up volleyballs) as best you could. I took very good notes as to who all of these dodgeball assailants were and vowed my revenge one way or another; luckily for me I wasn't a particularly main target but that didn't make me any less angry. Then out of the clear blue sky, the grizzly ole beast that dragged us into this sarcophagus to begin with apparently determined that we had suffered enough and bid his cronies to stop the massacre. They must've thought he was kidding as they continued their assault, now this guy wasn't the main gun, or the leader, or maybe not even the most notorious, but he certainly had inner brute strength and asserted that on his own brethren. As much as I wanted to stick around and watch this guy light into his own degenerates, it seemed much wiser to sneak through the door and head out into the hallway towards safety.

✍️   In today's world of constant monitoring by numerous staff members and also video cameras scattered throughout the school, this kind of assault could never take place, but in the 60's and 70's we were on kind of an honor system. There was not a lot of teacher supervision in those days; the teacher's took their lunch breaks pretty seriously back then. They had their own little hiding places to get away: there were two teacher's lounges, the smoker's lounge and the non-smoker's lounge. If you really needed to get a specific teacher during lunchtime you had to know if they smoked or not. I can remember walking into those teacher's lounges three or four times and the smoker's lounge was like being in the thickest fog you've ever imagined, you seriously had a heck of a time just seeing across the room. The smoke was so thick you just had to yell into the room and call out for whomever you were searching for. The teachers were always mad as a hornet when a kid popped their head into either of the teacher's lounges and always screamed at you to, "Get Out!"

There was also the coach's office where only the coaches could go. Often the projector would be up and running football or basketball film and it didn't take long to hear the coaches cussing about missed blocks or bad officiating. Players would be brought down to ice their ankles or sometimes to watch films with the coaches. I don't think it was too much of an issue for certain players to miss class if they were called down by the coaches.

Another hangout was the boiler room, Dude, the boiler room! The boiler room was an exclusive club made up of coaches, ex-coaches, or just cool teachers who lived by their own code and own set of rules. When I was a senior I was allowed entry into the boiler room, at least long enough to pop in and get one of the teachers if I needed him. This room was completely off limits to any and all underclassmen, but we always heard stories about what went on down there and they ended up being pretty accurate. Smoking in the boiler room was almost a pre-requisite, drinking a little premium hooch in the boiler room seemed to be pretty acceptable too. The smell of coffee, not the rich smell of some high-class Starbucks coffee mind you, but the coffee smell like from an all-night card party enveloped the place. Dirty jokes and premium cusswords were shared by all including the janitor who seemed to be an integral part of this club. I was honored to be able to hang out in the doorway and listen to these guys for two or three-minute sessions when I was a senior. Who could have guessed that ten years later I'd be on the other end, sitting in the boiler room at another school, telling stories with the janitor and other coaches during my lunch period; isolated from and indifferent to anything else going on in the school. The bell would ring and we'd put our teacher faces back on, but it was (is) always nice to get away for that thirty minutes of carefree paradise.

✍ Going back to our lunch system, it was unique and probably couldn't be done the same way in today's society. We had a very long open lunch, now when I say long, I'm talking about something close to an hour, which for high school lunches is a long time, and when I say open, I'm saying that we could leave the school and go anywhere we wanted to, and basically do about whatever we wanted to do as long as we were back by the end of lunch. It was really quite different than anything we'd ever experienced before where we were corralled into specific confined areas; basically we were told where to sit, what to eat, and what to do when we were done. No more. You had the option of a regular lunch inside the school if you chose to, but you didn't have to eat a specific lunch, we had an ala carte system that allowed us to pick and choose items. Sweet! We had never had that opportunity before, so we were going to take full advantage of it; I don't think we ever ate a vegetable at school our entire high school careers. They also had another ala carte line that was strictly junk food: chocolate pies, pecan pies, potato chips, Moon Pies, Fritos, chocolate milk, orange drinks. When I did eat at school, I only ate from the junk ala carte line. There was also another junk food ala carte opportunity out in the hallway too which was run by the Varsity C Club; basically they opened the basketball concession stand and sold pop and candy. Amazingly, we were in far better shape then, than today's kids who have Government Nutritional lunches rammed down their throats are today. Exercise. Exercise. Exercise. That's the difference. We were constantly on the move.

I will admit to about a two-week span one year when we thought it would be cool to challenge each other to eating dares. I know that I ate over 20 Milk Bone dog biscuits on dares at what I thought was a bargain rate of one dollar each. We ate raw eggs and would stuff whole hamburgers or whole packs of Twinkies in our mouth at one time. I know some guys talked about eating live goldfish but I never witnessed that, but I did see a couple guys eat bugs and another ate a live nightcrawler.

Mostly, unless it was raining or snowing out we ate our lunches away from the school. We had to walk, it wasn't like we could drive as freshmen so our choices were pretty slim; we had the IGA grocery store which was about a half mile from the school and we had Hall's Drive-In which was a little bit further and you also had to go up Brenton Hill which was a third of a mile long and was as steep as any hill you've ever seen in San Francisco or the Alps for that matter. We would gather up eight or nine of us and head out for our lunch; in reality the meal was inconsequential, half of the time we either wouldn't have money, wouldn't have enough money, or were saving our lunch money so we could afford to go to the dance that weekend or a lot of the guys were saving up for beer money for that weekend. IGA had a really good deli and the fried chicken was really good and the noodles were delicious. Most of the time when we came out of the store, someone would pull something out of their pocket and brag about the booty of candy, or pop, or doughnuts that they kiped. Even the kids that I knew who had plenty of money to pay for whatever they wanted, partook in the thievery. I honestly didn't steal much from the stores like some of our buddies, I don't know if it was a moral thing or if I just wasn't very good at it but I know a couple guys who could walk out of any store and have $50 worth of stuff jammed in their pockets, underwear, socks, you name it.

Hall's Drive-In was an ice cream shop, they sold other food as well but we only ever got the ice cream. We would walk a mile and a half total for an ice cream cone. On one of our treks back from Hall's Drive-In, we spotted one of our less than brilliant classmates. We came up with a plan as he approached; we snatched him up and dragged him off between a couple houses and there we cut a clothesline (I just happened to have my switchblade with me that my dad got for me and I was walking around school with it and no one seemed to think that was a problem) and we hogtied this student. We casually left him tied up and went back to school like it was something that we did every day. With about 20 minutes left in school, a list of names were announced over the intercom to report to the office, those names sounded pretty familiar and we all gulped as we walked into the office at the same time. There he stood, our little hogtied friend, who was stuttering, and spitting, and stammering, and pointing at all of us as we entered the office. He stood there drenched to the bone; it had started raining pretty hard after we got back to school. "That's them, that's them fu_ _ ers that twied to dwown me."

Jesus, I couldn't stop laughing then any more than I can stop laughing now. All of us were looking at the floor trying not to laugh and having no success at restraining our amusement at this poor, wretched, near drown soul who was trying to pinpoint his attackers in an overly animated, less than perfect pronunciation. However, the principal was furious and didn't seem to catch the situation nearly as funny as we did. We only got the board, in today's world we might have gotten kidnapping, hate crime, and attempted murder. Good gosh, it sounds absolutely horrible now, but back then it was just a funny little prank that was barely a blip on the school radar. There was a lot worse stuff going on.

Another good one we pulled at lunchtime was the time we picked up one of our gang's car and put it on the sidewalk. He owned a 1977 Honda Civic which wasn't a whole lot bigger than today's Smartcar. I think four of us picked up the car and put it up on the sidewalk; it was perfectly wedged between a big oak tree and some guy's cement retaining wall. There was no way to get into the car to move it; it was the perfect prank.

We all have some memorable, surreal experiences in our lives and I can tell you that one of the most memorable experiences that many of us witnessed during high school happened during one of our lunch breaks. Remember, I said that we freshmen had somewhat vowed that we had gone through enough harassment during junior high and we weren't going to take much more, (even though in reality a few of us went through a bunch more torment and torture for most of that first year of high school), well one of the greatest culminations of enough is enough occurred during the Spring of '76. One of our great freshmen warriors was scheduled to battle one of the sophomore's best warriors; neither were known as the scariest, or the best, or the toughest, but certainly no one was volunteering to mess with these guys either. Even fewer volunteered to mess with these guys after their epic battle. It seemed like most of the school headed down to Pine Field: the school's practice band field which was located about half of a block down and across the street from the High School; you could not see Pine Field from the school. For anyone who has ever seen one of the Clint Eastwood movies, *Every Which Way But Loose* or *Any Which Way You Can*; those movies may have been based on this fight. Our freshman champion was a Golden Gloves boxer who learned his craft from fighting at The Ohio State Fair and other venues across the state and he started off like he had never left the ring, he jabbed, and bobbed, and weaved, and peppered the other combatant's face over, and over, and over again. Blood streamed down his opponents face and I guess we thought that we were earning a victory for freshmen and other impoverished souls all over the world. But the sophomore's soldier of fortune wasn't chosen because he was a wimp and back he came, taking the battle to the ground and beat on the boxer for a lot longer than any of us thought possible. Unlike the 30 or 40 fights I'd seen before, this one just kept on going, and going, and going. A normal two-minute fight went 10, then 20, then 30 minutes. Then the whooping and hollering and cheering for the fighters turned into a near riot situation with guys getting chased around and others getting sucker punched. An all-out testosterone fueled Helter Skelter situation was occurring and me and a couple of my more ingenious buddies had safe, front row seats: laying underneath the school buses watching guys getting pummeled; we crawled deeper under the bus as the hoodlums came closer to us. I will admit that it wasn't our most heroic moment, but hey, these guys were jacked up on violence and when we heard our names being kicked around as potential victims, we figured that it may be a better idea to deal with these guys one at a time rather than all 35 of them at once.

The two fighters stood there, just exactly like in the movies and traded punches. Each punch seemed to take 15 or 20 seconds for them to gather up enough energy to swing one more haymaker. We lay under those buses waiting for one of them to stop, or give up, or drop to the ground knocked out. But after 45 minutes it didn't happen; their clothes where ripped to shreds, their faces were bloody swollen messes, and they ended by shaking hands and walking up to the school together, leaning on each other to have the strength to make it up the hill. We had heard the bell ring for sixth period several minutes earlier, but what the heck were they going to do, give 100 people detentions? We walked back to the school at our own pace and took our chances with the punishment; but who cared? We had just witnessed the most exciting battle since Ali-Frazier. Over 40 years later we still talk about it like it just happened yesterday.

✍ Of course the teachers had to eat lunch too and one of our teachers, a young, innocent lady without much teaching experience could not for whatever reason make it back to her Math class on time after lunch. This gave her class two or three extra minutes to casually sit around and talk, no big deal, right? Except that one of our classmates chose to use those two or three extra minutes to hide the teacher's egg timer. I suppose most Math teachers at that time used an egg timer to give us timed little quizzes or worksheets. You would spin the timer to the desired amount of time and then it would ding when it got to that time. This student hid that timer every single day of the school year, not just a couple times, not once or twice a week; I think he hid this thing every single day of the school year. So where can you hide an egg timer you ask? Well use your imagination and try to come up with as many different places as you can and then double that because this guy was inventive and fearless and there was no place he wouldn't try to hide this stupid thing: Under the teacher's desk, in the teacher's locker, in the teacher's desk drawers, under the teacher's stack of homework papers, under the teacher's chair, under student's chairs, in the back of the room behind a stack of books, in the ceiling tiles, outside on the window ledge, in the trash can, oh heck I can't cover all of the hiding places.

So we would all watch him hide it, she would walk in and we would all just kind of giggle (the kind of giggle you give when you know something that someone else doesn't know), and then she would start her lesson, but the whole time we would sit there in anticipation of this stupid egg timer alarm going off, we didn't know when it was going to go off, we didn't know how long it was going to be before she noticed it going off, we just knew that class was going to be interrupted and we were all going to start laughing. It got to where we didn't pay any attention at all to what she was saying; I'm going to say that is why I'm not exactly exceptional in Math, and neither is this guy. We all just sat there looking at each other, giggling like idiots, trying to guess when this stupid timer was going to go off. It was absolutely ridiculous.

Now you would think that this teacher would hide the timer before she went to lunch, well she tried, but this guy would root through her drawers until he found it. You might think that she would just ignore the timer going off, and she tried, but then we would say stuff like, "I think I hear an alarm, is that the fire alarm, should we leave?"

There were times when she would laugh, there were times when she would almost start crying, there were times when maybe the principal or another teacher would be knocking on the door and you knew she had to be hoping beyond hope that this daggone egg timer didn't go off.

No one ever told on this guy, we actually looked forward to it, we loved the guy's bravado; there were times when he would just get the thing hidden as she was walking in the door and he'd make a dive back to his seat. He'd also have the nerve to complain every time the timer went off, "Miss Such and Such, I really can't concentrate with that timer thing going off, you're gonna have to do something about that thing."

At that point we'd all absolutely lose it and then start chiming in ourselves, "Yeah, why do you set that timer every day and put it in weird places?"

Of course that wasn't the only teacher or only class where kids played pranks; let's go through a few of them: We didn't take a lot of field trips, and maybe it was because of stuff like this; we loaded up a bus full of ornery teenagers and headed to a beautiful arboretum. Looking back, I'm not even really sure why, I think the teacher was a History teacher; maybe she just wanted us to have a little beauty in our life or it was nice to get out in the spring and relieve our winter doldrums. Anyways, after our little excursion through Nature was winding down a few kids decided to splinter away from the main group and well... basically hide out in the woods. When we got back on the bus, the teacher counted and alas three or four boys were missing, so a few of us volunteered to go out and try to find them (knowing all along exactly where they were), so we went out and wandered around, found our buddies and sent them back to the bus while we stayed hidden. "Oh, I'm so glad that those boys found you."

"Boys? What boys? We were lost and just now found the bus. We didn't see anyone else. Do you want us to go out and see if we can find them?"

Well, the teacher didn't really have the option of going out looking for them herself and leave 30 kids on the bus by themselves. So she picked two of the boys that had just returned and sent them out to try and find the original search party.

We met up again, and ran the scam again. We came jogging back to the bus, panting and frustrated, "Mrs. Smith, we looked everywhere but couldn't find them, we're sorry."

"Well boys, they came back but we had to send some others out to look for you." She said.

So after another 15 minutes of waiting, even the bus driver knew what was going on and started laying on the horn. The teacher didn't send any more search parties and it was obvious that we had ruined any chances of getting the bus back to the school on time. And even though this revolving scam could have played out for several more hours, we ended it with an Academy Award performance in our efforts to find our lost companions. I don't think there were any more trips to the arboretum.

✍ Remember, this is the 60's and 70's that we are talking about, and the movies and magazines and books that you have seen concerning drug use during this time is completely accurate. If you didn't smoke dope, you definitely knew someone who did. It was probably harder to avoid being around drugs than it was to be knee deep in the whole drug culture. It wasn't like the whole student body was addicted to heroin or something but marijuana was heavily used and very easy to find. For the most part, once you were labeled as a non-user, you were pretty much left alone; but don't go walking into a party and expect to not see a group of kids passing around a joint.

There were a few kids in almost every class that were stoners, dopers, dopeheads, herbalists, druggies, or whatever you want to call them and these young misguided youths would often be excused from class under the veil of needing to go to the restroom but they would use the facilities to get high instead. You could smell the overwhelming herbal stench as soon as they cruised back into class. Everyone in class knew what they were doing and either the teacher's didn't care or were told not to worry about it, but they had to have known.

One time one of our most accomplished criminal duos asked to go to the restroom, the teacher thought she was being prudent by telling them that only one of them could go and when he came back, the other could then go. These fellas took their "restroom breaks" and turned them into 15-minute long departures from class. They calmly walked out to their car and tried to see how much beer they could drink; by their accounts they drank nearly a case. The first guy came back in and had the whole class looking at him, we knew he had been up to something, then he just laid his head down and went to sleep (nothing unusual there). When the second guy came back, this stirred the first guy and he wanted to go back to the "restroom", but the teacher balked, telling him he'd been gone too long the first time. He almost begged to leave, and just as the teacher was going to say No, what seemed like a gallon of Pabst Blue Ribbon came spewing out onto the floor. The smell was like the final hours of any Saturday night V.F.W., or frat party kegger gone wrong.

Another drinking situation happened during study hall. I was sitting next to a guy in study hall who was bragging about how much beer he and his crew had consumed before school that morning. The longer this whispering conversation went, the more he mentioned that he wasn't feeling very good. Then without any more discussion or even asking to go to the restroom, he grabbed the hooded sweatshirt of the girl sitting in front of him and puked an un-Godly amount of beer-smelling intestinal garbage into the hoody. Everyone within twenty feet started their own gag reflex, I was only two or three feet away and got some of this stuff on my shoes, and I cannot even imagine the disgust and anxiety this poor girl must've felt; something like that just doesn't go away without a few psychiatric sessions.

Once on the way to school we kicked up a mouse and somehow managed to kill it, probably bashing at it with a stick or something. I thought it might come in handy at some point in the day, so I shoved it in my pocket. Now ordinarily, I wouldn't have gotten within twenty feet of a mouse (dead or alive), but on this particular day I was rodent fearless (at least dead rodent fearless, I had used the patented stick to the eye test). I'm sure it wasn't the first or last time I had something disgusting in my pocket, but here I was, a high school student walking around most of the day with a dead mouse in my pocket. I've gotta believe that I pulled that mouse out several times throughout the day to show my buddies or to gross out some of the girls, then I patiently waited for the exact right moment, which surfaced toward the end of the day. One of our more experienced lady teachers had to step out into the hallway for a few seconds so I made my move; as I walked around the teacher's desk I could hear the other students in the class guffawing and holding back their laughter. I reached down and grabbed her gradebook and put the mouse inside it and made my way quickly back to my seat. The poor innocent teacher opened the gradebook, took an extremely deep breathe, and very calmly said, "Tab, could you go to the office and tell them what you did. And please take the mouse with you."

I don't think she had seen what I had done, but I wasn't going to fight it. I politely got up, grabbed the mouse, and headed to the office. "Sorry Mrs. Smith", is all I said.

I actually thought she handled it extremely well, probably better than I would today as a teacher. It seemed like the Principal must've thought it was pretty funny also, he hardly even gave me half a swat.

✍ There were punishments other than the board: being thrown out of class and made to sit in the hallway, detentions, if you were an athlete you were probably going to have your crime reported to your coach which meant extra running or push-ups or something, but one of my favorites was writing. Yes, I said that correctly, one of my favorite punishments; I actually liked writing out my punishment. *I will not talk in study hall, I will bring my book to class, I will not throw things in class, I will not hit Billy,* (insert your own crime here). One of my study hall teachers loved the way I wrote out my penance; I could write *I will not talk in study hall* 200 times on a quarter sheet of paper. He would sit there and actually count the sentences even though I had numbered them for him. You could tell he was amazed at my micro-writing ability, he would giggle and I think I made his day; at the end of the year he actually asked me if I would write him a few hundred sentences without having even committed a crime. I didn't mind, I liked to do it. I wanted to see how small I could write. Funny stuff now but I probably could've used that time more wisely. As a teacher myself, I've gotten mad at kids in study hall and made them write all of the A words in the dictionary, which certainly deterred their rambunctiousness.

✍ We did have actual classes and to my account I think we had some pretty good teachers. We had a typing classes of which was totally dominated by the girls, but we boys got pretty good by the end of it. It was probably the loudest class that we had, if you've ever been to a casino it had that same sound to it, kind of a constant erratic clicking and pecking with occasional dings thrown in. We used real typewriters and there was no backspace key or save key to bail you out of trouble, you did it right or it counted against you.

We had all of our regular classes like English, History (I remember talking about how the cowboys would jump on a steer and the teacher got up on his desk and took down a student he told to walk by, HILARIOUS), the Sciences (I remember grabbing the business ends of a hand-cranked generator and electrocuting ourselves in class) and then we had classes like Art and Home ec. (which all of us boys took as seniors as a goof and most of us spent half of the period either trying to eat as much food as possible or hit on the teacher to try and bump up our grade).

Study hall; what an oxymoron. The amount of actual studying that went on in a study hall, then or now, is shamefully low. I don't know if schools just don't have enough classes to fill an eight period day or if they think that kids need an extra 45 minutes included in their day to just unwind, but for the most part study halls aren't used in the fashion that they were designed. High school study halls weren't as wild and rebellious as their junior high cousins. High school students seemed to revel more in sleeping rather than throwing notes or spitballs around. Some of my finest midday siestas took place in study hall, albeit you didn't want to be so sound asleep that you didn't hear the bell and kids either left you or gave you some arousing slap to the back of the head on their way out of the room.

Girls seemed to get their work done in the first few minutes of study hall and then worked on writing their boyfriend's name in some sort of creative, flowery artwork. I suppose that girls that went through a lot of boyfriends also went through a lot of tablets of paper. I do remember a few girls who would put their head down and take a quick nap and I recall one that awoke to find her hair in braids (at least as good as I could – three sections, over, then under, then over, then under, yep I still remember).

Most boys didn't even bother to make the slightest attempt at finishing homework, again though we really didn't have a lot of it. For those of us who didn't or couldn't sleep you could always draw. We would draw pictures of muscled-up superheroes, or a drawing of a football helmet, or professional baseball logo, or some Rock Band album cover, or a sword, or a souped-up car, or maybe just the engine. I think most of us worked on drawing our name in block letters, trying to get the shading just right; maybe seeing what it would look like carved into Mount Rushmore.

We also had the option to go to the library during study hall. You would go to the library and put your name on the sign-in sheet, and once it hit a certain number (30 or 40 I suppose), those who didn't make it had to return to study hall. There was always some time in there that would be unaccounted for, you had to make sure that all 15-20 kids that didn't make the library roster would return to study hall at the exact same time. So basically you only had as much time to get back to study hall as the most uptight person. Mostly you made a long, serpentine walk from the library to study hall which bought you eight or nine-minutes. The library itself was not much fun, a lot of shushes, and I don't think you were allowed to sleep in there, so I didn't make a habit out of going to the library. Yeah, I suppose there were books in there, but I don't recall reading any of them. (There is no doubt by now, that you are thinking that I am a complete and utter moron; although I surely was anti-education as a high school student I can assure you that I am fairly well-read and am quite capable in any number of subject areas. This apathy was probably the case for several of us during these years; education wasn't something that was particularly stressed to us in our homes).

Sometimes teachers or coaches or janitors would come into study hall looking for helpers. Most of the time we didn't know what the job was, but we would quickly volunteer to get the heck out of the confines of study hall prison. We were like prison trustees, the more good work you did, the more freedom and responsibility you earned; but if you screwed off or created more work than you were worth you were sent back to study hall, never to be paroled again. One of the jobs that got you a Get-Out-of-Study-Hall ticket was to go down and work on the wrestling room. The wrestling room was built off of the weight room and was built by using study hall slave labor, not much different than the slaves that build the Great Pyramids. Kids were sent in to start digging a tunnel through a wall, there couldn't have been one proper building code rule that we followed. We dug with shovels, and spades, and seemingly spoons stolen from the prison mess hall. I don't know where we took the dirt; maybe we hid it in our pockets and dumped it out in the exercise yard. Your clothes got filthy, you got filthy, and it was great, you got out of study hall, you walked around filthy, you had a chance to miss a few minutes of your next class and not get in trouble for it, and you were working side-by-side with teachers and coaches who were almost treating you like an equal. (I feel like I'm re-writing *The Shawshank Redemption*). The wrestling room ended up being about 5'8" high, which worked out well for wrestlers who had to spend most of their time in a hunched over, stalking position.

This sort of building project was the way things operated back then, there wasn't a big discussion about things, and you didn't have 75 meetings, and discussion groups, before something got done. You just did it. A coach probably said, "You know I need a new wrestling room."

And the A.D. or Principal probably said, "Well, why don't you just get some kids from study hall to help you with it and we'll come in on the weekends and lay the block." The visiting bleachers at one of the schools I coached at was built by boys from shop class, and even though it was later discovered that it used no footers it still managed to last 50 years.

There wasn't a concern over building codes, or child labor, or how many exit lights or sprinklers had to be installed; and you know what? We all lived through it, we may have skinned up our fingers, or gotten our clothes dirty, but we felt pretty good about being a part of something. In today's world 38 lawsuits and a petition to remove the guy as coach would have been submitted to the school board, not to mention the half million dollar cost to build the facility instead of the 800 bucks that was probably spent back then.

We did stuff like that all of the time. Our junior year in track, the coach told us all to bring shovels to track practice, so we did. Our track was covered with two-feet of snow; his plan was to have us shovel the snow so we could practice sooner. All 40 of us started straight down the width of the track but after 25 minutes we had probably only managed to remove maybe ten-yards of snow, so he switched his plan to just removing the snow from the first two lanes (about eight feet wide). Well after three hours we had managed to get about half way around the track. We didn't exactly accomplish our intended goal but we each got a three-hour workout, we had a visual reminder of our achievement, and we had spent quality time learning how to work together. And yes we did get on the track a little bit earlier than if we hadn't shoveled. How is any of this bad? Why is it so bad to do manual labor? Amazingly we pay hundreds and even thousands of dollars for gym memberships and personal trainers but we look down our noses at the idea of shoveling snow (snow blower) or raking leaves (leaf blower) or mowing the lawn (riding mower), and that's if we don't hire someone to do it for us. We live in a lazy, lazy, lazy society!

Our track coach did a great job of taking kids who weren't the greatest athletes, didn't come from the best families, and just plain weren't given much attention and he showered them with caring. He cared about them and because of the attention he gave, he received the absolute very best that these kids had to offer. Track practices were tough, so tough that we had a special club for those of us who worked hard enough, the Atomic Rangers club; if you threw up in practice you became an Atomic Ranger, (funny now, not so much then). As a track coach now, it is amazing to look back at what we were able to accomplish because our equipment was completely inferior to today. We ran on cinders (no all-weather track), we used 5/8 inch spikes that could do some serious damage (today's shoes are so superior), we landed on triangular metal crossbars (as compared to today's rounded plastic ones), our nutrition was non-existent, at times we were told not to drink water because the coaches wanted to toughen us up (not in track, but certainly in football during these years); we were indeed Old School when it came to our sports. Concussions, bloody nose, knocked out for a second or two, suck it up and get back in there. Rub some dirt on it, you'll be fine.

✍   Girls' sports were just starting out. Many sports were GAA, or Girls Athletic Association and were not actually sanctioned by most state athletic associations. Finding quality coaches was difficult because most coaches wanted to coach the boys' teams and many didn't even want to be associated with girls' teams. There wasn't a great deal of incentive for girls to play sports during the 60's and 70's. Attendance at girl's contests was basically parents only, while attendance for any boy's contest was often standing room only. I am certainly glad that things have gotten better for girls' sports, not perfect, but certainly way better than they were 40 years ago.

✍   In the morning before class, students would gather together in their respective cliques and even though the hallways were really wide and you could easily avoid most unwanted confrontations; there were certain places that you probably should stay away from. There was a hallway for athletes, there were make-out corners (always kind of awkward), there was a dopehead hallway, and there was a senior hallway. On Football Fridays, the cheerleaders would take over the main hallway to sell a little spirit ribbon with a safety pin that would have some sort of slogan on it, *Kick the Colts*, or *Stomp the Blue Devils*, or whatever team we were playing that night. The ribbons cost a dime and you would pin them onto your shirt, some kids would pin 10 or 15 of these things all over themselves. I personally didn't care one iota about those stupid ribbons, but as you will recall I said the cheerleaders were the ones selling them. The intoxicating smell of a varsity cheerleader to a 15-year old boy was as energizing and magnetic as a bucket of chum to a Great White. I often had to borrow the dime, but it was worth it because I had come up with the perfect plan, "Could you help me with this? I can never get it to stay pinned to my shirt."

Dude, that was the perfect scam, I didn't just hand over a dime and get some stupid ribbon dropped in my hand, I now got the personal touch of a real-life, living, breathing, super-popular cheerleader, WOMAN pinning this goofy ribbon onto my chest which could take upwards of 15 seconds, and always ended with me thanking them and them feeling like they had helped some poor, unfortunate, mentally-handicapped kid followed by them smiling and telling me, "No problem, thanks for buying one."

Wave, smile, deep breath, take off this stupid ribbon once I get around the corner, repeat next week.

✍ During basketball season our basketball team wore team blazers. It certainly marked you as a varsity basketball player. When I first started coaching varsity basketball I would make my boys wear ties; the staff and parents would rave about how nice we looked but our kids were fidgeting around in these stupid ties all day long so I switched over to khakis and embroidered long sleeved t-shirts, our winning percentage went up, (but I may have just had better players at that time, either way, no sense messing with a winning thing).

Athletics were a big deal in the 60's and 70's, many a great athlete played during this time period. Most of us had played youth sports when we were younger but everyone didn't make the team once you got to high school. There were tryouts and cuts and a lot of kids that were pretty daggone good athletes weren't able to make the squad sometimes. I always say that because everyone in town played sports nearly every day when they grew up, that most of the gym classes of this era were as competitive as many of the varsity contests of today. Earning a varsity letter and wearing that letter jacket made you part of a very elite club and the athletes took that honor very seriously. Our student body took games very seriously as well, all of our contests were well represented with loud boisterous fans that cheered their team and at times harassed the visiting teams. There was a very small group of the student population that didn't attend the home games; it was just what you did on a Friday night.

The clothing of our time period had its own unique flavor. Some of us tried to keep up with the trends and some of us just wore whatever we had laying around. Unless I was going to a dance or the first day of school or something, it didn't make much sense to wear some of this stuff: bellbottom pants (can't tell you how many times I got those things caught in my bike chain or tripped on them playing basketball), Earth shoes, clogs, and platform shoes (our mothers were just glad to get us out of our tennis shoes every once in a awhile), tube socks and multi-colored socks with toes (those things made me claustrophobic), Paisley and patterned silk shirts (usually unbuttoned at least half-way down, we thought we were sexy), everyone had big thick belts with gigantic belt buckles that looked like they could've been WWF tag-team champion buckles, (the belts were so thick that they honestly wouldn't fit through the belt loops on today's pants), tie-dye and peace sign shirts (according to every tv show that I watch trying to depict the 70's, you'd think that everyone wore tie-dye shirts with peace sign patches all over them, but that wasn't really the case). I've got a picture of me wearing an orange t-shirt (which was our rival's school color, so I don't know why I had that on) and a pair of white painter's pants, so apparently that was cool at one point also.

I assume because of *Saturday Night Fever*, but a lot of us had leisure suits; actually girls wore polyester leisure suits as well. We must've bought them three sizes too long because of the platform shoes we wore with them. There were a lot of hot pants and crop tops and halter tops, I guess the girls were trying to keep up with us sexy guys with our bare chests and puka shell necklaces (we all know that girls could wear a burlap potato sack and be sexy). You may as well throw a mood ring in there too, the ring turned color supposedly according to your mood, but in reality heat is what caused the change. As I glance through a yearbook it is impossible to not notice the amount of flannel patterned shirts; boy, girls, teachers, everyone was wearing those things but didn't see a single tie-dye, peace sign, or smiley face shirt.

If you had earned a letter jacket, you wore it, regardless of the weather, regardless of the occasion; you wore that letter jacket until it fell apart or you graduated, one or the other. Same with your class ring; it was a huge day when your Josten's class ring was delivered and you basically never took it off unless you were spinning it on your desk or you were offering it to a girl (which meant you were "going together" when she wore it on a string around her neck).

Maybe the true defining fashion statement of the 60's and 70's wasn't our clothes, it was our hair. From behind, you couldn't tell the difference between the boys and the girls. If you were a guy you were going for long, feathered, Barry Gibb-looking hair. There were also a few guys that made the regrettable decision to get a perm, (yep, it looked as bad as you can imagine). A lot of the black guys wore big, blown-out afros; sometimes they would leave their pick in their hair, (which I know a lot of us white guys thought was cool as hell). If you were a girl you had three choices:

A) Long and feathered which looked exactly like the guys (except we called it Farrah Fawcett hair),

B) long and curled under, or

C) the Dorothy Hamill haircut (1976 Olympic Ice Skating Champion). Which was also Toni Tenille of Captain and Tenille's exact haircut as well.

We boys went from our moms giving us a bowl cut on the back porch to us making hair appointments at Reflections. I'm sure every town had a place that *styled* hair back in those days. Me and most of the guys I knew didn't have much styling, we just let our hair grow and combed it out of our faces the best we could. But I can certainly recall a few trips to Reflections where I got my hair cut by a pretty girl, who smelled really good, and rubbed up awfully close to me while she worked those scissors. I honestly wasn't overly concerned about how my hair looked when she got done.

✍ The senior hallway was a pretty cool place when you were a senior, not so much so if you weren't. You kind of waited patiently for those first three years to whiz by, if for no other reason than to have that Senior Hallway. Nothing really went on in that hallway that was overly amazing, as a matter-of-fact by the time you were a senior you were kind of too old to do some of the immature things that underclassmen did; (NOTE: I am not at all saying that I or most of my friends didn't do these immature things, but seniors in general didn't). In the mornings we would rodeo some of our younger classmates (leapfrogging, squeezing their head with our legs, and pulling them to the ground). We would also play human pinball with freshman that might wander through; you can imagine what human pinballing looked like, us pushing freshmen back and forth, bouncing them unwillingly down the hallway. I'm sure we dished out some non-threatening noogies, wedgies, Dutch rubs, Indian burns, and wet willies; but we did these lovingly, we weren't really trying to hurt or intimidate anyone like our predecessors. I think that for a large chunk of my senior year we sang Kenny Rogers' *The Gambler* as we stood in that hallway looking at all of the underclass girls walking by.

Being in education and coaching for as long as I have, it is usually easy for me to spot a freshman; not just their diminutive size and lack of muscle tone, but just the way they carry themselves in an awkward, unsure manner, usually trying like the dickens not to make waves or stand out for any reason. We certainly weren't any different. Low key was safe. Being a wallflower was safe. Letting others have the spotlight was safe. That first year in high school was certainly eye-opening; the upperclassmen served as role-models (one way or the other) as to what maybe we secretly aspired to become. Jocks had their followers, druggies had their followers, academicians had their followers, bandsies had their followers; I guess we could look at these older kids and see what we could potentially evolve into.

✍ Our class of students ran the gamut of possible career paths a person could take as we got older, but as freshmen we were just trying to survive and hang on long enough to become sophomores. Our dreams were mapped out in very wet cement and were fluid enough to change as easily as the wind. Having fun and being with our friends and making plans for the weekend were as far as most of us planned anything at that point. It would all change over the next few years and suddenly learning would become important, and colleges were really on the horizon, and moving out and making a living on our own was something that was actually going to happen. But it was kind of relaxing to just be clueless for a while, we didn't know it at the time, but we were as blissfully ignorant as we would ever be during that freshman year of high school.

As we got older our confidence grew, we certainly wouldn't have brazenly stood out in public singing to whoever passed by as freshmen and sophomores, if anything we would hide in the shadows and pray that we didn't get noticed. Our outgoing nature continued toward the opposite sex as well, although we kind of knew that getting together with girls in our own class was often next to impossible (at least for some of us), we finally weren't afraid to talk to them, and as seniors we had a seemingly endless supply of younger girls that were somewhat infatuated with us, or at least infatuated with the idea of being with a senior. And that seemed to work.

Every so often our confidence, arrogance, ignorance, bravado, or whatever you want to call it, got us in a pickle. New, young female teachers were just as much fair-game as the rest of the girls in the school; I remember printing up some very professional-looking Elevator Passes in print shop and selling them to unsuspecting freshmen and also to my new English teacher. I do recall refunding her money, but the other 15-20 scam victims were out of luck. By the way, we had no elevator in our school.

I was so full of myself, I thought that because I kidded around with this same English teacher that I was exempt from doing work until she pulled me aside and told me that if I didn't complete a book report I was probably going to fail the class. Since I had never taken the Evelyn Wood Speed Reading course; I had to use my street smarts. I got a B on the report that I turned in: *Hollywood Nights*, the romantic tale of a country boy who fell in love with a city girl and looked out over the lights of Los Angeles in the Hollywood Hills. Author, Bob Seger, who was also the singer of this hit song of 1978. I actually told her at the end of the semester that the report I wrote was based on a song and not a book, she laughed, shook her head, and told me that she thought the story seemed very familiar. I certainly wasn't the only one who used trickeration to get through a class or two, I'm sure that I had heard about stuff like this from older guys.

One of my most notorious bouts of bravado occurred toward the end of my junior year. Our school year was coming towards a close and we always had a big, formal election of class officers with the highest of which being Senior Class President. There was an assembly that allowed the winners to give a speech to the general public; basically it was a way to show off what we had learned in Government Class and promote the Democratic principles of our country. What a great concept, except when you are a snot-nosed, smartaleck kid being encouraged by a bunch of other rabble-rousers to throw a monkey wrench into the whole political system. We spent about a week sneaking down to print shop during lunch making gigantic posters promoting my running for Student Body President. I hadn't formally registered for the office and I didn't qualify for the office even under the most liberal of candidacy rules, but there were posters, big ones, all over the school promoting my running for office:

VOTE FOR TABLIDO NOVUS MUHAMMAD AS STUDENT BODY PRESIDENT YOUR WRITE-IN VOTE CANDIDATE.

Now my name isn't Tablido Novus Muhammad, but I still get an occasional Lido or Tablido when I see people from over 35 years ago. I flew under the radar because I didn't use my real name and I think that the teachers even thought it was funny; they knew it was me, but I wasn't hurting anything. Election Day came and there was to be an assembly after lunch to crown the victor, but instead of an assembly all we got was a call over the intercom saying that the assembly would be postponed until tomorrow. A knock came at the door of the class I was in and an office worker told the teacher to send me to the office. I wasn't real smart back then, but I was pretty good at adding and I knew that all of this added up to trouble for me.

"Tab, or should I say Tablido? Take a seat. First off, I'm not mad, but you and your buddies have really screwed this whole election up."

I knew better than to say anything and denying that Tablido was me would've only made the situation worse.

"Let me tell you about the voting. It appears that you won. Now I don't know if that's because you had so many write-in votes or because your buddies who were counting the votes were throwing away the votes for the other candidates. It really doesn't matter; you know that you can't be voted in because you not only don't have two years of student council, in fact you have no years of student council experience. Did you even know that we have a student council?"

"Not really sir." I admitted.

"I didn't think so. Anyways, you and your buddies really worked hard and I will commend you on what you were able to achieve, but..."

I knew that this BUT was not going to lead to anything good. I had already mentally prepared myself for three or four swats.

"I'm going to have to suspend you."

Holy crap! I sure in the heck wasn't ready for that. Suspended from school! Wow, I'm gonna say that the Old

Man wasn't gonna take that real well. The look on my face must've really shown through because the principal's next words softened the blow.

"I know your dad a little bit and I don't think this would go over real well at your house so here's what I'm willing to do. If you can keep this between us, I'm going to suspend you for the rest of today and all of tomorrow. I don't care where you go; just don't show up here, you've done enough damage for a while. I'm not going to call your house or send any suspension paperwork home. Get a basketball from Mr. Cox and go down to the park or something, just don't show up here tomorrow, ok?"

"Yes sir" and "Thank you" were the only things I could manage to whisper on my way out the door.

Chapter 5

Summers, Weekends, and Those Glorious Snowdays

Although we roamed all over town, we still had our general base camps in or own neighborhoods. There was still plenty to do right out in our own backyards. We were extremely fortunate in our particular neighborhood in the fact that we had 15-20 kids within a couple years of each other and The Children's Home was right across the street, so that could easily double our numbers. The Children's Home kids were somewhat restricted at times as to how far they could go and how long they could be gone, so we went to them and spent a lot of time at The Children's Home playing basketball, football, whiffleball, and we also went inside and played a lot of bumper pool and ate a lot of Freezee Pops.

I'm sure looking back now, that the kids that lived at the Children's Home were there because of some kind of unfortunate family situation, but honestly none of that stuff was ever brought up. We really never brought any of that stuff up with one another. Sure, we knew that there was a lot of yelling and screaming coming out of this kid's house or that kid's house, and we knew that when we saw certain kids' parent's cars driving towards us that things probably weren't going to end real well, but we didn't sit around talking about it. We didn't cry out for help. We didn't beg for therapy. I think we all figured that most of this stuff was happening to us as well, so we just sucked it up and moved on. We didn't exactly run home and have long conversations with our parents about the things that we did, or discuss the people we hung out with and their family structure. I really don't remember any conversations of any kind with my parents other than to answer specific questions that were sent my way, which actually wasn't very often. Most of us, (at least the people that I knew) weren't particularly close to our parents. Maybe that's why I've bent over backwards to be close to my kids; it would kill me to not be a major part of their lives.

In the 60's and 70's kids played outside, they were in their backyards, or on the sidewalk, or out playing in the middle of the street, but very seldom was a kid inside unless they were grounded, (and the whole grounding thing was rare; punishment was usually a swift kick to the rear or yelled at for half-an-hour, and then it was done). Usually the girls played with other girls and the boys played with the other boys, but there were always two or three times a week when all of us would meld together and do something. It didn't mean that we were boyfriend and girlfriend, we were just neighbors, we passed each other 20 times a day, and a lot of times we needed another person for a game so we asked them to join. We all got together sometimes and had dances in one of our basements or in our living rooms or in our driveways. I remember learning *The Bump* at one of these impromptu living room dances. I can proudly say that I was voted Best Dancer in my class and I'll bet that some of that knowledge came from stuff I learned in Bobby's living room.

One of our all-time favorite neighborhood activities was Kick-the-Can; everyone my age knows what I'm talking about here. We would get a can (remember, cans were solid back in those days and could take a pretty good beating) and a group of kids around dusk, 10-20 would do, and we would nominate some poor soul to be IT. In any game where there is an IT, you should probably try to avoid being the IT. In all of my years of playing Kick-the-Can I was only IT twice; the first time I almost started crying because after an hour I couldn't get anyone out and the second time I got mad and just went home without telling anyone. I would make up any excuse to not be IT. Anyways, the IT would close their eyes and count to 100 while everybody else would try to hide; you hid behind garbage cans, and behind cars, and between houses, and under cars, and behind trees, and in the bushes, basically anywhere that you could safely not be seen. It was coolest to hide real close to the can and watch everything that was going on. The IT would start to stray away from the can to search for the hiders, if they saw someone they would run back to the can, put their foot on top of the can and say, "1, 2, 3 on

Marvin behind the car." At that point Marvin would have to come in and sit and wait for someone to kick the can, which would release him to go hide again. If the IT went too far to look for hiders, someone would sneak in and kick the can. It was basically impossible to catch everyone. Often the game would be ended because the IT was being screamed for by their mom or dad. It wasn't anything unusual to hear parents standing on their porches screaming their kid's names at the top of their lungs. If you weren't home by the second or third scream, your mom or dad jumped in the car and went looking for you, which was never good. "Tab!", "Bobby!", "Kathy!" Wow, I can still hear those names being hollered out. Other kids had street light curfews, which meant when that street light came on, you better be hoofing it to get home. I remember me and another fella throwing rocks at a streetlight one afternoon in the hopes of knocking it out and giving us an excuse to come home a few minutes later that night. I also remember rewinding my watch (that I was given specifically to ensure I made it home on time) back an hour, and then showing it to my dad to prove the point that I was home exactly when he told me to be. It didn't work! I knew friggin' well it wouldn't but my buddies thought the idea was flawless.

We also played a game called Chase. It was pretty straight forward; one team chased another team until everyone was caught. Being fat and slow in our neighborhood would've been detrimental to every game that we played. Wow, the chase. We could fly back then, sprinting through the backyards, jumping over fences without any hesitation, scaling eight-foot walls, hurdling toys and dogs and fire hydrants, we were too fast for own good sometimes. More than once we were hit by cars (usually we just bounced right up and kept playing, no doubt scaring the living dog crap out of the drivers), clotheslined by literal clotheslines, or swallowed up by unforeseen groundhog holes. But that sound of the wind rushing past my ears was the sound of freedom and certainly one of the things I miss the most.

✍ I also remember our passion to jump over things; it's a wonder that we didn't have kids go on to the Olympics in high jumping, long jumping, and hurdling. Here are some of things we jumped, or at least attempted to jump (sometimes we didn't make it):

Creeks and streams – even if you made it across, sometimes the bank would be slippery and you'd fall back into the water. Always good for a laugh from your buddies.

Retaining walls – because of the hilly region I lived in, about half of the houses in town had some sort of retaining wall that kept the yard from shifting out into the street, they ranged from one to four feet. We could take one step and pop up onto the highest wall in town, but it took a few hundred botched attempts before you could actually master it.

Bushes and fences – many neighborhood backyards were divided by a string of bushes or a fence; in the middle of sprinting from a dog or other assailant we learned that it was easier to just jump over whatever was in front of us than to see it as a boundary. Sometimes however we didn't know what was on the other side of the fence or bush which might be a pile of bricks or a giant hole or maybe another dog waiting for us. I think that's why we spent a lot of time walking around town doing reconnaissance.

Sidewalks – we liked to measure our jumps by the number of sidewalk sections we could travel. Unlike real long jump where you land in the sand, the sidewalk was pretty unforgiving. There were also a lot of sidewalks back in the day that weren't in very good shape so we would try to jump over those bad spots or better yet, ramp our bikes off of them. (I know that one of those bad sidewalk bike ramping escapades ended with me wrecking and giving myself a blackeye the day before second grade pictures.)

Cars – yep, I wrote the word cars. We got pretty cocky when we got to be in high school and through a series of dares we figured out that a couple of us could actually jump over the hood of some little cars like an MG Midget, or possibly a Pinto or Vega. I will admit to getting so carried away with myself that I tried to jump over an MG lengthwise; I really thought I could do it and I'm still not so sure that I couldn't have done it on a track with some spikes, but I did not make it, I cleared the hood and even got up over the windshield but hit my tailbone on the trunk. I understand that humans no longer have tails (or maybe never have according to whatever belief you have), but we sure in the hell have tailbones; wow that hurt for weeks.

I will say that the one thing you didn't want to try to jump over, no matter for what reason, were fire hydrants; if there was something harder than a fire hydrant I don't know what it would've been. You were instantly and semi-permanently taken out of commission when you hit a fire hydrant. I recall (VIVIDLY), standing on top of a fire hydrant, both feet slipped out at the same time and... Holy Christmas Trees, I came straight down on the giant bolt thingy sticking up from the top. It was one of the very few times that my buddies actually came to my aid and didn't laugh at me getting hurt; amazingly I was able to reproduce after that accident. I went out of my way to not even walk near a fire hydrant after that for weeks and if anyone outside of our group ever started to climb on a fire hydrant in our presence we would basically all in unison, "DUDE! Get down off of that, just trust us."

✎ We also had community kickball games and whiffleball games. There was never a big fight over picking girls last or trying to not pick them. For the most part the girls of our era were pretty good at stuff and always gave a good effort. However, nearly every game ended when one of the boys hurt one of the girls. It was inevitable that we were gonna hurt someone, we played like every game was a tryout with the Yankees (actually we liked the Reds and Pirates). The girls would swear up and down that they would never play anything with us again, but they would forget in a couple days and we'd be back at it again soon enough.

✎ We spent a lot of time at the public pool when we were growing up. It wasn't anything to spend 60 days a summer at the pool. Cambridge's Municipal Pool, we just called it The Big Pool, was bought and paid for with government works money from the 1930's. It was built to survive a nuclear blast with its three-foot thick concrete walls. It had a sun deck, a high dive, a low dive, and a full-sized 20-foot playground sliding board in the middle of it. I don't recall how much it cost to swim there but it couldn't have cost too much because me and all of my riff-raff, no money between us friends went there almost every day. The pool would always open on Memorial Day and close on Labor Day. Now if you think about it, it's pretty darn cold around Memorial Day, so we would walk in, wait until it was rest period, climb on top of the lifeguard chairs and jump in. The lifeguards would come running out, blowing their whistles, yelling at us to get out of the pool, and we would take our time, often floating on our backs as we spit water into air, then we would climb out with an ovation from the other swimmers. The manager would kick us out for two weeks, which seemed just about perfect as far as the pool water heating up. I know we did that for at least three years in a row.

The high dive was always kind of hinky, it made your knees wobble a little bit being up there. You basically were just going to do a crashdive and get out. A crashdive was a dive where you jumped into the water somewhat horizontally, arched your back, and kicked your legs down as soon as you hit the water. The result was a big splash and the raising of your head out of the water almost immediately. We had it down to a science where we could probably crashdive into two-feet of water from a ten-foot platform and not hit the bottom.

But the low diving board was our real home. I've been swimming at a lot of places but I've never seen as many guys that could do acrobatic maneuvers off of a diving board like we could at Cambridge. Front flips, one and a halves, doubles, back flips, fronts with twists, gainers, spiders, and double turn arounds. Yes we smacked the water and got hurt a lot, but that's the only way we could learn how to master a dive. We were crazy competitive and if Eddie could do a double then I could do a double, and if Eddie could jump off the board and land in the five-foot section of the pool about thirty feet away so could I, (well I couldn't, none of us could except Eddie, but we all sure tried). We were allowed unlimited bounces on the board and some of the guys were absolutely fearless and would take five or six bounces, taking them eight or nine feet above the board before they finally decided they were going to go toward the water. One bounce was fine with me; I tried two bounces once, went too far forwards and scraped my back down the front of the board. That felt exactly as bad as it sounds, but it happened to all of us. Even the kids that didn't look like they could swim were doing one and halves; heck our heavy weight wrestler could out dive just about anyone from some other town.

The big slide was only put there to tease us. We wanted to jump off of that thing so badly but we were always watched very closely and threatened with a lifetime ejection if we jumped off of the top. You were also jumping from a height of twenty feet into about four feet of water so you'd better be able to do a really good crashdive. It didn't stop us though, eventually we all jumped off of the top of that slide but I think the event that got the slide taken out was when one of the older hellions, and this will be hard to explain the full athleticism involved here, slid down the slide standing up, like The Silver Surfer comic book hero and finished it off with a flip at the end of the ride. All eight lifeguards blew their whistles at the same time and we knew that we not only had seen history but that we probably would no longer see the big slide again; but that maneuver was really, really impressive.

The Big Pool wasn't all rainbows and unicorns; until you were about a junior in high school it was a little scary walking through the locker room area. There was a 100% chance of being rousted for money and if you told them you didn't have any and they saw you later with a Chick-O-Stick you were going to get frogged until you thought you were going to need your arm amputated. There were also the dunks and near-death drownings. It wasn't anything for some of the older guys to hold you under water for 30 or 40 seconds. I don't know what the heck the lifeguards were doing while we were being dunked over and over, gasping for anything resembling air when we fought our way to the top, but I'm sure there were more than a couple times when I could've used a little help. After taking in a pint or two of highly chlorinated pool water you were coughing that crap up for the next three or four hours. And I can vividly remember a couple fights up on the sundeck when guys were trying to weasel in on some other guy's girlfriend. The girls were brave; they cared so much about an even tan that they would untie their bikini tops and lay on their stomachs. The natural thing for us boys to do was to toss cold water on them and wait for the girls to jump up and hopefully forget their untied top. We were so stupid!

You could always count on a super tan by the end of the summer but that was after you survived at least one second degree sunburn that wiped out your shoulders, and chest, and nose. I'd like to have a dollar for every time my "buddies" slapped me on the back when I had a sunburn, "How's that sunburn coming?"

I know that they sold Coppertone suntan lotion in the stores back then (remember the ad with the dog pulling the bikini bottom down and exposing a great tan), but I can guarantee you that we never used any and we would stay at the pool for hours at a time. The best part of sunburns was trying to peel as big of a piece of skin off as you could once you started peeling. The worst part was trying to find a comfortable way to get to sleep or put that daggone flannel baseball uniform on over your sunburn. I think Noxzema was supposed to help, but I'm not sure it did much.

We also had another pool, which we called the Kiddie Pool. The Kiddie Pool was for little kids and truthfully we had no business being there. The water was probably only two-feet deep on one side and maybe three-feet deep on the other side with a bridge that went over the two halves of the pool. It was aesthetically pleasing to look at, not only for its architectural design but because of the lifeguards that worked there. The best looking girls in Cambridge worked at this pool and no day was complete until we patrolled past the Kiddie Pool to watch the lifeguards. Now mind you, we had absolutely zero chance of ever, ever, ever getting with these girls and I think we knew that; but I still like going to the zoo even though I know I can't pet the tigers. We would waste twenty minutes there, possibly wave to one of the girls on the way out and then start walking to the Big Pool, planning all of the things we were going to try that day.

✍   Of course we always spent a lot of time playing sports. As high schoolers we knew where all of the good games were being played and we didn't mind walking across town to be included in them. If it was basketball you wanted to go to The Courts, if it was baseball you went out to the Big Diamond or one of the Little League diamonds, if it was football you knew you wanted to go out to Pine Field on Sundays.

Pine Field Sunday football games were epic, legendary games which might draw up to 40 competitors. The hits were hard and many a player left with broken bones or was sent to the hospital to go get stitches, (I will admit to both of those). It wouldn't be prudent to wear your favorite shirt, chances were it was going to be torn off of your body, and you better wear the right shoes because if it was muddy and you didn't have cleats on you were screwed. There were guys you wanted on your team because they could help you win and there were guys you wanted on your team because you didn't want them to hit you. There were always a lot of long bomb passes and triple reverses. If you were fast that helped, if you were really fast, well that really helped.

I do recall one of our games in which one of our really fast guys wore the wrong shoes and kept slipping. Just when it looked like he was going to take off from the pack, he'd slip and fall and slam the ball into the ground and start cussing. On one of his plays he slipped, another player hit him under the chin, and he bit through his bottom lip. We decided we should go to the hospital once he started putting his tongue through the hole in his lip.

Another football-type game that we played that I'm sure wouldn't pass today's world of Political Correctness was Smear-the-Queer. I am positive that none of us gave that name a second thought, it didn't even register with us that it may have been inappropriate. I'm sure that we had homosexuals during the 60's and 70's, and we had no problem teasing each other with those types of slurs, but I'm not sure we actually knew anyone back then that was openly gay.

This was a very rugged game with limited rules and had no real winners or losers or even ways to keep score. Simply put, if you had the ball, you ran like hell, if you didn't have the ball, you tracked down and tackled the guy with the ball. If you've ever heard the term "Dog Pile", I'm sure it originated from playing Smear-the-Queer. Once you got tackled, there was a tremendous chance that everyone involved in the game was going to jump on top of you in one gigantic (and potentially rib-breaking lack of oxygen) stack of humanity. Once tackled the ball would squirt out and someone else would scoop it up and the process would start all over again. Honestly, I may have been one of the fastest, shiftiest, and most agile athletes in our group but that didn't particularly mean that I wanted to pick up that ball.

We didn't have a lot of equipment to play baseball with but we still liked to play. We would scrounge around the weeds and underbrush by the ball diamonds until we found a foul ball that someone else couldn't find. I know one time at practice, I ran across the street to hunt down foul balls from batting practice and stuffed a couple under a tree root and covered it with leaves, so we could have a ball later that day. Since we couldn't afford a baseball we certainly couldn't afford an aluminum bat, (the idea of spending $350 for today's baseball bats sickens me to my core, I'm positive our rent back then was under $200 per month and at least half of the time it was a week or so late). Aluminum bats were new at this stage and would ding up and dent very quickly, so we learned our craft with wooden bats most of the time. There was nothing better than the crack of the ball being shot off of that wooden bat. Unfortunately the wooden bats would do exactly that, crack. We would tape up bats and use nails to hold the bats together, and glue, and whatever else we thought would salvage what was obviously a broken and useless bat to 99% of the world. We grabbed our bat, grabbed our ball, grabbed our gloves and walked a couple miles out to the Little League diamonds. We split up the teams and the first pitch came in, I drilled it, knocked it a country mile and the bat split in half. We retrieved the ball, retrieved the broken pieces of the bat, and walked home. Total time of the game was, I don't know, two-seconds, maybe three. There was no reason to get upset about it; we probably had fun walking out to the park and even more fun walking back home talking about all of the different ways we were going to try to fix the bat.

We played a game called Indian Ball when we didn't have enough kids to play a full game of baseball. A batter would smack a ball into the outfield and the fielders would scramble to be the first one to run down the ball. After the ball was retrieved, the batter would lay the bat down in the grass and the fielder would throw the ball and try to make the ball roll up and hit the bat. If you could do that, you would become the next batter. It took an incredibly accurate and often lucky throw to hit the bat from 150-200 feet away through various lengths of grass, clumps of dirt, and ever-changing bat angles.

Although we'd sometimes go out to the city baseball diamonds and play homerun derby or actual games, most of the time we played baseball-type games in our backyards or in the local empty lots that we all used as our own personal playgrounds. We could just play catch for hours (it's not called "passing the ball", which I hear from kids today, that would be when you throw a football back and forth), if we had a third player we'd often start up a game of "rundown" or "pickle" to work on our base running and defensive skills. But I'd say that most of our fielding skills and throwing abilities came from taking a ball and throwing it repeatedly against a wall or set of cement steps. Although we tried many types of balls, the Super Pinky became the Cadillac of off-the-wall baseballs. I know I had a wall that I threw at almost every day for a half-an-hour or so, it had one discolored cement block that I would try to hit over and over and over. We also had a game in which we would make the ball hit the ground right in front of the wall and make the ball pop up into the air, the other player would have to catch it before it hit the ground. Short hits were singles and deep hits were homeruns. It was just a made up game, but you could find boys all over town playing it.

Whiffleball wasn't exactly baseball, but it was close enough for us. These weren't the whiffleball games that you might see today; we used doctored up balls and personally enhanced bats. The bats, which started out as normal plastic whiffleball bats were stuffed tightly with wet newspapers until they turned into concrete sleeves of destruction covered with a thin layer of plastic. Neighborhood whiffleball teams of five or six boys would invade into other neighborhoods and we'd battle it out. You were quickly given the home field special rules and then the game was on. Those home field rules might include: right of the telephone pole was a foul ball, no homeruns in left field because the German Shepherd would eat the ball, third base is the cherry tree, second base was always a pizza box or a hula hoop or someone's glove, if you hit the electric wires it was an automatic do-over, the game is done if we break one of Mr. Gray's garage windows. Big curveballs with three-feet breaks and fluttery hanging knuckleballs were the preferred pitches. Very few of us batted to improve our batting average, keeping track of our homeruns was the only stat that any of us ever cared about.

The Courts was one of the ultimate basketball courts in Ohio. It drew players from around the State to play in these basketball wars. If you didn't have some real game, don't come to The Courts, this was not the place to learn or practice, it was a place to showcase your well-honed talents. There were always plenty of All-State players, former All-State players, and guys that didn't even go out for basketball who would have easily been All-League players. You had to be able to make shots, you had to be able to handle the ball, you had to be able to not turn the ball over, and you had to be able to stand up for yourself both physically and mentally. You called your own fouls, so if you were timid and wouldn't open your mouth to call your foul, you were prey; these guys would knock you down, take the ball from you, and go score. If you barely touched them they would call a foul if you didn't stand up to them. If they saw you as a punk, you had no chance. Playing at The Courts developed many a fine basketball player in Cambridge.

If we didn't have enough players for a full court game, or if we had too many people and just plain didn't want to play a regular game, we played a game called Chicago. I've heard it called different things over the years: 21, cutthroat, barn ball (which was actually another game where I'm from). The rules of Chicago were fairly simple, if you had the ball in your hands you tried to score any way that you could, if you didn't have the ball in your hands you tried to stop the guy with the ball any way that you could. There were no fouls so the games got really rough. Grabbing the ball and shooting quickly was a way better idea than dribbling around too long because three or four guys would just attack you and take the ball from you. If you were fortunate enough to make a shot, you got to shoot unguarded free shots from the foul line, in Cambridge you got unlimited shots until you missed although I will admit to seeing that number capped off at three if someone was too good of a foul shooter, and there were certainly guys out there who could string together 19 foul shots in a row and win a game without anyone else even getting a shot. Now an unguarded foul shot didn't exactly mean that it was an un-interrupted foul shot; there was always a lot of coughing and yells right when you were releasing the ball and an amazing amount of boys had gas attacks right when you were ready to shoot. No doubt that Chicago is the number one reason why I can still drill foul shots one right after another today.

On one of those games of Chicago another player swatted at the ball in my hands and I turned away so he couldn't get the ball, instead he got his finger perfectly to the side of my eye and then behind my eye and pulled it slightly out of its socket. Needless to say I was in pain and stressed out beyond belief. It must've been serious because the game ended and me and my buddies walked home with me holding my eye in with my palm. After they figured out that I probably wasn't going to die, (maybe only be blind in one eye) they started asking me, "Dude, can you like hold your eye in your hand and see around the corner? That would be awesome."

At The Courts there was a spigot with a handle on it that drew up water. Sometimes you would just soak your whole head to try to cool down, but the unwritten rule was to hurry up and get your drink because if you left the water running too long it made a mud puddle. If you got real hot you could always climb the fence and jump into the Kiddie Pool or even dive into the Duck Pond. Sometimes the ball would roll down the hill into the Duck Pond and if you were the youngest guy at The Courts you knew that they were going to tell you to go in and get it. If you didn't have a ball you could always just walk across the street to Dan's house, walk in and grab a ball from the front closet. That's just what you did. Dan's mom would be sitting there watching tv and she'd say "Hi", and go back to watching her show while you were rummaging around in her living room closet. No one ever thought about taking anything other than the ball. Life was simpler and safer back then. We had the ability to interact with people and work out our beefs. We actually talked to each other and talked to strangers without fear. We didn't hide behind computer screens and cell phones and communicate with each other through electronic notes and pictures sent through space. I'll be honest, I'm glad there weren't instant records of the things we did; half of us would have ended up in jail over the crazy things that we did.

One of my worst memories of The Courts happened one summer night in 1978. The year was easy to remember because it was the summer of *Saturday Night Fever*. There was a Park Dance which was about 200 feet from The Courts, I was walking up to the Park Dance decked out in my new *Saturday Night Fever* suit, (oh yeah, I had one). One of my buddies was still at The Courts shooting around, I said, "Hey, give me the ball. Let me dunk one."

He tossed me the ball and I jogged up, planted to rise, and then my three-inch heeled, *Saturday Night Fever*, hard as a rock shoes slipped out from under me and I cracked the back of my head on the cement. I don't recall much more than that. My buddies walked me up to the dance and I came home an hour later than my curfew, of which the Old Man was already out in the car looking for me. He threw me into the car and took me to the police station because he thought I was drunk, (no real difference in someone who is bombed on alcohol or has a Grade Three concussion). My buddies heard about it and went to the police station to tell them what really happened. I did learn that I shouldn't try to dunk a basketball with platform shoes on. I probably should have been arrested for being an idiot, but not for anything else.

✍ ___YMCA.___ - The YMCA in Cambridge was a very busy, bustling place that always gave us plenty of activity options. There were certain times of the year in which we all but literally lived there; probably staying there for eight or nine hours a day, and then there were months in the summer when we wouldn't even walk within three blocks of the Y.

When school was cancelled for inclement weather, Christmas Break, or during weekends during the winter is when we got our true money's worth out of our YMCA memberships. Now all of us didn't have money for Y memberships so some of us had to get pretty creative on ways to get in. The Y director had a good heart and devised ways for us to pay off our memberships through some sort of menial labor. I know one time he gave me one just to shut me up, if I promised not to get into any more trouble when I was there, (I may or may not have gotten into a couple fights and also may or may not have "allegedly" cracked a kid's head open when I tried to throw him over my head King Kong Bundy-style into the pool and his head hit the side of the pool.) I know that at least once, me and a couple of my street urchin buddies agreed to be in a boxing tournament run by the Y, in exchange for a free membership. Apparently, it was worth getting our brains beat out in public for the usage of the YMCA's sporting facilities; yeah that sounds about right.

The Cambridge YMCA was awesome; it was an old mansion that had a gymnasium and swimming pool attached to it. The old Y mansion had a hang out area with a pool table, ping pong table, tv area, vending machines, an old piano, and an upstairs ballroom that we used for Y dances until our attendance numbers grew so large that dances had to be moved into the gym.

Most of us learned a few simple ditty's on the piano during those long afternoons we spent hanging around the Y on those cold blustery winter days. Ping pong ball rental was a dime and often that was too pricey; the chance of returning a ping pong ball in refundable condition wasn't very good. And most of us were pretty good around a pool table, so there were many competitive games along with some awfully creative billiard shots. It wasn't uncommon for the cue ball to go flying into the ping pong room, or the ping pong balls to go flying into the billiards room.

The Y's basketball court filled up quickly on those cold winter Saturday afternoons. A court that was meant to house 15 or 20 hoopsters, quickly swelled to 40 or 50 energetic players of widely varying abilities. The side hoops were attached directly to the walls, so we learned how to run toward the wall as fast as we could, put our foot on the wall and catapult ourselves up high enough to get some pretty amazing dunks. The catch was, that the gym would get extremely hot with the overload of active bodies and someone would always open the side door and let the cold air in, the mixture of the two created some of the slipperiest sweaty walls you could ever imagine. You can probably guess how the rest of this story goes: teenage boy runs full speed into slippery wall, teenage boy lies on the ground bleeding, and then the other teenage boys stand over said bleeding friend laughing hysterically.

The Y had a pool and we had a swim team that was pretty good. I remember a couple of my buddies that were on that team and they talked me into coming to one of the practices; they knew that I basically lived at The Big Pool in the summer so joining the swim team seemed like an obvious progression. But alas, my swimming skills consisted of a modified dogpaddle from wherever I landed from my dive and back to the ladder so I could get back into line and dive again. I vividly remember swimming laps for 45 minutes, getting passed by kids ten-years younger than myself, so I asked my buddy when practice was going to be over and he responded by telling me that it hadn't started yet, all we were doing up to then was only a warm up. I dragged myself out of the pool and left with a much greater respect for the swim team.

That was one of my first experiences of "walking a mile in someone else's shoes". I guess I figured that getting to swim year-round would be awesome, but I didn't have the slightest clue as to the amount of work that group put in. We've all done that, especially when we were younger, discounted the work involved in certain activities. I know that I've had enough different jobs and coached enough different sports to give everyone the respect that they deserve; nothing is ever as easy as we think it's gonna be. There are trials and tribulations involved in everyone's lives. As young, dumb, naïve kids it's easy to poke fun at those who are different than us, but eventually we all learn that life is hard for everyone.

The Y also had its own gymnastics team, and when my daughter was five I enrolled her right away. They spent a lot of time working on very specific skills and some of our gymnasts went on to have some pretty impressive careers. A lot of times, some of the equipment would not be put away when the gym was scheduled for basketball so of course that gave us boys a free chance to try out some of the equipment. Honestly, we weren't that bad at most of it but it usually took all of two or three minutes before one of the directors would come flying into the gym and give us a good scolding for messing with the equipment. The same thing happens when I leave any equipment out in my gym classes, I guess life has come full-circle.

✍ We played a lot of games right out in the middle of the street. We'd throw a baseball around or play tag football right in the middle of Gomber Avenue. When one of us saw a car coming we'd yell, "Car", and everyone knew to slide off to the side and let the car go past. The cars that were parked on the street got hit by various balls, skateboards, bicycles, motorbikes, and teenagers. Until you've knocked your knee into a '65 Impala bumper as you were trying to make a one-handed over-your-shoulder catch you've never really felt pain before. Every once in a while the owners of the cars would come out and yell at us, but usually only if the car was brand new (which didn't happen much in our neighborhood). There was a guy down the street that had a Shelby Cobra and I know we didn't know much about cars back then, but we had sense enough to stay away from that beauty when it wasn't in the garage (which wasn't very often).

Sometimes we'd get so involved in the game that we didn't even notice cars coming down the road and occasionally they sat there waiting for us to clear out, giving us the horn and yelling at us to, "Get the hell out of the street you little bastards." I'm sure that we politely got out of the street, apologized, and gave a friendly wave to them as they left.

Many street games were halted when a ball went astray and ended up down in the storm sewer. Every so many feet there were storm sewer drains along the side of the road. If a ball went under a car, well that was an easy fix for someone to crawl under the car and get the ball or Frisbee, but the storm sewer was a completely different animal. There were a few guys who lived for the chance to go down through the narrow little slot and retrieve whatever went down there, but like I said, it was a pretty tight fit. You could always lift the manhole up and go in that way, but we were always worried about a car coming along right then and sinking a tire down that hole (it's a wonder we didn't take the manhole covers off just to watch that happen). Eventually we all ended up going down into the sewers just to say that we did it; Jesus, I can feel my claustrophobia kicking in just thinking about sliding down through those storm drain holes and crawling around in the sewers looking for Frisbees and whiffleballs and whatever other cool things that popped into the view of my flashlight. On one of those, (we'll call it my FINAL) trips into the underground recesses, I came face-to-face with a possum (yeah, I suppose they are officially called opossums but I just would never, ever say that). A possum is probably all of eight-inches tall and might weigh six pounds soaking wet, but go ahead and meet up with one of those little S.O.B.'s face-to-face in a sewer with your only weapon being a flashlight and when it starts that crazy infernal hissing and starts coming right at you with the hair on the back of its neck standing straight up, let me know how brave you are then.

✍ We also kept occupied with non-traditional sports; some were store bought by our parents and others were ones that we invented or tweaked to fit our environment.

Tetherball – The game of tetherball is pretty basic, one player tries to hit a ball that is "tethered" to a rope around a pole, while the opposing player tries to stop them with the goal of wrapping the ball around the pole in the opposite direction. It was marketed as a relaxing backyard game that the whole family could have fun with, we however had other plans. Our tetherball games were one-on-one fights to the death where we collected bragging rights by hitting our opponent in the face with the ball as many times as we could with as much speed as we could possibly generate. That whole family thing was out; first of all I don't remember any of our parents ever being outside with us to play some backyard game (or do much of anything with us for that matter), and I couldn't imagine any teenage girl wanting to join in a tetherball game after they watched us play it for a few minutes.

There was no such thing as an old tetherball kit. Tetherball had too many potential breaking parts for it to have a very long lifespan. The pole was sturdy enough for a casual game but it was not designed for our rough play followed by our swinging on it like Batman coming down the Bat pole; we would break it in half, bend it out of shape, or usually just pull it out of the ground. The ball was sturdy enough, made of some sort of industrial-grade plastic, but alas the tether itself could not withstand the G-Forces we placed upon it. It was inevitable that the rope was going to break and that the ball was going to go flying off at supersonic speed toward someone's face. But while it lasted, we got our parent's full money's worth out of tetherball sets.

Croquet – The fact that they actually sold croquet sets without a warning label similar to what you might find on a machine gun or bazooka was amazing. Croquet in theory is a wonderful game that is a mix of skill and strategy, but the reality of it was that you were handing over three-foot long wooden mallets and wooden croquet balls as big as softballs to energized teenage boys. The game which was only supposed to resemble golf but on a much smaller scale turned into an all-out pursuit of one of the games' most obscure rules: *Sending* an opponent's ball. *Sending* meant that if you could hit your ball and cozy up against your opponent's ball you would put your foot on top of your own ball, swing your mallet as hard as humanly possible, hit your own ball, and through energy transfer send your opponent's ball flying off of the course. Flying off the course is a vast understatement; we tried to *send* the other person's ball down the street, out into the highway, through our neighbor's picture window, into the path of an oncoming semi, name a place as far away from the course as you can think of and that is where we were trying to send our opponent's croquet ball. However, *sending* a croquet ball wasn't always a perfect science, it was a 50-50 venture. 50% of the time you would indeed *send* your opponent's ball flying well off course; it was always a glorious achievement that made everyone that was playing roll on the ground laughing except for the guy who was chasing his ball down the street. But the other 50% of the time, we either slammed the mallet into our own foot which caused varying degrees of pain ranging from barely felt it or "Jeez maybe I should go to the Emergency Room", or we broke the mallet handle which would often cause the head of the mallet to go flying and you can probably begin to imagine the potential destruction that a one pound wooden projectile the size of someone's shoe could cause travelling around 60 mph.

I always pick up and examine the croquet sets when I'm at Walmart, I've even put a set in the cart, only to turn around and put it back on the shelf. The thought of a croquet course set up in my yard sounds so fun, but the reality of me and my son sending each other's ball flying toward the highway, into the pond, through the windows of the Florida room, or perilously close to the dogs' heads makes me second guess that purchase every time.

Jarts – Now here's a safe, family-friendly game where absolutely nothing could go wrong. Not! Jarts or lawn darts are giant four-pound missiles with a plastic body and a huge metallic head with a six-inch pointed spear at the end. The object of the game is to loft these projectiles high into the air and have them stick in a circular scoring grid. Well, they stuck alright, they stuck in yards five houses away (you could really wing these things), they stuck in people's feet, they stuck in the cat, they stuck into the dog, and after about two seconds of investigation my suspicions were confirmed; there are at least three confirmed deaths where a jart stuck into the top of some poor souls head.

Tennis – About every two years we would get hopped up from watching tennis on tv. We had some pretty cool tennis characters during our generation and although I'm not a big tennis fan, I would've paid to go see some of these guys: John McEnroe, Bjorn Borg, Arthur Ashe, Jimmy Connors, Ilie Nastase. These guys were characters, three of the five were psycho rabid dogs and two of them were the coolest cucumbers you've ever seen in any sport. Anyways, we would scrounge up enough money to go buy a racquet and a can of tennis balls and then we'd head out to the tennis courts. I think we could've been good tennis players if we only could've served, ...or returned a serve, ...or hit a forehand without knocking it over the back fence, ...or hit a backhand shot that didn't drive into the bottom of the net, ...yep I think we had lots of potential.

For whatever reason it always took us about eight dollars' worth of new tennis equipment (note the price and also note that I do not at any time divulge how we came up with eight dollars) to remember just how bad we were at tennis. It was too slow, it was too methodical, it was too grown up I suppose; regardless of what it was, it just wasn't for us. So on our way home from the tennis courts we suddenly were reminded of what the tennis racquets were good for, hitting stuff. We would hit pine cones, rocks, dirt clods, tin cans; if we could lift it we hit it. We hit things for distance, we hit things for accuracy, we hit things (bugs and such) to kill them, we hit things at houses, we hit things at cars, and we hit things at each other. These wacky tennis racquets were awesome to hit things with.

Polo – We obviously couldn't afford horses (although the Old Man got suckered into buying a racehorse one time that I'm pretty sure ate better than we did) so we improvised by using our bicycles. The remaining croquet mallets that had somehow managed to survive Croquet Day were great to knock the ball around with. I'll bet that people just shook their heads when they drove by and saw a dozen boys riding around on bikes swatting at an old kickball with croquet mallets, golf clubs, and baseball bats acting like they were real polo players.

Swing sets – If a family owned their home and had at least 40-square feet of backyard it was mandatory that a swing set be installed.   The swing set came in a box with lots of nuts and bolts, and hollowed-out poles, along with some chains and plastic seats. Most of them also had a sliding board and ladder that needed attached as well. Total construction time on one of these sets according to the instructions was probably around an hour and a half; but the real amount of time after not reading the directions for the first hour, starting over, losing three or four bolts, putting the wrong bolt in the wrong hole twelve times, putting the poles in upside down, and trying to use a flathead screwdriver instead of a Phillip's really changed the time spent assembling this piece of moving architecture. But our father's favorite part was always digging the holes, getting out the bags of Quikrete concrete mix, and cementing in our swing sets. In theory it should've worked; each pole was held down by an 80-pound man-made stone the size of a car engine. It was then buried two feet into the ground. But when the swing set is designed for 75-pound kids to casually swing back and forth and 150-pound kids used the swings to try and propel themselves into the trees that were 30 feet away, the whole swing set theory went down the drain. Sometimes the poles couldn't handle the weight and force put upon them, sometimes the chains couldn't handle the weight and force put upon them, the sliding board had no chance at all, and inevitably the poles would come out of the ground and the swing set would tip over.

Weight Lifting – I think we all had the 110-pound poured concrete into plastic weight set. Each set had one long bar and two smaller bars along with a set of cast iron collars. Half of us (probably the guys with basements or garages) also had the ultra-sturdy bench press set that was constructed of metal which was about two levels sturdier than aluminum foil and held together mind you with wingnuts.

I know for about six or seven years, I would lie in bed every night and bench press that old gray concrete 17 ½ pound plate. (Maybe I should start doing that again, I was in pretty good shape back then.) It was cool for us to put all of the weight on the bar and see if or how many reps we could bench press it. I did watch a drunk guy one time at a party load the bar with weights from two or three sets easily lift the bar and when he tried to put the bar back onto the bench press rack, he missed and the weights went straight back, crashed to the floor, and knocked the electric out until we could reset the panel.

The weights would always begin to crack and the vinyl would split, leaving crumbs of concrete all over the place. The bar which was registered to hold right at 110 pounds would bend if there was 111 pounds of weight on it. The clamps would always disappear and if we went two or three months without using them they would rust and become worthless. The bench was too fragile and was so narrow that if you had a waistline larger than 28 inches, you would barely fit on the bench. Some of the benches came with a leg extension piece that rattled and shook when you tried to use it and made the screws come loose on the bench. It was always just a matter of time before the whole thing fell apart. You could always go out to the dump and find 20 or 30 old broken down benches lying around out there.

Boxing – Growing up in the Muhammad Ali/Joe Frazier time period, we were very boxing literate and knew our way around a pair of boxing gloves. Sometimes in high school gym classes, disputes would be handled by both boys throwing on a pair of boxing gloves that the gym teacher kept in the back of the equipment room. I remember when my gym teacher had listened to one of the kids mouth long enough and both of them put on the gloves; he let the kid have the first three or four wild swings and then POP! He busted the kid's lip and I stood there trying to hold back a good laugh.

We had older boys in our neighborhood who either were busy trying to avoid us and act like we were a disease or were busy trying to be bad influences and teach us things we didn't need to learn for several more years. But there were a couple of them who took us under their wings and tried to work with us on sports stuff. They taught us how to throw curveballs, how to shoot a reverse-lay-up, and how to handle ourselves in the boxing ring. One of these guys ended up being the Ohio Valley Toughman Champion (TWICE), he was eight inches taller than us and had a reach that was double that advantage. But he'd show us some moves and let us spar against each other. He would pay us a dollar to spar with him, always allowing us to get a few good punches in before he unleashed on us. In one week he broke my nose (TWICE). Each time I'd think I was getting somewhere and even managed to make him back up a couple times and then out of nowhere this punch would come in that felt like I was blind-sided by a Buick, knock me on my butt, and I'd sit there bleeding like a stuck hog, while my buddies worked to get the gloves off of me so they could have their turn. Now think about that last statement, (They would work to get the gloves off of me so they could have their turn). The lure of earning a dollar was too much for us to ignore, despite the knowledge of certain injury.

Skateboards and Go-Karts – In no way did kids of our generation resemble what you may picture as today's skateboarders but most of us at one point owned some sort of skateboard. We really didn't do any tricks and we didn't have our own skate parks or anything like that but we liked to go down the steepest hills we could find and see how fast we could get going before it all ended in a big head-over-heels crash. I can still vividly recall how the skateboard would start wobbling like crazy and we'd try like the dickens to ride it out, somehow thinking that we could stabilize what was an obvious train wreck. There wasn't any good way to land one of these full-speed crashes; we wore no helmets, no knee-pads, as a matter-of-fact we probably were in shorts, a tank top, and a beat up pair of Converse. At an estimated 35 mph, the crash was going to leave a good bit of your skin on the pavement.

We certainly couldn't go out and buy a go-kart, (don't get me wrong, I'm sure there were plenty of kids that could go out and purchase a go-kart, it just wasn't any of us). Our go-karts were built from pieces of scrap that we collected from anywhere and everywhere. These weren't motorized metal monsters, they were wooden crates solely powered by gravity. The concept was pretty simple, a couple of us would go out and rummage through garages (maybe our own or maybe someone who lived on the block and just happened to leave their garage door open), and we'd come back with miscellaneous stuff that we thought could be used for a go-kart: a couple 2x4's, a hand full of nails, some rope, a few of those U-shaped nails, and anything that resembled a tire. Every group had their own mechanic who would piece this machine together and come up with some sort of chariot that would at least make it TO the hill of our choice.

The steering system was almost always a rope attached to both sides of the 2x4 axle. The seat was anything that we could semi-attach to the frame (lawn chair, seat cushion, milk crate, cinder block). The tires like I said were anything we get our hands on (lawnmower tires, Big Wheel tires, tricycle tires, tires from a dolly), they didn't even have to match, as a matter-of-fact, if they matched...well, it was impossible, so there is no sense talking about four matching go-kart tires. The braking system was your standard Fred Flintstone, drag your feet on the ground, and hope that you didn't roll out in front of a moving semi, go-kart braking system.

The average number of trips down the steepest, most dangerous hill that we could find was 1.5. 1.5 means that only half of the time did the go-kart even survive its maiden voyage. All of the trips started out really fun. The steering worked for the first few feet, the tires all stayed on for the first few feet, and we didn't have to worry about stopping yet; so everything was peachy. But then gravity really started to assert her strength and the go-kart picked up speed very rapidly, as it went faster it had more of a mind of its own and we had less and less control over what we wanted it to do. At some point the steering gave out, either the rope broke or one of the tires up and fell off. The speed was now way faster than what you had anticipated and things were coming at you like you had hit warp speed but forgot to attach your seatbelt. Parked cars, moving cars, pedestrians, dogs, trees, houses, intersecting streets, fire hydrants; the list was pretty long as to what we were flying towards. After several panicked attempts at steering you quickly resorted to Flintstone brakes, which worked pretty well when you were coasting on a flat surface, but cranking down a 30% grade quarter-mile stretch of City Street, Flintstone brakes were utterly useless. The only method of stopping at this point was to somehow manage to crash this wooden missile into something that would stop you without killing you. So after watching all of this, we were all still willing to take another voyage if we could salvage enough moving parts.

Mumbley Peg – This is one you don't see every day. Two kids (obviously boys, girls were way too smart to do 3/4's of this stuff), stood with their pocket knives (or screwdrivers worked just as well) about ten feet apart, spread their legs a little bit and threw and stuck their weapon into the ground between their opponents feet. In some versions you throw your knife at your own feet, but that seemed stupid when you could throw it towards somebody else's foot.

I couldn't pick up a knife or screwdriver without throwing it into the ground and making it stick; if there was a nightcrawler or grasshopper on the ground that could be used as a target ...well, all the better.

Buck buck – You talk about a game that was crazy; I'd say that most people have never even heard of buck buck. You needed a big group of 15-20 fully wound-up participants to play this game, you split the teams (usually according to neighborhoods or the buddies you hung out with) and then it went something like this: One person on the team would grab a pole or tree or telephone pole or goal post, that guy would bend over and hug this pole or post like his life depended on it, then another player would grab around his waist (basically in an L-position) and the rest of the team would connect on. So here you have eight or nine guys bent over hugging on to each other's hips with the first guy latched onto a telephone pole or something. The other team's only job was to try to break that human chain (and trust me, this was the only team having fun). You would break the chain by sprinting as fast as you could, propel yourself as high and as far as possible and come down onto the defending team and break their grip. The defending team knew you were coming and would yell and try to rally each other, "Hold on. Hold on doggone it, don't let go." Which was real easy to yell if you weren't the one getting pummeled? The offensive team brought as much pain and punishment as they possibly could, landing with all of their body weight directly onto their opponents backs, necks, heads, and that crucial arm hold. And it wasn't like you were Roy Rogers saddling up to jump on Trigger, no, no, no, guys were flying in the air like Jimmy "Superfly" Snuka mashing an elbow down into their opponents spine or backs of their heads. Concussion, what concussion? What kind of pansy would complain about a mere headache? I never even took an aspirin until I was darn near 30.

A lot of teams would save their best buck bucker for last. They probably used their flyweights in the beginning of the line-up and saved their big boys for the end. So if the pole huggers could withstand the punishment delivered by the first seven high flyers, (and also hold up their weight because the buck buckers didn't get off once they landed on the defenders) then you knew the anchorman was coming after you, and he might be a couple, three hundred pounds.

When we were college aged, we rounded up about 30 guys at 3:00 in the morning and played this game against a palm tree on a Fort Lauderdale beach. I stood there and gave an interview to the local news reporter who said he'd seen a lot of things throughout his years of covering Spring Break, but this may have been the coolest thing he'd ever seen.

Slip and Slide – There was an actual slip and slide game that you could buy, but I'm pretty sure that we did this way before those hit the shelves. We originally started it as a way to practice our sliding into bases and we would actually have a guy stand at the end with a glove and we would throw a ball to them and they would try to tag out the incoming slider. We took whatever long pieces of plastic that we could find or we would just start spraying down a section of the yard. We would completely soak the area with a garden hose and then we would start sliding over it, the more we slid, the slipperier it got. We slid on our butts, we slid on our sides, we slid on our bellies, and we slid on our backs; at times we got going pretty fast. If there happened to be a bump on the course, they we'd go flying and sometimes land well, and sometimes not so much. We would occasionally hit tree roots or rocks or possibly crash into a sticker bush or the edge of a garage; each trip had its own distinct opportunity for injury. The Pete Rose (diving headlong at full breakneck speed) dive was everyone's favorite and honestly it's amazing there weren't more serious, "hey-look-at-my-new-wheelchair" type injuries.

Our town was surrounded by the Appalachian Hills so you never had to go very far to be engulfed with the beauty and dangers of nature. We could go months and never even notice the wooded areas surrounding our homes or we could run off for a week and spend nearly every waking hour goofing off in the woods. We found a lot of ways to stay busy on the outskirts of town.

I've mentioned fishing and hunting with my dad, but as I grew older I ventured out with my friends to try my hand at these manly sports. We'd grab a couple poles and head down to the creek with a loaf of bread to make dough balls to use as bait. Our goal was to snag one of the giant carp that lived in the slow moving creek water. Over the years we caught several of them but mostly we would just watch our dough ball fall off of our hook and then we'd resort to screwing around catching crawdads with the end of a stick. Every once in a while we'd catch one of the big 40 pounders and spend half-an-hour reeling him in. Of course once we caught one of these giants none of us wanted to actually touch him... because he was a cruddy, filthy, bottom-feeding carp.

Our hunting expeditions didn't go much differently. We would walk four or five blocks through town carrying shotguns or 22 caliber rifles and a pocket full of ammunition and end up down at the creek. None of us actually had a hunting license, nor even knew what animal was in season. Our ignorance didn't particular affect our trip, our primary goal was just to shoot something; if we killed something other than ourselves, well, that was a bonus. Heaven forbid that we saw a stray cat; I'm positive that it would've been history. Groundhogs, (chuckers as we affectionately called them) had no chance if we saw one. Squirrels, chipmunks, birds or any other tree dwelling animal was fair game. At some point we'd end up shooting other things like fish in the water, or dragonflies, or frogs, and then eventually move on to inanimate objects like tin cans, or pop bottles, or rotted logs, or big ant hills. At some point, it just really didn't matter what we were shooting at; we had bullets left over and it would be a crime to go home with ammunition, so we had to shoot something.

I will admit to trapping a few times and I will also admit to not being very good at it, (except for in town, I had a tremendous knack for catching the same cat night after night in a box trap). There were several guys who trapped all winter long and always came home with muskrat, beaver, mink, and fox. They knew how to kill them, clean them, and stretch the fur. I don't know how much they made, but it was spending money; way more work than what is was worth but I always thought those guys were pretty cool. On my personal trapping attempts, when I did catch something, the damn thing was still very much alive, seemingly rabid, and very much wanting to bite me. It had no intention of sitting still long enough for me to shoot it in the head with my 22, and as a matter-of-fact they always tried to eat the barrel of my gun. It always looked so easy when I went with my trapping friend; he didn't seem scared of this thing at all. Well, I guess I'm just a pansy because I sucked at it. To this day I'm still afraid of cows, so you can imagine how I felt about snakes and wild animals with teeth that were legitimately trying to bite me. About the only animal that I'm not particularly afraid of are dogs, except Collies, I was bit in the... you know what, by Laddie the neighborhood Collie, on two occasions, same spot (don't ask).

Of course spending hours on end down in the deepest, thickest woods north of the Amazon Jungle we easily came home with enough mosquito bites to give us malaria, horsefly and deerfly bites that looked like someone put a marbles underneath our skin, and plenty of debilitating poison ivy that would often saturate our skin so intensely that we'd earn a trip to the Emergency Room. Everyone my age can remember getting poison ivy and our mother's going to the closet to get the Calamine Lotion to spread all over our bodies. It went on pink and ended up drying a kind of ashy white, but at times it was the only thing that helped. Sometimes I would dig and claw at my breakouts so badly that I was put into a Clorox bath. Now I'm not real smart sometimes, but I've gotta believe that sitting in bleach (unless you're Michael Jackson) couldn't've been very healthy for us. Not scratching was not an option. We would get poison ivy so bad that it would swell our eyes shut (that was usually the Bat-signal to take me to the Emergency Room). Even if you didn't go down into the woods there was still the possibility of getting poison ivy; almost every household had burning barrels in those days. Big 55-gallon oil drums that our families burned our trash in. It would eventually fill up with things that didn't burn completely like bottles, cans and such. They filled up with heavy ash and the barrel would rot out at the bottom and you knew at that point you needed a new burning barrel. Anyways, people would clean out the weeds around their house, throw them into the burning barrel, and if there happened to be poison ivy mixed in with the weeds, voila, 50 neighbor kids would catch poison ivy through the air, (sounds like a horror movie).

The woods were also a prime hideout for older teenagers to go down and drink or smoke dope. I imagine there was some romancing down there too since no one, and I mean no one but kids ever went down there. The only time we ever saw an adult down there was when we were walking out of the woods and a bum, a real-life hobo popped out from behind a tree and got drilled in the face by one of my friends and we set a new world record time of getting out of the woods. The guy that hit him wasn't a violent guy or anything, it was just a knee-jerk reaction; the bum was like a foot from him when he popped out from this tree, and the kid just instinctively swung, it just happened really fast. I'm positive that we told people a murderer was in the woods.

Sometimes we would go through the woods and start walking the railroad tracks. The first few times we didn't even particularly know where we were going to end up, there just seemed to be a lot of neat things to see and do along the way. There were always a couple guys that wanted to turn around and start heading back and then there were always a couple guys that wanted to go until they saw ocean water. But the majority of us were just followers, if the bulk of the group turned around so would we, if the bulk of the group kept going, then so would we.

On our most daring railroad track adventure, we walked what I now know to be about 14 miles. On our trip we stopped at the local sawmill, climbed up on some sort of machinery and jumped down about 15 feet into a giant sawdust pile. Did it itch later? Yeah, but it was pretty cool while it lasted. We had heard about other kids who spent time out there and thought we'd try it.

One of us had some shotgun shells in our pocket, (I know that seems odd, but at any given moment it would be impossible to guess what might've been in our pockets). We had the bright idea that if we saw a train coming, we would put the shells on the track and see if they would shoot. Well, sure enough a train did come down the tracks, and we put the shells on the track. I don't know if it shot or not, but the shells certainly were crushed and luckily none of us went home with any shotgun pellets in our butts. We also put those great big railroad rocks on the track, we had the idea of thinking we could derail the train and somehow that would be cool. My goodness, when I write this stuff out on paper, we were far dumber than I remembered. I also recall that after the train went by, we waved at the engineer then threw those giant rocks at the coal cars it was pulling behind it.

By staying on (or close to) those tracks we discovered The Reservoir, Apex, and Coal Ridge, three of the greatest illegal swimming holes in Southeastern Ohio. Apex and Coal Ridge were old abandoned strip mining pits that were reclaimed and filled with water. The legends were that both of them were bottomless and that scuba divers had tried to find the bottom but ran out of air in their tanks. Regardless of exactly how deep they were, they were pretty friggin' deep; deep enough to jump off of 30-foot highwalls and not worry about hitting the bottom. The water was crystal clear, you could spit into the water from up above which attracted bluegills and then you'd try to jump on them. I will admit to going fishing at Coal Ridge, getting in a pinch and having to go to the bathroom, and I mistakenly wiped my butt with poison ivy. Talk about being miserable for a couple weeks.

✍ I would be remiss if I didn't tell this story. The Reservoir was pretty far from town, we could walk there or ride our bikes but it would definitely had taken a while, so we heard that one of the older neighborhood guys was going out there so four of us hitched a ride. The Reservoir had an old wooden bridge that linked up to a brick tower out into the water. We would walk across the bridge, climb a couple window sills, and shimmy up to the roof of the tower and then jump off into the water. We were all in the water when one of our gang was walking across the bridge, and just like a friggin' Scooby Doo cartoon or Indiana Jones movie, the old rotted boards gave way and he crashed through catching himself with his armpits but his legs dangled in midair. The four of us who were below in the water laughed hysterically, none louder than myself. I felt compelled to shower him with joke after joke about him dangling there with his legs churning like he was walking on a cloud. The bridge walker took exception to all of my joking and tossed my clothing, shoes and all into the water. Well, that didn't seem funny. I retrieved my clothes, what didn't sink and proceeded up the bank to punch this kid, but our driver in his infinite wisdom (mind you, this is a guy who crashed his car trying to drive with ice skates on) decided that falling through the bridge was indeed funny and that he had no right to throw my clothes into The Reservoir. His punishment would be to walk home, (again, this was a good five miles). We got in the car and I'm sure we waved at the guy who was now walking. I went home, ate supper, and left the house to meet up with my buddies and here comes the dangler. He had spent the last hour and a half thinking of what he was going to do when he saw me, five miles worth of fury boiled inside him. So what did I say, "Hey, how was that walk home?"

Crack! I took a shot right to the mouth. Well, he thought he was in the right, and I thought I was in the right, so let's go at it right here and now in the middle of the street. I don't know why no one stopped us, I don't know why no one jumped in, but several adult neighbors stood on their front porches shouting their encouragement while we stood in the middle of the street and pounded on each other for about ten minutes. I do recall it was the first time I tried a dropkick and it landed successfully. So here we were, two fifteen-year old kids fighting out in the middle of a fairly busy city street. We had quite a number of cars backed up on both sides of the street and the next thing we knew four police cars came rolling up with sirens on and the whole nine yards. They threw us into the back of two separate cruisers, drove us around the block and dropped us off at our houses.

My dad found out later that night that I was in a cop car and had been in a fight with Rusty. Rusty was a big tough dude and the idea of getting into with him now seems pretty friggin' brave, but I held my own, with both of us getting some pretty good shots in. My dad's only response was, "Why didn't you hit that sumbitch with a 2x4?"

He wasn't worried about my well-being, he didn't care what the fight was about, and the idea of me being chauffeured around in the back of a cop car didn't bother him. His concern was the fact that I didn't try to permanently maim this kid with a piece of wood. That sums up my childhood, and this era about as much as anything I can think of.

✍ When we got older many of us even took up golf. We only tried it a couple times while we were in high school and if I wrote about things we did after high school I know that I'd need an attorney. However, there is no way that I can talk about the dumb things we did growing up and not mention this one: Like I said we took up golf, now most people have never seen golf played in the manner that we played it; golf etiquette was non-existent, golf attire was non-existent, and golf equipment was also non-existent. We played 100 mph, using three or four Mulligans on each hole; we could easily run out of balls by the third hole. We played so fast, actually running to our ball, that we could play 18 holes in a little over an hour. If we lost a ball into the woods we would either just ignore it and act like it didn't happen or go into the woods and search and search and search until we came out with 30 or 40 balls. Our golf attire was usually shorts and a tank top until the courses started making us wear shirts with collars, then we began putting polo shirts in our golf bag and putting them on at least until we got out of sight of the clubhouse. For the first three years that we played only one of us even had clubs so we would all have to play out of the same bag. I just carried the five iron around with me; it seemed easier than switching clubs every time.

Anyways, I could easily devote an entire chapter to our golfing escapades but I will just give you one story, but it's a good one. Golf was kind of expensive and just paying for the balls that we lost would have prohibited us from playing very often so we thought about where most people lost their golf balls and came up with the water hazards. Sure the woods collected their share of stray hooks and slices, but a lot of times the golfers would wander in to retrieve them, but no one ever went into the ponds. There had to be a gazillion balls in the bottom of some of these ponds that lay right in front of the greens. "I know the perfect hole; half of the golfers at the Country Club hit their balls into the water on this one hole." One of our crew said excitedly.

"The Country Club? Dude, I've never been out there, you sure we should go out there to get 'em?" I asked.

"Yeah, I'm telling you it's perfect." He answered confidently.

That seemed good enough for me. We loaded up some stolen empty five-gallon pickle buckets from McDonald's, a couple flashlights and we set off for the Country Club in the dead middle of the night. We kicked our shoes off and walked out into the pond using our feet to feel for golf balls. It took all of 30 seconds to realize that this was the best idea we had ever had. You didn't have to walk a foot before you felt the smoothness of a golf ball underneath your foot; we simply submerged ourselves, reached down into the water, grabbed a ball and tossed it up on the bank. This went on for another two hours before we stopped and that was just because we didn't think we could fit all of the balls into the four, five-gallon buckets.

The only catch to the whole system seemed to be what we called the Black Lagoon Mud that stained our hands, feet, and all but ruined our finger and toenails. The mud on the bottom of the ponds stunk to high heaven and didn't completely wash off for a couple weeks. Three of us stood there that first night with about 500 golf balls, enough to supply our golf jones for a year or more, and then we got greedy. "This stuff is awful, let's go down and wash it off down at the pool."

Now mind you, I had never even driven past the Country Club before so I certainly didn't know they had a pool, let alone where it was, but this guy had spent time there and seemed to know his way around so, "Yeah let's go."

I had never been to a Country Club before that day but I've been to a few since and have a pretty good clue as to their overall demeanor and all I can say is that I bet we were the talk of the Country Club for weeks.

Remember, I had darn near lived at the Big Pool for the last ten years so I knew my way around a swimming pool. As soon as I saw the pool I made a beeline for the diving board. Of course we didn't think much about the Black Lagoon Mud that we were leaving behind until we were ready to leave. Wow! It looked like an avalanche of mud had come crashing through the entire pool area; little muddy footprints were everywhere; black footprints on the sidewalk, on the deck chairs, on the diving board, just everywhere. But the good news was that the Black Lagoon Mud was washed off of us so we merrily walked back across the golf course, collected our buckets of golf balls and went home to tell all of our buddies how much fun the whole ordeal was. Well something that fun couldn't be ignored for very long, as a matter-of-fact we gave it exactly 24 hours; we came back the very next night.

We parked in the same spot as we had the night before (about half of a mile from the course), we had our McDonald's green five-gallon pickle buckets just like we had used the night before, and we made our way down to the same pond that we had had so much luck with the night before. And just like the night before, we found ball after ball after ball. We were working on matching the number from the night before when all of the sudden we heard a dog barking, a barking dog on the Country Club golf course seemed a little odd, and then we saw a flashlight bobbing up and down. So there we stood in the middle of a pond, on private property, in our underwear, with our clothes on the bank, with 500 more golf balls laying on the shore and what had to be a very determined security guard complete with what appeared and sounded like a loyal and energetic bloodhound. As the guard started yelling for us to come out, the dog started howling, which gave us a little opportunity to at least whisper a plan to one another, "Duck down. Swim over there by the cattails, I've got an idea." Our leader whispered in a drill sergeant tone.

I know I didn't have any better plans so I followed him over to the reeds and cattails with just my nostrils, eyes, and forehead out of the water. "Here. Take one of these reeds and break it in half, we'll be able to lay on the bottom and breathe through it."

For Crying Out Loud, are you kidding me? That was his friggin' plan. I knew full well this wasn't going to work, yet there I was lying almost totally submerged with a daggone reed in my mouth just exactly like we had seen it done on at least ten cartoons. But for some reason the security guy couldn't find us with the flashlight and the water must've thrown off our scent to the dog. We actually had a chance to get out of this without going to jail. And then...the biggest bullfrog in the history of bullfrogs jumped right onto our leader's back. I don't know if he thought the guy grabbed him, or if the intensity of the situation panicked him, but he shot out of the water like he was on a hopped-up jet ski. He ran past the security guard at such a speed that I'm sure the guy thought it was just a rush of wind. Then the dog, which was also frozen for a split-second, began dragging the security guy behind him and bellowing to the world that the hunt was on. Me and the other guy in the water didn't know exactly what to do, so we started collecting the balls into the buckets along with our clothes. "Do you think we should wait on him?" the other guy asked. (I know, you're probably thinking, really? You stayed to get the golf balls? Well, that is what we went there for wasn't it?)

"Nope. If I know anything, I know that Tom will make it back to the car...EVENTUALLY!"

So we ran to the car, lugging all of our golf ball hunting gear. The whole way we back to the car we could hear that crazy dog, bellowing and baying and howling. But as we sat in the car waiting for our buddy, becoming more nervous as time went on, we noticed that the dog's howls were less frequent and certainly less purposeful. I have heard that you can run a good hound dog until it just plain up and dies. I don't know if that is what happened or not, but I do know that the howling stopped right about the same time that Tom showed up at the car. He slid into the driver's seat and we all drove into town in our underwear (not the first time that we did that, nor would it be the last time either).

✍ Regardless of golf courses, railroad tracks, and trips into the woods we were still primarily city kids. We had a thousand places to go and a million things to do in the city. Each neighborhood was a little different than the other, but they were all a little bit the same as well. There were places and things that were uniquely ours and places and things that we all shared. Playing chase through the backyards of Gomber and Highland Avenues, playing basketball at Park School, and sneaking into Mr. Hamm's barn were things that belonged to the kids in our neighborhood. But climbing on the cannon at the Courthouse, or carving your name into the covered bridge at the City Park, maybe even climbing on the old fire truck that was set up for us to play on in the park, or riding the taxidermied bear that sat out in the front of Bair's Furniture were things that all of us shared.

We had plenty of stuff to get into when we ran around downtown. Here were a few of the downtown options that we enjoyed as kids of this era (those not from Cambridge can insert their own proper nouns in, but most likely the stories were very similar):

The Courthouse – Yes this was an official government building, but we still ran around in there goofing off. We would ride the elevators and wander around the hallways looking for who-knows-what. When we got in a pinch, the Courthouse was usually open late at night and we could run in there to use the restroom. There was an old cannon out front that we would climb on when we were little kids.

Eating establishments – There were several downtown eating establishments to choose from. I will name a few by their real names, not to bring attention to Cambridge but to allow those not from Cambridge to insert the names of your own hometown eating establishments.

We had a downtown bakery, Kennedy's Bakery which was (and still is) one of the finest bakeries in the Eastern United States. The aroma that came out of that building was the start to many a great morning. Every kid in town at some point in their lives got their birthday cake made there.

There was a downtown hotel, The Berwick Hotel that had its own restaurant. It always reminded me of what I assumed a 1960's Las Vegas or New York City mob restaurant would've been like. Dad used to take me there at 5:00 in the morning to get breakfast before taking me to work with him painting houses. I think half of the guys were coming in to get breakfast and the other half were on their way out from drinking at the bar.

We had department store restaurants like S.S. Kresge's and Newberry's with big long cafeteria counters. Sometimes you didn't mind going shopping with your mom if you thought you might be able to get some food from one of these Five and Dime early department stores. When we got older and had a little bit of money in our pockets, we'd get a Kresge sub and fountain pop.

Of course Cambridge had the Coney Island (and still does) which sold a little bit of everything but were famous for their coney dogs and strawberry pies. I remember as a little kid sitting in the booth flipping through the jukebox selector that hung on the wall at every table. I probably wasn't going to be given a nickel to play a song, but I still liked to look. My dad would ask me what I wanted and he'd get upset if I didn't say a coney and a piece of strawberry pie; maybe that's why I still try to order the feature item at places when I go out to eat.

We also had the stereotypical drive-in restaurants of the 60's and 70's that either walked out or roller-skated out to your car with big trays of food that they hung on your car window. (Maybe car windows were thicker and stronger back in those days, but I'd be scared to death to allow a tray of food to hang on my driver's side window). Orr's Drive-In sold a heck of a lot of pizzaburgers and A & W sold a boatload of root beer back in those days.

Stores of every kind – We didn't have a Walmart, (although Bargain City was an awfully close substitute) but we had a lot of specialty stores downtown that you could go to and find whatever you needed. We had sporting goods stores, shoe stores, women's clothing stores, men's clothing stores, furniture stores, Penneys and Sears, a music store, hardware stores, paint store, barbershops, greeting card store, pharmacies, grocery stores, newsstands, bars, jewelers, I guess we had just about everything covered; we even had Al's Novelty which as a kid was one of our all-time favorite places to visit. Al's had everything that a goofy teenage boy thought that they just had to have: magic kits, every kind of penny candy known to man, magazines (Mad Magazine was one of our favorites with the three-fold hidden puzzle on the back), rubber chickens, x-ray specs, sea monkeys, junk plastic toys, Mexican jumping beans, even pet rocks (what a stupid fad); I can't even remember all of the only-valuable-to-13-year-old-boys stuff that was in there, but we loved it.

Entertainment – There were also plenty of places downtown or near downtown designed to give us entertainment options. For the most part we needed a little bit of money to pay for these entertainment options but by the time we hit high school we had figured out ways to "earn" money. Although there were certainly groups of kids that seemed to spend all of their time at these types of places, most of the kids I knew didn't have the desire or the funds to hang out at these places all day.

Every couple years a new video arcade would open up downtown. I suppose on paper it was a great start-up business idea but in reality a bunch of teenage kids (many of whom were complete riff-raff) came in and hung out in your establishment for a couple hours trying to see how long they could take to spend the 75¢ that they shared. We would however go down there every once in a while and play some of the favorites of this time period like: air hockey, Space Invaders, pinball machines, full-sized PONG, foosball, skeeball,

Asteroids, and Death Race. We grew up during the Dawn of Video Games where a black and white screen with stick figure graphics was considered pretty cool. The 80's video games were the ones that people remember the most with legends such as Pac Man, Galaga, and Donkey Kong; and now if the video game doesn't look exactly like a real person, shooting a real bazooka, with real-looking brains splattering on the screen kids won't even buy them.

Roller Skating during our era was a big thing. Watch the movie *Roll Bounce* to get an idea of what it looked like to combine roller skating and great dance music. Our parents grew up with a roller rink in Cambridge but it wasn't around when we were kids so we had to travel to the next town over to go skating. There were kids who would make the drive every week and there were others of us who thought making that trek once or twice a year was plenty. Most of the things I mention in this book have evolved and changed dramatically since the 60's and 70's, but every roller rink I've ever went to for the last 40 years is exactly the same as the ones we went to as kids. The same music, probably the exact same skates, traveling around in the same oval, with the same velour mushroom shaped ottomans to sit on to change your shoes.

Cambridge had two bowling alleys and they seemed to be pretty popular places, especially on the weekends and even more especially on Saturday mornings. Saturday mornings were league days for youth bowlers. I never joined the youth bowling league but I got plenty of bowling experience going with my friends and occasionally with the Old Man. The Old Man bowled in a league which gave him a free pass in the middle of the week to go drink, smoke, cuss, and carry-on with some other guys with similar plans. He was actually a pretty good bowler, he would talk about when he was a kid and worked as a pin setter at the bowling alley. Good Lord, I remember sitting in the house on Sunday afternoons watching Earl Anthony and Dick Weber battling it out on ABC's Professional Bowling Tour.

The bowling alley always had a special ambiance that mixed family-friendly with a backroom all-night poker game.

Any sport where you can smoke and drink while you play, probably isn't really a sport. And there was plenty of smoking and drinking going on at the bowling alley, not necessarily by us kids, but the adults that hung out there had no problem contributing to the delinquency of us minors. None of us had our own bowling balls or our own bowling shoes like all of the Saturday morning bowlers; we just guessed on a size and rummaged around the ball racks until we picked up something that felt about right without getting our fingers stuck in the holes.

When you combined six or seven teenage boys at the bowling alley, you had the ingredients for complete stupidity. Between heckling, bowling out of order, using each other's bowling balls, hiding each other's bowling balls, cheating on the score (the score didn't just add up by itself like it does today, you actually had to know how to keep score), and making crazy throws we actually got pretty competent at bowling. It wasn't anything for some of us to bowl 200. After about two games we got bored and started doing crazy shots and trick shots, my trick shot ended in splintering off a piece of my ankle bone (which is still floating around somewhere) when I tried to throw a twelve-pound bowling ball between my legs and connected on my ankle bone instead.

The local pool hall wasn't a place where every kid went, most kids wouldn't have even considered going down those steps into the pool hall, but it actually seemed safer than every single square foot of the junior high building. You kind of had to build up your courage before you walked in, once you entered the pool hall, there were no other exits and you just hoped that the clientele were on the up-and-up, but all of the older guys down there always treated us great, but we liked to tell stories to our buddies who were too chicken to go down there with us about how rough and scary the place was. The pool tables were premium, slate tables and in the back of my mind I always had that 1% fear of tearing the felt on a break, but things always worked out fine.

We also had a music store that gave lessons for almost every imaginable instrument and a dance studio that taught all forms of dance. I always wanted to play an instrument and so did a lot of my buddies, but I neither had the money or the confidence to break away from my crew and tell them I was taking guitar lessons or piano lessons or whatever. It was always difficult to break away and do new things, the fear of being teased for a couple days had the power to control us and keep us from fulfilling many of our true dreams.

I remember the Old Man coming home one time with an electric guitar; he was going to join a band. Mom and I knew that was never going to happen, but what the heck we were going to say about it. Through the years he came home with a wide variety of...*things*. Most of these *things*, were obtained through questionable methods: bets, trades, pawned items to keep a night of drinking going. The electric guitar wasn't anything; I woke up one morning with a full-sized pinball machine in my room. There was another time he came home with a motorcycle, (of which he couldn't ride and on his sole voyage ended up laying it down in the middle of the street with traffic coming right at him). I'm pretty sure that we got at least two cars from guys needing money, (a Gremlin and an old Chevy II).

It wasn't like I was the only kid on my block that this stuff was happening to. I might have had it a little worse than some of my friends, but each of us had some sort of pitiful story that we could tell if we wanted to.

We didn't have Cineplexes or other multi-screen cinemas, we had a real theatre; an old time 1500-seat monster complete with balcony. It played the one hit movie of that time period, it staged the annual Christmas play, it put on the annual dance recital, and every year it hosted the Lion's Minstrel Show. If there happened to be two hit movies at the same time, tough! You would have to wait a week or two and if the theatre owner didn't like the movie, then I guess the whole town would do without it. We had some great hit movies during this time period in which we stood completely around the block waiting in line to hope that you got in to see the show. It was a good idea to get in line for the 7:00 p.m. show and then if you didn't make the cut, you were all but guaranteed a seat at the 9:00 p.m. show. *Jaws* and *Star Wars* were the two mega-hits that hit our town and the rest of our country like a storm. People were waiting hours and in some cases camping out in front of theaters trying to get in to see these movies. I remember watching *Rocky* and we had already done a good bit of boxing by this age, so it really spurred us on even more; I know that we woke up every day for a week and swallowed down a raw egg.

The era of kids before us would go to the movie theater every Saturday afternoon. I think they watched a lot of westerns: Hop-along-Cassidy, Roy Rogers, and the Lone Ranger were a few. As teenagers growing up we didn't go as often and films were changing; there was very few contract actors that put out 20 movies a year, the 70's especially was known for big budget block busters that took ahold of the entire country.

Sometimes we would pool our money, send in one of our buddies to legally pay to get in, and then the rest of us would all sprint down to the fire exit door and wait for him to sneak us in. If we waited more than five minutes or so, we just figured that he couldn't figure out a way to get to the door so we left and he would watch a movie alone, (but for free). Back then the concession stand had reasonable prices that we could all afford, (all didn't particularly include us sometimes). I don't know when the whole 900% mark-up thing started but it wasn't during the 60's and 70's. The balcony only was opened up when they sold out all of the lower level seats, and for good reason; once the doors to the balcony were opened up every ornery kid in town made a beeline to go up there. Having a seat in the balcony was a license to throw popcorn, and M&M's, and JuJu Beans down on the lower level movie goers. We were pretty sneaky, so the chance of getting caught was pretty slim.

✍ Yes, we also took dates to the movies as well but it wasn't a regular thing by any stretch of the imagination. When we were old enough to worry about dates, we mainly took them to the Drive-In movies. The Drive-In movie theatre was a whole other animal; it was a culture and secret society all to itself. We would load up the biggest vehicle we could locate on "Carload Night", and when it wasn't "Carload Night", we would stuff as many people as we could into the trunk. Once inside we would drive to the back of the parking lot and let our stowaways out of the trunk, (apparently I didn't have claustrophobia back then).

It was a good place to take a date because you were alone, you had room to stretch out a little bit in the car, and you were usually there to see a double or sometimes triple feature set of films. There were always several dating cars at the Drive-In and I don't know how much movie was actually watched by these young romantics. Even if you went there with a carload of boys, there was always a carload of girls that had driven there as well, so it was pretty common to find a "Drive-In Friend" when you were there.

I know that I never stayed for a triple feature and staying all the way through the second movie was just as rare. One of the few movies I can really remember watching at the Drive-In was *Halloween*. We had eight of us in a station wagon and I remember that when Michael Myers first showed his face on the screen, we had a guy that was in the front seat jump all of the way to the back seat in a flight of terror.

You had to drive up close to the speaker pole and hook the heavy speakers onto the inside of your driver's side window. Some people brought lawn chairs and some others brought blankets and sat on top of their cars. There was also a playground that was right in front of the screen. The concession stand was always a little seedy and I'm gonna guess that it was outside of the jurisdiction of the Health Department, but that didn't stop us from getting popcorn, and hot dogs, and candy there in between the movies.

The Drive-In also became the site of weekend drinking and weekend fights. It wasn't uncommon to hear about three or four fights that took place out at the Drive-In. With all of the girls that were out there and the fun that we had watching movies with a group of half a dozen buddies, getting hit in the mouth and rolling around in the gravel parking lot just didn't sound very appealing to me. I will say that one story was kind of funny, well funny now, but probably not so much to one of these kids: A young fella came running up to one of the tougher hellions of the Drive-In and was holding his nose. With blood dripping through his fingers he pointed over to a group and said, "That guy punched me in the face for no reason."

Well, it didn't take much prodding for this hellion to walk over to the group and without saying a word, blasted one of the boys and broke his nose with one quick shot. He walked back over and told his bleeding buddy that he had taken care of it. His buddy said, "Yeah, but it was the other guy standing next to the guy you hit."

So this tough guy walked over for a second time, put his arm around the guy he had just punched, told him he was sorry, then without a word turned around and broke the other kid's nose (the one he was supposed to hit in the first place). That was too much craziness for me. Even though the police would always drive through once a night, flash a spotlight at your car, and then drive out. That was as much supervision that took place out there. Remember, this was before cell phones, so if you wanted to call the police on someone, you had to get out of your car, probably walk right past the culprit you were going to rat on, ask the Drive-In concession stand people if you could use their phone, make the call, then walk past the culprit again and go wait patiently over by the front entrance for the police to come out, then at that point you would talk to the police and then walk the police back to the car that was causing the trouble. Call me crazy, but that seems way more dangerous and complicated than just either dealing with the problem yourself or getting in your car and leaving safely.

✍ In the 60's and 70's if we had a problem we had to be able to think on our feet. We didn't have cell phones where we could instantly call for help or Google an answer as to how to fix our car or what the weather was going to be later that day. We had to be able to walk up to strangers and ask for their help, we had to be able to knock on someone's door and ask to use their phone, (most of us were supposed to keep a dime in or pocket or in our sock so we could use the payphones that were scattered throughout the city), we had to be able to flag someone down and ask for a ride, or ask them to jump our car. We learned how to fix our bikes, or knew to just walk them home when they were really broken, we certainly weren't going to waste an emergency call to our parents to come and pick us up because of a broken bike. If you called home, there better darn well be one heck of an emergency, (I once bandaged myself up after getting a kids tooth stuck in my forehead when we were playing Smear the Queer, which easily could've taken six or seven stitches); then a few hours later went to sixth grade basketball practice with my self-bandaged head that made me look like the fife player in the *Spirit of '76* painting.

When we were older, almost all of us knew how to fix the 20 most common things that could go wrong with our car. You could look inside our trunk and know that we could get out of a jam if we needed to: a jack, four-way, a box of various tools, a jug of water, a gas can, a blanket, a full-size tire (not a donut), a flashlight, and a hanger (to reconnect our tailpipe or muffler if it happened to break free).

We were all pretty self-sufficient, if we didn't come home for supper our parents didn't freak out and put out an Amber Alert, they just assumed that we ate at someone else's house; if we were hungry we'd eventually come home and eat. I can guarantee that the total of my conversations at my house some days consisted of, "I'm going out." And ten to twelve hours later, "I'm staying at Bobby's."

✍ I suppose there were lots of reasons why we stayed overnight at our friends' houses: we didn't want to stop whatever we were into at that time, we wanted to be able to stay up a little bit later than we could at our own houses, or the place we were staying just had more lax rules than we had at our own homes, we truly just enjoyed the company of our friends, but I'm sure for many of us it was that we just weren't overly thrilled about the idea of going back to our own homes. The older we got, the more we stayed at other people's houses; we also got sneakier too, I'm sure that there was a high percentage of us who played the "I'm staying at Joe's house" while Joe was telling his parents that he was staying at your house, which gave both parties a free pass to stay out all night. (Sounded fun but was pretty stressful worrying all night about getting caught.)

In the summers of the 60's and 70's, staying overnight meant sleeping out; there couldn't be a bigger oxy-moron than the term sleeping out. In all of my experiences of sleeping out (which were quite extensive) I can guarantee that there wasn't much sleeping going on.

Every kid on our block had a tent and a sleeping bag. I'm no good at it now, but back in the day I could put up or tear down that little two-man tent in absolutely no time at all. Right before dusk on dry summer nights, you could always spot teenage boys (and a few girls) walking down the street carrying their rolled up sleeping bags on their way to some backyard camping destination. We tried to angle the tent so we could get in and out as inconspicuously as possible, it was always best to hang out in the backyard until we knew our parents were in bed. Remember, this was before air conditioning was a common creature comfort so almost everybody had a loud box fan in their bedroom window thus we had no problem sneaking in and out of the tent.

Once we had escaped the confines of the tent, our world opened up like never before. Whatever house laws or city ordinances that tethered us in the daytime, quickly disappeared with the setting of the sun. The familiar streets and back alleys that we walked every single day of our lives turned into new exotic locales for us to meander and explore for the next five or six hours. We seemingly walked every corner of town during those hot, humid summer nights, I'd hate to try and estimate the mileage we tallied on those nights, it'd have to be in double figures. Sometimes we walked down the lighted sidewalks and other times we'd cruise right down the middle of the streets; for no reason we might cut between houses and stroll along the unlit alleys and backyards. We had no particular place to go but still we pressed on, if something caught our eye we'd stop to check it out, if we sensed danger or saw a cop car coming, we could vanish into the darkness like a wisp of smoke. In a city of 12,000, somehow we knew something about nearly every resident; we may not have known their names, but we knew who had a big menacing dog chained up in their backyard, and who was going to be sitting out on their front porch, or who might give chase if we did anything stupid around their house. We definitely knew where every girl our own age lived and which ones had protective dads that we didn't want to mess with. We knew which backyards had fences and which ones had clotheslines, or creeks, or rose bushes; we knew the escape route from every possible location in the whole town, along with the meeting place if we got split up. Getting caught (by anyone for anything that we happened to have done) really wasn't going to happen, we were fast, we could run all day, we could jump, we could climb, we were fearless, and we certainly knew the lay of the land; the streets belonged to us and that sense of belonging was never as strong as it was in the middle of the night on one of our sleep out adventures.

There were times while out on our midnight adventures that we would be chased by stray dogs; to avoid being bitten we figured out that if we jumped up on a car, the dog could not follow us, (I don't know why they couldn't or wouldn't jump up on a car to attack us, but I'm glad they didn't). We got pretty good at jumping on cars, so good in fact that it became a regular thing to do without a dog chasing us. We could run on one car or a string of five or six cars. It usually caused little to no damage to the cars, aside from definitive footprints like when you find cat prints on your car some mornings. Although, there was the time when one of our crew was running along and then suddenly disappeared... moral of the story: Don't do car runs across a convertible !

Invariably our midnight strolls would always lead us past a list of at least a dozen girls' houses that we may or may not have actually had a chance to talk to. We liked to try to find out when the girls were also sleeping out so we could have some kind of late night rendezvous; it all sounded awesome in theory and we boys would get wound up tighter than a watch spring, but in reality it never materialized. The idea of one of us boys actually going out with a girl that had friends that wanted to go out with all of our goofy friends was as mathematically improbable as hitting the lottery twice in a week. The best we could hope for was to find one of these groups of girls sitting out on their front porch (under close observation from their parents in the living room) and we would sit and talk and act silly and joke around for a couple hours until they had to go inside, leaving all of us boys with unfulfilled delusions of grandeur. Sometimes when we were trying to get these girls attention we would speak into the fan that was in their windows, of course it came through the other side sounding like a robot and probably scared the crap out of them. More than once we talked into the fan of an angry dad.

The heat of the night often lured us towards the Big Pool. There was nothing more invigorating than a moonlight swim and it wasn't too hard to dare each other into making it a nude midnight swim. The ten-foot fence and breaking and entering laws probably deterred most normal people from believing that they had the right to swim in the Big Pool anytime they wanted to but it barely even slowed us down; we could scale that back fence, strip down, and be in the pool in less than a minute. We knew enough to not make too big of a scene, no dives from the board, no jumping off of the lifeguard chairs, just calmly get into the water and swim around. If we saw headlights or heard voices, we would duck down and keep as quiet as possible, the adrenaline factor sometimes would be off the charts as people walked their dogs past the pool or drove along the road near the pool. However we were well past a simple adrenaline rush the night that the police parked right behind where we had climbed the fence and shone their spotlights out over the water. I don't think they had any suspicion of us being in the water, but they sat there for what seemed like an hour which was probably only five minutes. Eventually they left and we made our escape.

We also made a lot of trips through the cemetery when we slept out. I don't know what the infatuation was with sneaking around in 40 acres of crypts, headstones, and mausoleums, but we did it quite regularly. In fact it was one of our favorite make-out places as well, (I can't believe the amount of girls that agreed to romantic liaisons in the middle of a cemetery). In the dead middle of the night (no pun intended), it took a certain of amount of bravery to go very far past those somewhat ominous gates. But before I brag about our late night courage; in all honesty the slightest movement, be it from a rustling leaf or a squirrel scrambling up a tree had us making a hasty exit to the safety of...well, anywhere other than the cemetery.

Another thing that we liked to do when we were sleeping out, especially when we had a big group of seven or eight of us (the more that joined our group, the lower our IQ's dropped and we did dumber and dumber things) was to dare each other into going streaking. Streaking was the fad of taking your clothes off (you kept your shoes and socks on) and running. I can't tell you how far a streaker was supposed to run or where they were supposed to run to, it was different based on the situation. Sometimes we streaked and ran around someone's backyard, or around a house, or past a group of girls, or if we were really feeling brave we might try to make it the length of the block. We had some streakers run through the cafeteria during lunchtime in high school, got caught and I believe they got expelled. Streaking became a national epidemic with nude runners appearing at about every sporting event that you can think of. While we were running down the street naked, we never came across the police but that was all you could think of as you were jiggling down the road. The general rule while streaking, was to jog along and act like nothing was going on regardless of who, or how many people were watching.

At some point (usually around 3:30 or 4:00 in the morning) we would find our way back to the tent, crawl into our sleeping bags, and pass out on the cold bumpy ground. Half of the time we were absolute zombies the next day until around 2:00 in the afternoon, and then we'd just start the whole process over again. I guess that when we got to be 19/20-years old it was pretty normal for us to stay out all night running around and make it into work the next day without too much difficulty.

✒ It probably didn't take you over 200 pages to figure out that we were not angels. There were a heck of a lot worse deviants than me and the guys I hung around with. There were real, stone-cold, psychopathic criminals that lived in my town who as youngsters were busy practicing their future adult criminal activities. But most of us were just kids, kids who didn't particularly have a lot of supervision, kids who had tough home lives and wanted to vent those frustrations into ornery, ill-conceived, brazen actions that kids often make.

It was much easier for us to get away with some of our ridiculous actions than it would be in today's society; there were no cell phones taking pictures and videos of every second of our lives, there was no You Tube, or Twitter, or Facebook, or Vine, or Snapchat, or ...(this social media crap is mind-numbing). So when we did something stupid it was usually only seen by three or four people, not filmed and potentially seen by millions on the internet. And the more we got away with stuff, the more stuff we did, and the more stuff we did regularly the better we got at it; so before it was all over with, it was basically impossible (especially in our minds) for us to get caught doing our dumb, childish, juvenile antics.

When I write these things down ...well, I ain't gonna lie, it looks bad. It wasn't like we did all of these things in one day, and it wasn't like I did all of these things myself, remember these were misguided activities that kids of our generation did. At no time am I justifying any of the actions that I'm going to admit to, but let me just preface this with the fact that very few of our families had any money, we were out on the run for hours at a time, we were fit, fast, and unafraid of getting caught. Not unafraid because we didn't fear the consequences of the police knocking on our door, we all knew that our parents would cave a permanent dent into our skulls, but unafraid because we really, truly thought that if we took off running there was no police officer in the world that could ever catch us.

✍ Here's some of the goofy, crazy, (probably criminal) things that we did through the years:

Pop bottles – pb's as we called them were something that we always were looking for. Regardless of where we were, who we were with, or what we were doing we were always on the lookout for pop bottles. I've been told by others that I could spot a pop bottle in someone's garage from a mile away, probably a little bit of an exaggeration but not by much. Why pop bottles? Pop bottles funded every activity that we did during our entire childhood; if we wanted to go to the movies (let's go steal some pop bottles), if we wanted to go to the dance (let's go steal some pop bottles), if we wanted something from the store (let's go steal some pop bottles), if guys wanted beer money (let's go steal some pop bottles). In the 60's and 70's there was a deposit on every pop bottle that was sold, people would drink their pop and return their eight-pack back to the store in an empty bottle bin that was usually in front of the cash registers. There was a nickel refund on each bottle until I think about 1975 in Ohio and then it was raised up to a dime per bottle. When it rose to a dime, I really thought that I was going to give J. Paul Getty (the richest man in the world at that time) a run for his money.

How did we get these bottles? Well, in the beginning we just walked up and asked people if they had any old pop bottles that they didn't want. That plan worked about 10% of the time. Then we had the idea of telling people that we were collecting pop bottles for the Boy Scouts; now mind you we weren't dressed in anything resembling a Boy Scout uniform and we had no literature or anything to give them about our collection. That plan worked about 20% of the time. But we saw an awful lot of pop bottles in people's garages and on their back porches that we weren't getting through dialogue, so we decided to just plain take them. Sometimes one of us would ring the front doorbell and then run away while another of us would take the pop bottles. Eventually we got so arrogant with it that we would just walk into a garage like it was our own and walk out with the bottles. One time there was a back alley unattached garage that had several eight-packs of bottles in it, but a guy was having a cookout in his backyard, we crawled in the garage and took out four or five eight-packs of pb's and walked right past the guy who waved at us while he was cooking his hot dogs.

One of our most cocky displays of pop bottle thievery was when the Pepsi guy was hauling in full bottles into the front door and was hauling out cases of empty bottles out the back door to load onto his truck. As soon as he loaded the empties onto the truck, we grabbed them and walked into the front door with them. The Convenient Food Store ladies weren't stupid; they knew darn well that we didn't drink that much pop. But they'd pay us that 80¢ per eight-pack and we'd be rich, at least for a few minutes.

I can still hear those clanking pop bottles in my mind as we'd run down every back alley in Cambridge. We could each carry six eight-packs if necessary, I remember that we'd stuff an eight-pack under each arm and then we could hold two eight-packs in each hand. That was $4.80! Which in those days was big money.

While we are speaking about pop bottles let's discuss pop machines for a second. Most early pop machines held bottles of pop in which you pulled open a long slender door that exposed the top of bottles and you paid your money (10¢ to 25¢) and pulled out what you paid for. If you knew what you were doing you could jimmy the bottle around and occasionally get a free one to slip out. Eventually most pop machines started using cans instead of bottles. Through urban legends we heard about a way to get free pop out of the canned pop machines, so we tried it. We poured salt water into the coin slot and sure enough, the machine began to kick out cans of pop and nickels like a slot machine. There was some chemical reaction with the salt water and the nickels that made them fly out of the machine. I know that there were guys that did this all of the time, once was enough for my group, the process was really loud as the machine was clinking out nickels and shooting out cans of pop like you'd see in a cartoon, and it went on for a long, long time, we weren't crazy about crimes that took longer than a few seconds.

Ok, so I guess I have one more story related to pop but this time it's about the delivery trucks. We would often hang out around the back of grocery stores, it was a good place to sit and eat the Ho Hos or Oreos that we'd buy throughout the day (no doubt from stolen pop bottles). Anyways, the delivery drivers would be done with their deliveries and would drive off; through a series of dares we eventually started hitching a ride on the back of the delivery trucks. The trucks usually had a wide platform on the back to stand on and there was always a handle or two that you could grab. We would jump on the truck unbeknownst to the driver and ride on the truck until it was just about ready to pull out onto the road and then we'd jump off. One day instead of jumping off before the truck turned onto the main road one of our hellions stayed on; the rest of us started whooping and hollering as we ran down the sidewalk following the truck. The delivery truck got up to legal speed pretty fast but the guy hanging on the back didn't seem overly concerned. A street light was coming up and if that light hadn't turned red, I'm not sure how far this guy would've had to go before he was able to bail off. We sprinted to catch the truck and congratulated our brave rider like he had come back from a moon landing.

Food – Well, we had to eat didn't we? Although we didn't spend a whole lot of time worrying about our next meal, we still had to eat every once in a while. Chances are that we were as skinny as we'd ever be, probably under seven percent body fat, but the fact that we were running around all over town jumping from one activity to the next forced us to get some nutrients into our bodies. In the summer and fall we ate pretty well on fruits and veggies that we found as we strolled through the back alleys. I'm pretty sure that the tomatoes which were staked up two feet from a guy's back door were supposed to be off limits, but alas a rosy red tomato staring right at us when we just happened to have a salt shaker in our pockets, would have been a crime if we didn't eat it. We did eventually find out that messing with 45-year old guy's prize tomatoes wasn't worth the hassle.

If the vegetables seemed to be somewhat claimed by the owners, fruits were another story. We had heard about tales of Johnny Appleseed planting apple trees all throughout our area so we just assumed that apples were community property. I didn't even really like apples but free was free and a couple apples tasted pretty good when you were hungry. Eastern Ohio must be a geographical paradise for fruit because other than pineapples and coconuts, you could find just about every imaginable kind; you just had to know when and where. Strawberries, blackberries, peaches, cherries, and grapes were all available somewhere in our town, most right in our own neighborhood. It ends up that strawberries didn't grow naturally at all and the planters of said strawberries would get really irate at us when they saw us pulling them off of the vine. The grapes had a pretty long lifespan and could be found closer to the fall, the cherries had about a five-day window of ripeness where we were fighting the birds for them, the blackberries were always found near the woods and no one cared or even knew we were eating them, but the peaches could only be found in one tree that we were aware of, and that was in a neighbor's yard right behind my house. When the peaches started to get ripe they would fall to the ground and didn't last long after that, they rotted quickly and were swarmed over by bugs and bees for their sweet nectar. But we could always count on about three days' worth of peach feasting which usually included a couple bee stings.

There were guys who were pretty good at stealing food from stores, I guess I figured it was way easier to steal pop bottles and just pay for the food than it was to steal food from the store. My thought process went something like this: I had a lot of different exit options if someone saw me stealing pop bottles, but if I got caught sticking a Snickers down my pants I only had one exit.

We also stole food from our own homes. If we happened to pop into the house with our friends and saw a fresh batch of cookies, homemade pie, or nice-looking cake sitting out on the counter it was pretty common to dig in and wipe out the baked goodies. Of course 90% of the time, our mothers certainly hadn't spent an afternoon baking desserts for our hobo friends. But it wasn't like there was a way to contact our parents if we came home and they weren't. We couldn't use our cell phone and call to see if it was ok to eat the cookies, as a matter-of-fact we weren't really encouraged to use the home phone unless it was an enormous emergency.

There were a lot of large families back in those days so when groceries were purchased they were planned out in an attempt to feed five or six kids. Thus a twelve-pack of Fudgsicles, Dreamsicles, or Popsicles was supposed to equal out to two treats per child. But if you were the first one to discover the box in the freezer, you would grab it, walk out the back door, and start distributing the frozen goodies to all of your crew. It made you immensely popular with the kids on the block, but your siblings whined so much and got you into so much trouble, a lot of times it probably wasn't worth it. Often though, you were just trying to steal it before your sister could because she was going to do the exact same thing that you had done.

If we got thirsty we had all the water we could drink; there was an unlimited supply of garden hoses and spigots on the side of people's houses. If we were in the woods, we'd just cup some creek water into our hands (once the water was in our hands it didn't look nearly as brown). If we were playing downtown we could get a drink from any number of businesses that had water fountains. A bottle of water wasn't even in anyone's thought process at this point; as a matter-of-fact I think I cussed for three straight days the first time I had to buy a bottle of water.

Sometimes even when we paid for food we stole it. There was a local pizza shop that had a buffet once a week and kids would go in there and just gorge themselves to the point that they were ready to puke. We had scored on a particularly large pop bottle heist and walked into the pizza buffet with plenty of coins burning a hole in our pockets. We jammed the jukebox full of quarters to play the same song over and over again; every patron in there was subjected to Earth, Wind, & Fire's *Serpentine Fire*, (no reason that song was chosen other than the fact we thought it would drive everyone crazy). Three of us ate 100 pieces of pizza; we scooped up full plates of pizza every time they came out to fill the buffet table. The other patrons finally complained enough that we were thrown out and asked not to return. We left so sick we could hardly move. I think some of the people inside were rooting for us while others wanted to kill us.

✍ Let me quickly go back to using the phone and coming home to an empty house. You had either a rotary dialed tabletop phone or a phone attached to the wall; each had an extremely long cord connecting the receiver to the actual phone. There was no caller ID so you had to actually answer the phone to find out who was on the other end. When you answered the phone you were expected to answer it in a friendly and businesslike manner, "Hello, Jones residence, Billy speaking." Once on the phone you would have a huge amount of wrong numbers, prank calls, and if you stayed on the phone for very long you had party line issues. Party line, what the heck is that? Your phone was on the same telephone line as several other people and if they picked up the phone they could listen to your calls and vice versa. Sometimes if you heard them on the line you would tell them to get off the phone, other times they would tell you to hurry up so they could use the phone. If you got mad at someone or if someone was giving you a prank call, you could slam the phone down and it would give a serious ring to the caller's ear, (can't do that with a cell phone). The phone was made out of two-inch thick industrial strength plastic so it was virtually impossible to break it.

When we got older and started talking to girlfriends and boyfriends we would often stretch the phone line across the living room and into our bedroom to allow us some privacy for our important conversations, "I'm not going to hang up first, you hang up first."

"Well, I'm not going to hang up first; you'll have to hang up first."

"Nope. We'll just have to stay on here all night. Hahaha."

So after 15-minutes of playing who's going to hang up first, you hear, "I'm tired of tripping over that *&^damn phone cord, hand up the &^%$ing phone."

"Jenny. I'll talk to you later, I gotta go !"

As far as coming home to an empty house, there was usually a note laying on the counter, or by the phone, or taped to the refrigerator. I'm at Aunt Sally's house. I will be back at 5:00 or Stay home until I get back and leave the cookies alone. There was always a handwritten list of the most used phone numbers next to the phone, so if you really wanted to find your parents you would start down the list until you miraculously found them. Usually when you found them in that manner their response was, "What's wrong? Are you hurt? Did you catch something on fire?"

✍   Drinking and Drugs – With all of the great things of the 60's and 70's, this is one that I'm not at all proud about. I never drank and I never took any type of drugs; I am gonna say it is because of watching my dad and I just never wanted to be anything like him in that category. And in fairness to him, he jumped all over me when I did anything that even looked like I may follow his path. Although I didn't get involved in drinking I suppose I helped enable some of my friends; I'd help them round up pop bottles for beer money, I'd drive them around so they could drink in the backseat, and I'd babysit them when they were about to do dumb things or when they got sick.

During the 60's and 70's the legal drinking age for beer was 18, so that meant that every senior and half of the juniors were able to legally walk into any place that sold beer and stroll out with as much as they could carry. So it wasn't real hard to find someone you knew that was a year or two older than you who would buy you and your buddies a case of beer. When you went into bars you were carded and stamped either 18 or 21; 18-year olds could only purchase beer, but 21-year olds could also purchase hard liquor. It wasn't real hard to have someone over 21 buy a shot of something powerful for some 18-year old, it wasn't like anyone in the bars was watching too closely. You could also have situations where a senior and their teacher might be sitting in the same bar. Potentially awkward; I'm pretty sure a lot of the teachers in those days drank at bars a few miles away. You also had a lot of fake IDs, you didn't have to do a lot of changing, just adjust the birthday by a couple years. It was real easy to be dancing in a nightclub with a girl, walk her out to her car, and see a high school parking sticker on the bumper. Whoops.

It was a weekly ritual for my buddies (and most of the rest of the town) to buy beer, drive around town, and then go to the Y-dance or City Park dance. Most guys would save their lunch money so they could have enough to buy the beer and get into the dances. If you weren't 18 and didn't have someone to buy beer for you there were other choices. There were bars and carryouts that would sell you the beer without too much hassle as long as you carried yourself in an adult manner and didn't look like you were ten-years old. If they asked for ID, you'd quickly make up a story. We had a place called the Buddha; it was in a section of town affectionately called The Bottom. The Bottom was primarily black, and it was at the bottom of the hill going out of town, the bottom of the economic rung, and the bottom priority for the police to worry about. Worrying about what went on in the Buddha was not high on anyone's list, so we'd go down there on Friday and Saturday nights. Before anyone ever went inside, there would always be some kind of verbal pact, "If I don't come out in five minutes go get the cops."

The guys left out in the car were probably as nervous as the guys that went in. There were always a couple guys standing around and we always felt like they were staring at us and making plans for our demise. We'd lay money on the counter and ask for a case of Little Kings or Genny Cream Ale, then the owner'd give you a look and maybe ask, "You old enough to be buying that?"

I'm pretty sure he was just messing with us, he was gonna sell us the beer regardless, he just wanted to see if we were gonna pee our pants. We played ball with these guy's kids or nephews so they knew exactly how old we were; I figure they thought if we were brave enough to walk in there and ask for beer they would go ahead and sell it to us.

After we purchased the beer, we would drive around town or drive out Eighth Street Road and they would drink and throw the bottles out the window while we had Wild Cherry *Play That Funky Music* playing on the eight-track as loud as it would go. Throughout the years, I'm sure that some of this nation's finest young men and women died in accidents related to those Saturday night drinking episodes; Lord knows we had plenty of close calls ourselves through the years.

Girls didn't seem to be big beer drinkers but were pretty quick to chug down some Boone's Farm, Peach Schnapps, or any type of sweet fruity drink they could get their hands on. These drinks were somehow usually stocked at where these girls were babysitting or boys were put in charge of trying to obtain these drinks for them, which were ten times harder to get our hands on because you had to be twenty-one. In times like these it was easier to just pay one of any number of guys in town who could just walk in and steal a bottle. These guys were masters and really excelled in their craft.

I am positive that there were hard drugs during the 60's and 70's but all I can attest to is the abundance of marijuana. I know that this time period is known for hippies and perpetual drug usage but I honestly didn't know one hippie, (although the Old Man called everyone who had hair longer than a drill sergeant a "&^%$ing hippie"). But if you wanted some pot, you could ask for some in any class you went to and at least five or six people in every class could sell you whatever you needed. There were dope deals in the parking lot, dope deals in the bathroom, dope deals at lunchtime, dope deals in homeroom, dope deals right in class if the teacher wasn't paying attention, dope deals at the park, dope deals in the back alleys; I don't know if there was a dope kingpin that all of this money eventually funneled into, but if there was he had a serious bank account. If you didn't want to be involved you just turned and walked away, you learned places to avoid, and unfortunately you lost friends through the years because they got so involved in the drug world (or I guess you could've gained new friends if you were a druggie and you hung out with all of your new druggie friends).

It was funny because almost all of us had watched our dads or uncles or grandpas roll their own cigarettes, (I think it was called Bugler in a greenish blue package). The Old Man didn't roll his cigarettes very often; he was a Lucky Strike man to the tune of three packs a day. Now we had kids going to the store to buy rolling paper (I think those guys used e-z wider) and rolling doobies instead of tobacco cigarettes. You could always spot a stoner by the impression of a Bic lighter in their pocket (unless it was firecracker season, then we all had one). Of course no respectable adult smoker would go anywhere without their stainless steel Zippo lighter. I remember my dad changing out the flint and refueling the lighter fluid; he would get mad as hell when he couldn't find his lighter, (I think he'd rather had lost his car keys than his lighter).

✍ I will break these next less than ideal activities into three categories: Throwing stuff and other dumb things, dumb things we did at work, and dumb things we did in the snow. I've got no recourse but to just label them dumb things; that is the least incriminating way that I can phrase it.

Throwing stuff and other dumb things – Clear back 170 some pages ago I talked about throwing stuff, we were obsessed with it. We couldn't walk down the street without finding something to throw; it may have been a rock, it may have been a stick, it may have been an apple, or a cherry, or a grape, or any other fruit that we happened by, it may have been a football, or basketball, or baseball, it may have been someone's hat, or shoe, or baseball glove, it may have been a tulip bloom, or a bolt that we found lying on the road, or a dead mouse, or a good dried up dog turd; as you can see it didn't really matter what we threw just as long as we were throwing something.

Like anything else, we practiced so often that we got good at it. Would it been more beneficial to have spent that time practicing the piano, or violin, or some other artsy-fartsy craft? Probably. Could we have made better use of our time if we had been practicing our reading, shoot maybe even crack open a Bible to see what all the hoopla was about on Sundays? Probably. But we didn't. We spent our time throwing things at things. Inanimate things, live things, stationary things, moving things, junk things, expensive things, worthless things, important things, things up close, and things far away.

You're probably waiting on some examples and some stories, so ok, here we go: By the time we got to high school, we had become far too proficient at throwing things at lowly, stationary, inanimate objects; we seemed to only get thrills out of calculating trajectories for impossible moving target tosses that could potentially turn into some kind of adrenaline pumping high speed chase through the neighborhood backyards and alleyways. I find it amazing that we never caused any real damage and that we never got caught.

We were smart enough to not throw solid things (except snowballs that turned into ice comets) at moving cars, but everything that wasn't made out of solid stone apparently was free game. We would walk around in groups of three to ten, and I can guarantee you that the more people that joined our group, the wilder things we were going to try. Sometimes we would hide behind big six-foot high hedges a few feet from the road and lob mushy apples or tomatoes at passing cars. If we heard tires lock up or saw brake lights we lit out of there like cockroaches when the lights come on. Other times we'd go for longer throws that were hard to connect on, but when we did it was pretty dramatic. The toughest throws were from the top of the Children's Home Hill down to Wheeling Ave, which was probably 100 yards, but straight downhill, so it was more like a 40 yard throw. There was little to no chance of hitting a car, so we patiently waited for a semi to come by and we'd pelt apples or snowballs into the trailer.

Once we thought it would be funny to throw snap-n-pops at a biker. Snap-n-pops were little packets of gun powder I suppose that were glorified caps that you could throw on the ground. The biker rumbled up the street and I suppose on a dare, one of us fired a snap-n-pop right into the side of the neck of this big, burly, tattooed, no-doubt-in-the-world-that-he-was-going-to-kill-us biker. He watched us throw something at him, so he knew he hadn't just been stung by a bee. Luckily he didn't lay the bike down, but he parked it pretty quickly and started a pretty thorough search for us. In our infinite wisdom, we hid underneath our buddy's front porch and watched his frantic pursuit through the diamond-shaped holes of the latticework. I think it was probably one of the few times that we ever really considered turning ourselves into our parents so that they would save us from being turned into dog meat, (our parents probably would've done worse, but this guy was pretty mad and pretty scary).

The greatest throw I've personally ever made was on a Halloween night. We were in the biggest group I've ever been in and things were getting wilder as the night went on. We were throwing eggs and a car went by, a Volkswagen as I recall, and a guy was yelling out the window trying to impress the girls he had in the car. So here was a car travelling 30 mph, it passed us, and I threw an egg that caught up with the car, went through the driver's side window, and splattered on the INSIDE of the windshield. Our whole group erupted into celebration and a couple minutes later, here comes this guy running down the hill towards our very massive group of Halloween hellions. He is yelling and screaming and wanting revenge for the egg that was literally on his face; we encircled the guy almost exactly like the scene from *Karate Kid* and this guy gets into some wacky Kung Fu stance. We all kind of tensed up and I was more than willing to step up and handle things but then one of our members says, "Who do you think you are Bruce Lee? There's 20 of us, get the f_ _ _ out of here" At that point the tension was immediately relieved and we all laughed and high fived our way right past the guy.

✍ Before continuing on with throwing, I will touch on our Halloween escapades. We trick-or-treated with pillow cases, when we filled one we ran it home, dumped it on the table and went back out to reload. Trick-or-Treat night was a solid two hours long and started at 7:00 p.m., so it was plenty dark when we finished. I figure we went "begging" until we were at least 17, and by then we had it down to a science. We sprinted for two straight hours and could cover...I don't know, probably seven or eight miles worth of neighborhoods. We came home with enough candy to keep us in confections for the next two months: Snickers, Milky Ways, Three Musketeers, Hershey Bars, Baby Ruths, Reeses', Tootsie Rolls, Fifth Avenues, Butterfingers, Candy Corn, Charleston Chews, Chocolate Coins, Pop Rocks (which supposedly if mixed with Coke in your mouth would explode), Clark Bars, Mounds, Almond Joys, Krackles, Mr. Goodbars, Kit Kats, M & M's, Mallow Cups, Mild Duds, Sixlets, Pixie Stix, Whoppers, Bit-O-Honeys, Black Jacks, Caramel Creams, Chuckles, Wax Lips, Wax Pop Bottles, Sweet Tarts, Sugar Babies, Mary Janes, Royals, Blow Pops, Tootsie Pops, Safety Pops, Fireballs, Jawbreakers, Lemonheads, (this could go on all day). We also took in a lot of apples and popcorn balls in those days; you didn't have to worry about most of us sucking down a razor blade hidden in an apple, because they went straight into the trash. Our costumes were made for speed instead of fright factor, so we would dress up in the cheapest mask money could buy that didn't hinder our breathing.

Of course Trick-or-Treat was split into two sections, treats (the candy we hauled in) and tricks (the pranks we pulled for the two weeks leading into Halloween). Yes we soaped windows, yes we advanced to paraffin (don't know where we even got that from), yes we threw corn at metal storm doors and windows, yes we threw eggs, yes we threw tomatoes, yes we sprayed Silly String, yes we sprayed shaving cream on parked cars, yes we put firecrackers (including M-80's) into mailboxes, yes there were guys who stole fire extinguishers from apartment buildings and businesses (no, I never did that, it just didn't seem worth the risk), yes there were kids that pooped in bags and lit them and rang a guy's doorbell (no, I never did that, it sounded too much like arson if no one answered the door), we certainly rang doorbells and ran or hid in the bushes, but in reality we kind of did a little bit of Halloween stuff year-round, so we didn't get overly cranked up about it.

At times we got carried away with water balloons as well. When it got boring throwing them at each other and at the neighbor girls, we quickly moved on to throwing them at cars. Our most infamous water balloon toss, (I'm laughing as I'm writing this), was in broad daylight as we walked right down the sidewalk. Without any real warning to the rest of the group, one of us fired a water balloon into the side of the face of a guy driving a Red Cadillac convertible who was smoking a great big two dollar cigar. I can still visualize in slow motion like it was from a *Jackass* movie, the water balloon blasting this local big wig's chunky face, and his face wiggling in waves as the cigar went falling into his lap. It's amazing that he didn't hit a tree as he was reaching down trying to get this burning cigar out of his lap, probably wondering what the heck hit him, as his car was weaving up onto the curb. We really didn't even run, we just sort of stood there and watched this guy's car lurch side to side and end up resting near the sidewalk. Big shot huh? Not in our neighborhood.

✍ Of course we could find plenty of other dumb things to do that didn't involve throwing stuff. I wish we could've harnessed our imaginations and creativity into something positive, luckily we had sports to keep our interest 90% of the time, but boy that 10% down time was nothing short of complete reckless abandon.

We played in the rain, we played in the snow, we played in sweltering 100° heat, and we played through blizzards and at least one tornado. I never see kids out playing in the rain anymore; I always thought that was pretty refreshing and not one of our parents ever complained about us playing in the rain (probably because that was the closest thing to a bath that we took outside of the Big Pool). We played in the street, we played on garage, and church, and school roofs, we played in old abandoned buildings and ramshackle barns, we played on downtown fire escapes, we climbed trees and telephone poles, we swam in pools, creeks, ponds, and strip pits. We played in the mud and we played in the leaves that we raked for the sole purpose of diving in them. All I can say is that Tetanus must not be a real thing because we were always stepping on old cruddy nails and cutting ourselves in 1000 different ways. When we were little our mother's would put that old crappy mercurochrome on it and everything would be all better even though it stung more than the original injury.

We were obsessed with speed and we were fascinated with the power of gravity. The Children's Home Hill was one of the steepest grass inclines that we could find, it was roughly 120 yards long with about a 60° angle that ended with a four-foot high drop that would catapult any object (or person) directly out into the middle of Wheeling Avenue (one of Cambridge's busiest, fastest moving thoroughfares). Yep, that sounds like the perfect place to test Mr. Isaac Newton's theories.

We tried rolling just about every imaginable object that you can think of down that monster hill. I can't drive by that hill today without looking to the top and just shaking my head. We stole a guy's spare tire one day, rolled it a block and half to the top of the hill, gave it a little shove, and then stood back and watched gravity do its best. The tire wobbled slowly in the beginning, then straightened out on its own, as it picked up speed it also started to bounce, first a few feet, then a few more, and then before it was over it was only hitting the ground every twenty feet or so. We watched it get to the end of the hill, shoot off of the retaining wall, hit once in the middle of the street, then land with a crash into some lady's shrubs. It was basically one of the most awesome things we had ever seen. We wanted to up the ante and put one of us inside an empty tire, but either decided against it or couldn't find an empty tire that day. So we settled for bravely retrieving the original tire (broad daylight, complete nerves of steel) and going for launch number two, which I believe didn't hit the shrubs as softly or at all for that matter and narrowly missed a car, (which I'm sure added to our frenzied excitement).

✏   We had a terrible habit of messing with For Sale signs. We discovered that we could run by and kick them and the sign would pop out, and we'd hit the same houses over and over nearly every night. I remember the day one of our gang kicked a sign that turned out to be metal and I believe he broke his toe. We paid a little bit more attention after that. We would also uproot the signs and move them to other properties; I can only imagine the potential calls that Realtors received from our pranks, "Yeah, I was calling about that yellow house on Beatty Avenue, I think it's 1314."

"I'm sorry, but I can't find that in our listings. Let me check on that and get back to you." Click of the receiver; yell to the back of the office. "Hey Dave, those little S.O.B.'s moved signs around again last night."

✏   The town of Cambridge had and still has one of the best city parks that you can find anywhere. The Duck Pond is the gateway to the rest of park, it had a floating fountain in the middle that I'm sure gave plenty of aesthetic beauty to the patrons of the park. What a good place to stick a pink flamingo. About every other year someone would swim out there in the middle of the night and plant a yard ornament pink flamingo on the fountain base. It must've been a pain in the butt to get out there and take it down because sometimes it stayed out there a few weeks.

The Duck Pond was surrounded by weeping willow trees of which in the summer we would grab a big handful of the vine-like branches, swing out as far as we could and propel ourselves into the less than chlorinated water. I remember the day we stopped doing that when a policeman cruised up and gave us a detailed list of all of the things we could catch from swimming in the Duck Pond, (I think maybe he was just jealous). Of course in the winter, we would dare each other to cross the (potentially) frozen waters. The Duck Pond was pretty big and you sure in the heck didn't want to get halfway across and fall through the ice; luckily that never happened. There were however a few really frigid winters in which the Duck Pond froze so solidly that the city allowed public ice skating on it.

I remember being picked up by my friend one summer day and he wanted to drive out by the park in his lift-kitted Chevy Luv truck. Cruising the Park was something that every Cambridge kid did, and I'm sure they did it in every park, in every city in the U.S.A. We saw some guys we knew so he pulled up to the side of the road, they walked towards the car, excited to see me and Joe and then all of the sudden, Joe hits his wipers and water squirts out horizontally and drenches these poor victims. He had rigged up an extra motor to his windshield wiper fluid reservoir, filled it with water, and aimed the sprayer to the left and right, and it now shot a good twenty feet. We must've sprayed thirty unsuspecting park walkers that afternoon. Crazy Joe.

✍ Dumb things we did at work – The quarter a week savings account that we started in elementary school had long since dried up. At some point we all got jobs, they may have only been jobs around the house or jobs we did for neighbors but most of us eventually needed more money than pop bottles could bring in, or the money we could get out of piggy banks with a butter knife, (the pennies came out so easily but the quarters just wouldn't come out of the slot). Although we got a lot of work done for the pay that we got, it just wasn't in our nature to keep our noses strictly to the grindstone; we found a lot of ways to "entertain" ourselves while at work. Here are some of the jobs that we had during the 60's and 70's (which are probably similar to those of today):

Mowing lawns – There were a few guys in town who as teenagers had very organized and probably profitable lawn care businesses. That however wasn't me and my crew. In a pinch we would walk around the block with a lawnmower from our homes, look for a yard that looked like it needed a little work, and we'd knock on the door and ask if they needed their lawn mowed. Every once in a while someone would accept, but it was only going to be a onetime deal,

A) once we had some money in our pocket we weren't concerned about anything other than how fast we could spend it, and

B) the quality of this "lawn mowing job" was so poor, no one would ever hire us back anyways. No, exaggeration, we would literally run as we pushed the mower. A lot of times if there were two of us, one guy would sprint down, make a U-turn and basically do a handoff to the other guy. We could mow a quarter acre lawn in about eight minutes; no trimming, no collection of the cut grass, and if a flower stood between us and the finish line it was history.

Raking leaves – Wow, raking leaves was real work! There was no easy way to fly through this job, although I'm sure we did it 50% faster than the next fastest person in town. You also had the lure of jumping in the pile of leaves; we were fired from more than one leaf raking job for piling up the leaves and then taking a brief time-out to dive head first into our awesome pile of fall remnants.

Shoveling snow – Even though this falls into our next category of dumb things we did in the snow, it was a job, so here we go. "When we were kids, we had to walk three miles to school in five feet of snow". Well, honestly, in the winter of 1978 that really wasn't that much of an old wives tale. It snowed and snowed and snowed so we had plenty of opportunities to make money shoveling sidewalks and driveways. I suppose we made $30 each that winter, which really wasn't too bad, except that the average for kids who went out to shovel that winter was probably closer to $150, (didn't matter, we had other stuff to do). My dad looked outside after one of the big storms and must've seen kids my age walking around with snow shovels so he got on me to get off of my butt and go make some money. So me and my pals hit the streets (literally, because walking on the sidewalk wasn't going to happen, there was too much snow) and searched for some snow shoveling business. The first place we stopped at had an old guy that was obviously physically unable to remove three-feet of wet heavy snow from his sidewalk and driveway. We dug, and threw, and cleared a beautiful swath that looked better than every walk on the block. He invited us in and sat us down to some hot chocolate that he had made for us. I was more concerned with getting paid and moving on to the next job so I could keep the Old Man off my back and possibly even make him proud of me for a change. Five minutes turned into twenty, he kept telling us we had to get the chill off so the *sugar water* would quit dripping from our nose (I always kind of liked that line). Eventually I got my buddies' attention and we made our way to the door, I figured we had at least five dollars each coming for this huge and well-done job; but alas he held out his elderly shaking hand to us with a very lonely one dollar bill attached to it. His eyes looked down at the floor and his disappointment and embarrassment started to well up his eyes. I took the money, looked at it, returned it to his hand, and told him, "Here you go. I think you gave us too much, the hot chocolate was plenty."

None of us said a discouraging word as we hit the streets to find another, maybe even paying job this time. Yep, I was asked how much I made that day, I don't think he was overly impressed with the five dollars that I eventually drummed up, but I know that I had earned a lot more than that, but I didn't dare try to explain the whole *sugar water* scenario to him.

Nightcrawler Hunting – When it was knee deep into fishing season (Cambridge is surrounded by several great fishing lakes), we would go nightcrawler hunting. I know the Old Man would pay us a quarter for every dozen nightcrawlers we'd bring him; other times we would actually try to sell the nightcrawlers by the side of the road, (which I doubt if we sold three dozen in three years). To be a good nightcrawler hunter you needed a few things: an old can or Icee cup to put the worms in, a flashlight, a little bit of rain or dew, and some patience. After a rain or when the dew was on the ground, big juicy nightcrawlers (worms) would start to come out of the ground, for the most part they wouldn't come all the way out of their holes, so that made things way harder. You would walk around and shine the flashlight out at an angle because if you shined it straight down on the crawlers, they would see the light and dive back down into their hole (no lie). Eventually you would see about half an inch of shimmering, slimy, pinkish worm sticking out of the ground; at that point you would sneak up on it (good gosh this sounds stupid), reach down as slowly as possible and try to grab the worm without ripping it in half. A lot of times you'd catch the little critter but he'd have a pretty good grip on the inside of his hole, at that point you had to tickle it (people must think I'm making this up), you would actually tickle it until it came out of its hole. On a good night you might be able to get six or seven dozen nightcrawlers, but two dozen was a more realistic number. I remember when I was moved out of the house and old enough to know better, I was a fisherman of some local renown, and I needed nightcrawlers, so I had heard that you could shock the worms out of the ground. I took an old toaster that we had and cut the toaster off from the cord; I plugged the cord into the garage, stuck the bare wire into the ground... and SHAZAM ! I had knocked the crap out of myself with enough electricity to put down a horse. No worms came to the surface, but I did see those little cartoon birds flying around my head for a few minutes.

We also hunted (caught) lightning bugs when we were real little. I remember that we would punch holes into the top of a Mason jar to give them oxygen, but after about four days of no food or water the jar smelled awful.

Construction jobs – As we got older sometimes neighbor guys would ask us if we wanted to make a little money helping them with a home improvement project. I know that once I graduated, I painted for twenty years in the summers and weekends, a skill learned from my dad. I couldn't hold a candle to his painting skill, but most people couldn't hold a candle to the amount of paint I could put on in a day either. Sometimes guys would hire you just to be a gopher, *go-fer* this and *go-fer* that, but I know one time about six of us got hired by a guy to dig a footer and lay some block. He told us all he could pay us was a dollar an hour, but we could have all the pop we wanted. We ended up getting fired for drinking our weight in pop in a three-day period, and later came back and stole our weight in those empty pop bottles for non-payment on the work that we had done. (The place is condemned now by the way; our footer work didn't help).

Regular jobs – Our parents worked at places like National Cash Register, March Electric, Cambridge Glass, Champion Spark Plug, or in the coal mining industry but our first jobs were more fast food, grocery store, or gas station-type jobs. At one point three of our crew worked at Domino's Pizza and between dough ball fights and bombing the delivery car (that had no windshield wipers) with giant half gallon cartons of Pepsi, it is a miracle that any of us got a pizza delivered. One night my pal drove behind the daily newspaper building and told me to get out and grab one of the bundles of newspapers, it seemed pretty illegal but I did it anyways. We drove away with a stack of 150 newspapers and pulled over a couple blocks later, "Go ahead and get those scissors out of the glove compartment." He said.

"Ok. But what are we cutting out?" I quizzed.

"Domino's ads on page nine. Don't stop til we get 100 of 'em." He retorted.

"I still don't get it. Did the manager tell you to cut these out? I asked still puzzled.

"Oh, hell no, and don't tell him we've got these. Look, the coupon is for three dollars off every pizza, so if you turn in a three dollar coupon for every delivery, and keep the three dollars for yourself, I figure we can make an extra $50 a night... unless you don't want an extra $50 a night."

"No, I definitely want the extra $50. What page did you say, nine? Let's get cuttin'."

If your buddies worked at a restaurant, you pretty much expected to get something for free, and if you worked at one of those places you spent the majority of your time trying to figure out how to hook up your crew if they came in. One of our crew worked at a the corner ice cream shop, I would walk in and ask for pretty much the most expensive thing on the menu of which he would then start adding things to the order, so a banana split would have four bananas in it plus a pint of chocolate sauce and 35 Marciano cherries and probably a coney dog thrown in the bag just to keep it company. I would rattle around a few nickels and dimes so the owner would think there was some kind of actual exchange and then he would open the cash register and give me a couple dollars' worth of change. It was a glorious system.

I know that I worked at McDonald's through college and one time gave my buddy a whole case of Monopoly open ups. I'm pretty sure we thought we were gonna win a 'Vette or trip to Vegas or something, but after sitting in a parking lot for an hour opening these stupid things, the only prizes we won were about 50 free French fries and 30 or so Big Macs.

One of our crew worked night shift at the truck stop. These big rigs would come pulling in and this guy would come flying out, hurdling over garbage cans and giving new meaning to fast service. The truckers loved him and would call on their CB radios, "Yep, ole Timmy's working. I think he broke the record tonight, washed my windows in less than a minute."

All I know is that we had free oil changes for the next two years from the two months that he worked out there.

✍ Dumb things we did in the snow – When we were kids in the 60's and 70's we had snow and at times, plenty of it. Sitting inside playing board games wasn't particularly high on our options as I've mentioned earlier. Our parents tried to talk us into staying in because the weather was so bad but by 9:30/10:00 I think they were pretty ready to get rid of us. We didn't even come in to use the bathroom, every boy in

America used to write their name in the snow. Funny stuff. Lucky for me I had a short... name.

In today's information right now world, we find out about school cancellations a couple minutes after the Superintendent makes their decision. We even have a one-call system in which everyone in the school district gets the same message over their phone and also through a text, (although it is always nice to see your school's name scroll across the bottom of the tv screen). But in the 60's and 70's we counted on the radio to deliver important messages, like, "Cambridge City Schools will be closed today." And honestly in the winter of '78, we heard that announcement for weeks at a time.

The blizzard of 1978 was a historical snow Armageddon. A series of "Perfect Storm" events lined up and dumped feet (not inches) of snow on the Midwest (but primarily Ohio) for several days. The subsequent snow drifts were so high, that if I wrote it here in the book, our young readers wouldn't believe what I wrote. I can remember how the snow plows would bury parked cars every day and in the Bargain City parking lot, they would plow the snow in a couple spots up against the lights in the parking lot and we thought we could walk up the side of the piles and change the light bulbs. (If you Wikipedia, the blizzard of 1978, you can get an idea of what it was like.)

We were out of school for so long, (and I honestly don't think we made up any of those days), I would be hard pressed to believe that it didn't slightly affect the knowledge that we were supposed to have learned in high school. I would also be hard pressed to believe that we cared; we had all day to run around in the snow and we took full advantage of that.

Each day would start with twenty minutes of preparation to adequately be able to battle the elements for ten or twelve hours. It was pretty normal to put on a t-shirt, a thermal shirt, a flannel shirt, a sweatshirt, a hooded sweatshirt, and then your letter jacket or a parka. A pair of jeans over a pair of sweatpants kept our legs warm; and three pair of tube socks and something that resembled boots kept our bottom half warm. A toboggan (now called a sock hat) and a couple pair of cheap thin cloth gloves and we were ready to head out the door, go to the garage, and either get our sleds or our intertubes.

Some of the pieces of our wardrobe made sense and some of it probably wasn't what most people would've thought was the best cold weather outfit. Wearing only two pair of pants kept us warm but still allowed us to move freely. The thin cloth gloves made it easy to make and throw snowballs and also to hold onto things like sled ropes, eight-packs of pop bottles, or shovel handles. Our fingers and toes were the only things that got really cold when we were outside all day; we were constantly on the move, but anytime that we stopped for a few minutes we realized just how cold we were. Wintertime was about the only time that we ever really went home in the middle of the day; it allowed us to throw our wet clothes over the heating register. It always felt pretty good to start round two with some freshly heated dry clothes.

The first few days of what turned out to be the never-ending winter of '78 we made snow forts, they weren't great but they served the purpose of a place to hide behind while we pummeled each other with snowballs. After a few weeks of near-continuous snow and freezing temperatures our original quickly formed two-foot high walls of snow turned into igloo-quality impenetrable citadels while crudely built snowmen turned into snow behemoths that lasted well into March.

Sledding sounded so fun, and maybe for some kids it would have been, but sitting on a sled and scooching your feet along trying to make it move and finally getting it to hopefully slide down the hill a few feet was a little bit below our standards. We escalated sledding to a much higher form of adventure; my dad drove me down to the tire store and we came home with the biggest tractor intertube that they sold. Once it was fully pumped up it could hold nine of us at the same time (although four or five was the norm). It was a no-brainer that we were going to return to the Children's Home Hill, and there we started to mold our very own bobsled half pipe. Every trip we made grinded out our course a little bit further down the hill, it got slipperier, and slipperier, and faster, and faster. It also took us closer and closer to the end of the hill or as a normal person would say, the three-foot drop off that could potentially shoot us off into the middle of the busiest thoroughfare in town.

I could only hazard a guess as to the overall speed that we generated on these intertube bobsled runs, but I would guess around 40 mph. The intertube was so big that we could sit on the outside, have everyone face each other, and put our feet in the middle of the tube. Everyone would lock arms or grab hold of the coat of the person next to you and then the trip would begin; slowly at first, but picked up very quickly, slowly spinning as it went. It was the spinning that was the problem; because only one or maybe two of us could actually see how close we were to the drop off, it was their job to scream at everyone to jump off of the tube before eminent disaster happened, (someone grabbing the tube before it went flying into the street as they bailed off was a bonus). The more rides we made down the hill, the more exciting (and dangerous, which for us was about the same thing), it got; our inevitable goal was to see how far down the hill we could go before we bailed off. Someone smarter than me would have to do the math, but basically you had let's say five boys weighing about 150 pounds each, travelling down a 120 yard, 60° incline path of ice, speeding along at 40+ mph, ready to vault off of a three-foot retaining wall, what would be the total distance traveled? I'm not smart enough to solve that problem with a calculator, but I can tell you from experience it ends up being upwards of 20 feet. It was an absolute miracle of miracles that we didn't get hit by a car. None us of would give in and jump off of the rubber ice rocket. It was one of the many times when we just stood there for a second, stared at each other, and then in unison, "Holy S%^% !" That just about summed it up.

Of course we still had our throwing fetish in the winter so the natural thing for us to throw was snowballs. When the wet and heavy snow fell it was what we called "packing snow" which made for the densest, most hazardous, and certainly the most destructive type of snowballs. If you were a kid and didn't get jacked in the face with a snowball, you must've lived in Florida, because it was a daily rite of passage to take one in the puss. You always resisted running home in tears because you knew that you'd be cooped up inside for the rest of the day and probably be banned from "playing with those little bastards" again, (which never worked by the way, we would just tell the said "bastards" to not come to the door for a few days and that we'd meet them at their house).

When we tired of throwing snowballs at ourselves we moved to throwing at random people on the street: some kid carrying groceries in from the store, the mailman, some guy walking his dog, some lady carrying a laundry basket to the Laundromat, whoever happened by, we weren't picky about our human targets. I guess we weren't overly picky about our non-human targets either: pop truck, beer truck, bread truck, Hostess Ho-Ho truck, U.S. Mail truck, gas tanker, random station wagon, some old lady in a Vega that couldn't drive in the snow, some punk teenagers in a Chevelle trying to be cool, again it really didn't matter what our target was. Hitting a door with a snowball made a very distinct noise and when it was hit by several snowballs at once was like a slot machine jackpot going off. It was hard for people to stop and see what had just happened because of the icy, deeply rutted roads; most people didn't even know they were hit (unless we splattered a snowball on a side window or up against the windshield) so they just drove off. Occasionally someone would slam their brakes on after they got hit like they had ran over a deer or something, well it wasn't like they could just get out of their car, leave it running in the middle of the road, and give chase to bunch of kids they couldn't catch anyways, they couldn't exactly drive home and call the police because by the time the police showed up we might be seven or eight blocks away, so... I'm not sure how we could've been caught back in those days. Today, someone would've taken a picture of us with their cell phone, called the cops immediately from their cell phone, and the guys in the group would've bragged about our actions on Twitter and we'd been caught within a day and a half. Kids did this all over town and I don't recall anyone every being actually caught, close calls maybe, but caught, never. I've heard of guys pelting a cop car from a safe distance and having no problem getting away with it, (I guess we were either smarter than that or weren't that brave). It was funny because even the guys who didn't know much about cars could spot the headlights of a cop car from a block away. When the police force got new vehicles, it always took us a couple weeks to get the new headlights memorized.

✍ Another somewhat comical thing we did in the winter was to go caroling. Now after all of the stuff I have put in this book, I imagine you think Christmas caroling would be the last thing you would have expected from us but we did sing on people's porches, but certainly not how normal people did. It started out as a dare, like 99% of the dumb things we did; "I dare you to go knock on that door and start singing a Christmas song."

"I ain't doing that. What'll ya give me?"

"The rest of the Oreos in the bag. There's like half a bag left."

"Ok, but I ain't singing no Christmas junk. How about *Black Betty*?"

" Awesome. But you won't do it, there's no way you'll do it."

"Bull^%^&. Just have those daggone Oreos ready."

And that is how it started, (that conversation was a blueprint to any dare we ever did), one of us walked right up on some random old lady's porch and started singing *Black Betty* by Ram Jam. This was anything but a Christmas song, but the lady stood there, smiled, and invited him in for hot chocolate while the rest of us jabbed each other in the ribs from across the street and all but rolled on the ground laughing at this guy's moxie. The next day, all of us joined in what would be the hippest group of Christmas carolers ever assembled, singing some of the grooviest songs of the late 1970's.

✍   Another pastime of ours was to gather at one of our friend's house (whose parents both worked first shift), and we played cards; saying that we played poker would put a bad name on poker players, but it was our first go around at playing cards for money. Of course the money was pennies with a nickel max bet and the games that we played were as wild as we were: 357, In-Between, Jacks or Better Trips to Win, Night Baseball, Indian Poker, Texas Hold 'em. But since the dealer got to pick the game each time, we would make up rules as we went, and often forget what was wild, usually with the dealer winning the hand on some last second forgotten rule. A typical game might be, fours are wild, eights get you another card, if you show an Ace you get to punch the person to your right in the arm, a one-eyed Jack gets paid a nickel by everyone, and if you have a black Queen you have to give your wild cards to the person to your left. That was a very typical game. You often went home with as many bruises on your arm as you did pennies in your pocket.

✍   One of the main things that was always on our Snow Day agenda was to go to the YMCA. I talked about it earlier in the book. I can only imagine how the Y workers would cringe when they heard that school was closed and they were soon going to be invaded by 50 or 60 of the most hyperactive rambunctious teenagers that the town had to offer. I know that we would track in snow and keep the janitor busy all day long trying to keep the floors safe and dry for the actual paying members of the Y. We were looked at as the Delta Tau Chi fraternity of *Animal House*, and yes most of the time we were on Double Secret Probation.

Chapter 6
Music and Dances

✍ There isn't a day that goes by in which I don't hear a song that takes me back to the days of my youth. Powerful. Powerful is the only word that describes the impact of music. Those songs from the 60's and especially the 70's (based on my age), have so many special meanings to me; each song of that era means different things to different people. The first kiss song for me is probably different than the first kiss song for you, the song that reminds me of the day I got my driver's license for example is probably different than the one that reminds you of the same event, the songs of that era are basically the soundtrack of our lives. We know the scenes based on the music that is playing.

The songs of this time period ran the gamut as far as genres of music: hard rock, country rock, pop, folk, disco, funk, soul, reggae, country, power pop, and soft rock. There was something for everyone and there were a lot of ways for us to listen to it.

Eight-tracks – Yep, we were the ones that started and also finished the eight-track cassette revolution. The eight-track wasn't our finest invention, but it was one of the ways we listened to music back in the day. The cost of a cassette was similar to the cost of buying an album, they were about as big as a VHS movie but only about half as reliable; every eight-track I ever owned was eaten by the player. Once it was eaten, you had a good 30 minutes worth of hillbilly engineering trying to get the tape out of the machine. You may have owned a large Hi-Fi system that included an eight-track player, a record player, and some decent speakers, or you may have just had a system with no record player, or you might have even had a portable eight-track player (late 70's/early 80's), and many of us had eight-track players in our cars. No one had very many of them in their cars, again imagine cassettes the size of VHS video tapes; so where in the heck were you going to store something that big.

✍ I will be honest, I don't know exactly what an eight-track cassette cost back in those days because I never technically bought one, (this is kind of trick statement), but like most of everyone that I knew, I did however purchase thirteen of them. Thirteen eight-track cassettes cost exactly 1¢, at least through the Columbia House music club. You couldn't pick up a tv guide, teen magazine, or Sunday paper without finding the very alluring, darn near hypnotic Columbia House ad. Big, bold, red letters ANY 13 FOR 1¢; whew, we had to investigate that. You were allowed to pick any thirteen records or eight-tracks from their list and all you had to do was tape a penny to the entry form and send it in, afterwards you only had to purchase five more at regular price over the next two years. How on Earth could this be a bad deal? Well, let me explain to you how this ended up being a bad deal:

A) It was easy to pick six or seven good choices from their list, number eight and nine were kind of iffy, and ten, eleven, twelve, and thirteen were records that you were never going to listen to, as a matter-of-fact you often purchased these for your mom as a Christmas present. Even when you found an artist that you liked, they wanted to sell you their forgotten and unknown album, not the one that had the hit songs that you knew and loved.

B) They sent you the Record of the Month, every month, and it was never a record that we actually wanted. You didn't have to order it, it just arrived. Remember, we were thirteen, fourteen, maybe fifteen years old and had no idea how to send something back in the mail, nor did we have the funds to do it if we did know how.

C) The regular price of the five records we had to purchase to fulfill the contract were close to double the Bargain City prices (of which we could not afford). So what happened was, you kept talking your mom into returning the Records of the Month and she gave you a good scolding to the effect, "If you ever sign up for some dumb s*&^ like this again, I'm gonna make you figure out how to pay for it."

Then Columbia House started sending monthly reminders, then bi-weekly reminders, then weekly reminders that you needed to fulfill your contract or they were going to ... going to what? You were fourteen-years old. There wasn't anything they could actually do, and at some point both you and your mom figured that out. If they wanted the eight-tracks back, that would be fine, load up the Ohio Players, Barry Manilow, Peter Frampton, Steve Miller, Aerosmith, Ted Nugent, Barbra Mandrell, Boz Scaggs, Johnny Mathis, Grand Funk, Steely Dan, Chuck Mangione, and Helen Reddy and send them back; you've only listened to three of them all the way through, two of them were eaten by your eight-track player, and four of them are still un-opened. If Columbia House reads this, I'm sure that I'm going to get a bill in the mail from 1976.

✍   Records – Ahhhhh yeah vinyl. You'd be hard-pressed to find anyone that lived in the 60's and 70's that didn't own a record player. Record players ranged from really cheap $15 Bargain City specials to very expensive systems that had amps, and receivers, and giant speakers that would barely fit in a normal bedroom. Every record player I was ever around always needed a penny (or a couple nickels) taped to the arm to hold the needle firmly down onto the record; without the extra weight the tuning arm would bounce all over and the record would skip. Basically, the cheaper your record player the more coins you needed to put on top of the needle, (I figure mine was about a three nickel record player).

The records were either LP's (or albums as we called them) 33 1/3 or singles (the small records) which were also called 45's. A lot of people collected albums and kept them in nice, neat, orderly crates; but alas, with no money of any kind it was hard for most of the guys in my neighborhood to collect much of anything. I wanna say that albums cost around five dollars or six dollars and 45's cost right around a dollar.

If you thought that eight-tracks were easily damaged then we don't even want to talk about records. Records had to be handled very, very delicately and if the record player was bumped while playing a record, it could be detrimental as well. In short, records got scratched; the scratch may only cause a single song to skip or it may have ruined the entire record.

Albums had a tiny little hole in the middle and 45's had a much bigger hole in the middle. If you were around in those days you know that we had a little plastic converter that you had to have to play 45's. Originally, records played at 78 rpms (revolutions per minute), but I don't think I ever saw a 78 record, but it was still an option on your record player. A single was called a 45 because that's how many rpm's it played at, and albums played at 33 1/3 rpms. Probably the funniest thing I ever witnessed was when one of my more animated buddies was doing a funny little dance in front of his friends and someone decided to start changing the speed of the record player. This guy went from dancing normally to a high speed version and then down to a super slow-motion version based on the speed of the record. About ten of us sat there in stitches; Jerry Lewis, Jim Carrey, or any other famous comedian couldn't have matched this guy on this night.

✍ TV – Unlike the 24/7 musical options we can find on the television today, in the 60's and 70's we were very limited. For the most part we just happened upon the music we encountered on tv, but it was our only chance to see what a lot of these groups looked like.

In the 60's and 70's there were literally dozens of variety shows on tv: The Tonight Show, Dick Cavett, Merv Griffin, Dinah Shore, Smother's Brothers, Hee Haw, Laugh-In, Ed Sullivan, Sonny & Cher, Donnie & Marie, The Mandrells, Red Skelton, Saturday Night Live, Andy Williams Show, Porter Wagoner Show, (really it was easier to name the people who didn't have their own show). On most of these shows there would be a scheduled musical group that would perform; sometimes we knew ahead of time because it would be announced on a previous show or we may have even been able to find out through reading the TV Guide. I know that

KISS was going to be on a Halloween special of some kind once and I missed half of Trick-or-Treat waiting to see them.

✍ I'm going to take a second and talk about TV Guide. It was by far the most read book in my house and I would guess it probably ranked second in the country as most read, right behind The Bible. It wasn't like you could watch any show, at any time like you can today; it was important to know if The Six Million Dollar Man was a re-run or not, or what show was going to be on Wonderful World of Disney this Sunday night. I always did the crossword and most of the time I drew glasses or moustaches or devil horns on the actor on the cover of the weekly magazine. There was also an Art Instruction School ad in every tv guide, more memorable as Draw Spunky or Draw Me, and there would be a picture of a pirate, or a clown, or a dog or something; you were supposed to draw the picture and send it in for evaluation. I know that I sent one in as a senior in high school and was called by their Minneapolis office to set up an interview, so they we indeed real.

✍ Another show that played non-stop rock and roll, (no pop music here) was Don Kirshner's Rock Concert. It only aired every other week, and it didn't even start until 11:30 so it was pretty rare that we caught an episode, but there were some characters at school (be them few and far between) who raved about how great this show was. In reality, it was one of the few chances to see hard rock groups play without going to a concert, (which really would have been an anomaly for kids in this time period).

And now the biggies; the two television shows that defined music in our generation were *American Bandstand* and *Soul Train*. These shows gave us the most current hits and often a glimpse towards what would be a hit in the near future. I'm going to go into a little more detail over the next few pages about these shows, but for now all I will say is that they were extremely important for us.

✍ Radio – Listening to the radio was still our number one source of musical enjoyment. Radio in the 60's and 70's was a much more powerful media source than it is in today's world. We used the radio for music, local weather, local sports, local news, local talk shows, and a few national programs. Throughout the day, in between all of the local programming, the dj's would play music; some of it we liked and some of it we didn't, but regardless we never strayed too far from our hometown radio station. Eventually more and more stations started programming specific genres of music to capture a specific fan base.

Radio reception was very inconsistent; sometimes you could pick up powerful stations that were hundreds of miles away, while other times anything other than the local station that was five miles up the hill wouldn't come in at all. Sometimes if you held your little transistor radio just right, the station would come in perfectly, so you twisted and turned and held it above your head just to hear that one song you'd been waiting to hear all night.

The local stations had times when they took requests and then they would play the number one requested song at the end of the show; we would sit there anticipating, guessing, and betting each other as to what the number one song was going to be. I think Olivia Newton John's *I Honestly Love You*, was the most requested song in our community for five or six months in a row; when all of the teenage girls started calling in to request a song they were a force to be reckoned with.

Even though I've talked about other radio broadcasts, there was really only one: Casey Kasem's *American Top 40*. Casey Kasem (who was also the voice of Shaggy on Scooby-Doo), hosted the weekly radio countdown of the 40 most popular songs in America. Kasem would intertwine obscure facts about each artist into the music; there were also long-distance dedications that were often pretty sappy, (at least through the ears of 16-year old boys). The lower the number, the bigger the hit, so after three hours, a whole lot of commercials targeted at teens, the number one song would be revealed followed by his signature sign off, "*Keep your feet on the ground and keep reaching for the stars.*"

✍ We loved music so much, that most of our Saturdays' revolved around it. Here was a typical Saturday when we were 16 or 17-years old: Wake up around 8:00 and watch a few cartoons and maybe grab a bowl of cereal (Count Chocula, Frankenberry, Lucky Charms, or just some regular old Corn Flakes would be nice), then out the door. Go find some friends that were awake, if they weren't awake, a lot of times their parents would tell you, "Go on up and wake him up, he needs to get up anyways." Then after a few grumpy minutes your buddies would finally manage their way out of bed and then out of the house. It would've been pretty normal at that point to jump on your bikes and ride around town or grab a basketball and shoot a few hundred shots. At some point we had to start paying attention to what time it was because I think at Noon, *American Bandstand* came on and we didn't want to miss it. Dick Clark's *American Bandstand* was our blueprint as to how we should dress, how we should dance, and what music we should listen to. Of course since Bandstand was filmed in Los Angeles and we lived in Appalachia, Ohio it usually took a while before any of those fashion trends hit the shelves of Bargain City.

Each week *American Bandstand* would play some of the most popular hits of the day along with having a musical guest play their newest song. Most of us didn't pay too close attention to the music; it was the dancers that we wanted to key in on. Were there any cool moves we could learn? Do I have anything in my closet that looks like what they've got on? By the time we were 16 or 17 we were probably watching the show just to brag about being better dancers than most of the ones on the show, (which I really believe we were), or maybe we just needed to learn what new acne medicine Stridex was selling that week because the commercials only centered around teenagers.

American Bandstand was more than educational enough for 90% of the white kids out there (this is sounding racist, but hang in there for a second), but 10% of us wanted to learn more advanced dance moves and we could only find that on *Soul Train. Soul Train* hosted by Don Cornelius was "*The hippest trip in America*", Don even said so. While *American Bandstand* (and Dick Clark especially) was the whitest of white shows, *Soul Train* was centered around African-Americans. The dancers were black, most of the acts were black, even the commercials were geared towards the black community (I know I never saw an Afro Sheen commercial anywhere else than during *Soul Train*). The *Soul Train* dancers were so different than the Bandstand dancers; they were doing wildly athletic moves and seemed to be completely oblivious to anything other than letting the music infiltrate their bodies. And that infiltrating music was different as well, R & B, soul, and funk pounded out beats that were made for dancing; they weren't pop songs that people danced to, they were dance songs that may or may not have even made it to radio play, but every decent disc jockey (including ours) knew about these danceable tunes.

Soul Train dancers were doing splits, the bump, the robot, and the famous Soul Train Line where two dancers would dance their way through two lines of dancers before the next duo of dancers would start their procession; each one trying to out-do the previous dancers.

When *Soul Train* and *American Bandstand* were over it was time to listen to the radio and *American Top 40*. You could just listen to it while you were doing other things (laying out to get a suntan, playing basketball, swimming at the beach or Big Pool) or you could sit through the whole three hours using your little handheld tape recorder making your own Top 40 mix tape. Making a mix tape wasn't like hitting a button and miraculously music appeared on your computer or phone or iPod. You had to sit in a quiet room listening to Casey Kasem talk about the songs and then at the exact second that the song started you had to push record and play at exactly the same time. Of course you had to have your tape recorder sitting up next to the radio speaker and then you had to hope that no one walked into your room, or the neighbor's dog didn't start barking, or the phone didn't start ringing because if anything like that happened it would be on your mix tape. I don't know how many times I sat there waiting for the number one song in the country and I missed it because I had to go to the bathroom, or run to the store for the Old Man, or supper was ready and it wasn't like I could've said, "Well, hold on I'm taping this song." Or a lot of times the friggin' tape would run out half way through a song.

✍ Once that final song played it was time to start getting ready for the dance. It was really the only time I hung around the house all week, I couldn't just pop in and tell the Old Man I was going to the dance, I had to ask (mainly because it put me out past my curfew by an hour). So I would hang out watching tv for a while and maybe even take a bath (which wasn't a for sure thing for us boys back then), and after waiting around until it seemed like the right time I would spring the dance question on him, "Dad, can I go to the dance?"

Now this wasn't like it was a mystery that this question was going to come up because unlike today's world that only have Homecoming dances and The Prom, we had dances every weekend, usually Friday and Saturday nights. Every once in a while he would say no, which really threw a wrench in things. If he said no, I would sit in the chair across the room, stare at the tv without blinking and start the loudest series of sighs you can imagine. Eventually I made him so mad that he would repent, "Jesus *&^%$, just go to the dance. You better make sure you're back here by 11:00."

Of course the dance didn't end until 11:00 and the Y was about a mile and a half from my house, which meant I could run home in about eight minutes; anyways I had won the battle of wills and I would worry about getting home on time later.

✍ Girls would often get ready together, it certainly took them longer to blow dry and then curl their hair than it did for the boys to get ready (although many a boy including me, had a blow dryer in their room and knew how to use it). I suppose while one girl got ready the other ones were sitting around in bean bag chairs or on the waterbed looking at Tiger Beat and

16 magazines reading up on Donny Osmond, Leif Garrett, and Shawn Cassidy. Many a teenage girl's room was splattered with pictures cut out from these magazines.

Of course teenage boy's rooms were completely different. Instead of the light pastel colors the girls enjoyed, the boys tried for total darkness. Black light posters (even if we didn't have a black light), a lava lamp gave off all of the light we needed (maybe we just didn't want our mom's catching us with our hidden Playboys). If you were brave enough to pull it off, you stuck the Farrah Fawcett poster on your wall (I certainly didn't claim to be that risqué), and many a teenage boy had a strobe light or a revolving disco ball in their room as well. There were always weights under the bed and probably a BB gun in the corner (just in case a pigeon dared to fly close enough for a shot at him). Our tennis shoes were always stuffed under our beds as well; I don't know how many times I got yelled at for leaving my bio hazardous rotten egg-smelling shoes in the living room.

Sometimes when we got together in our rooms we could sneak the phone in and make prank phone calls. This was before caller ID, so it was virtually impossible to get caught (unless you just kept calling the same house over and over and they had the police put a trace on the call). Most of the time during our prank calls we couldn't even get through the first few words without giggling out the rest of the sentence. With a roomful of your friends trying to hold in their laughter, it was next to impossible to do this without laughing. As teenagers we didn't have a lot of real good ones, actually a lot of times we would just call a girl that we knew one of our buddies liked, wait for her to answer, and then hang up. But here are a couple that I can remember doing:

"Hello" Stranger.

"Hello?" Us.

"Hello, are you there?" Stranger.

"Hello? Is someone there?" Us.

"Hello. Yes, I'm here, can you hear me?" Stranger.

"Hello?   (moving the phone away and yelling across the room), Damn it Martha, someone's doing one of those damn prank call things again." Us.

"No, no no. You called me. Hello? Are you there?" Stranger.

This would go on as long as we could hold it together without breaking up into laughter.

Of course we would order pizzas and send them to houses across the street so we could watch the ensuing fireworks:

Knock, knock, knock. Door is answered. "Pizza for Jones, that's $8.50.

"I didn't order a pizza, you must have the wrong Jones."

"Jones, 1220 Gomber Avenue, right?"

"Yeah, but I didn't order a pizza."

"555-1382, right?"

"Yeah, but I'm telling you I didn't order a pizza. Hold on a minute. (Leans back inside the house), Marge, did you order a pizza? (Gets answer) I'm telling you we didn't order a pizza."

"Well, someone's buying this pizza. It's your name. It's your address. And it's your phone number. How can that happen without you ordering this pizza?"

The local pizza delivery places had so many of these calls that they just got written down in the books as a prank call and then eventually eaten by the pizza employees.

✍   With the dance starting at 8:00 p.m., around 7:00 p.m. probably about a third of the kids going to the dance were out the door, driving around in their cars, looking for beer. Obviously that number is just a guess, but I'm actually trying to lowball that percentage; it may have been closer to half. For as much drinking that was going on, there were very few drinking related incidents: I can't recall anyone getting sick from alcohol at a dance, I can't recall anyone falling down or being incoherent at a dance, I can certainly remember some fights but... hey, girls dancing with boys, jealousies, it's just human nature there were going to be some fights. I guess some of that goes to the fact that these drinkers were swilling down pretty much a bare minimum of alcohol; it was possible that a carload of five or six partiers were splitting a case of beer, so four beers each must've been just enough to make them think they were buzzed. Buzzed enough to be courageous enough to get out on the dance floor, buzzed enough to ask a girl to dance, or buzzed enough to ask a girl out.

Walking in the dance right at 8:00 wasn't the cool thing to do, (even though I always wanted to be there when the doors opened). If you were cool, you pulled into the YMCA parking lot around 8:40; it was important to drive around town (no seatbelts, slippery vinyl bench seats, taking turns as fast as possible to skid your passengers from side to side, and the music up as loud as it would go), through the park a couple times, probably a Chinese Fire drill (where everybody gets out of the car at a red light and runs around the car and gets back in before the light changes), maybe a trip out some of the country roads, and then get rid of all of the physical evidence of an hour's worth of drinking. Apparently our parents never got in our vehicles because the smell of spilled beer was easily definable weeks after the fact.

There were a few other times when we had eight-tracks that we listened to on these Saturday night, rites-of-passage adventures that were not music, they were comedy tapes: Bill Cosby, Cheech & Chong, and Richard Pryor were the main comedy tapes of our era. They had to be smuggled into your vehicle or sometimes we listened to them behind closed garage doors; they talked about things we weren't supposed to talk about (especially Richard Pryor and Cheech & Chong). We would hoot and holler and poke each other, "Shhhhhhhh, listen to this part, it's hilarious."

We had seen these comedians on tv but they sure didn't talk like this. Censorship was alive and well during the 60's and 70's and I believe those people took their jobs pretty serious. Today's comics use the "F" word like most of us use oxygen, but back in those days it just wasn't done.

As soon as one dance ended we were mapping out our strategies for the next dance. Another dance meant another opportunity; another opportunity to do things we didn't do at the last dance, another opportunity to do things better, another opportunity to do things differently. A thousand different factors played into the success of each and every YMCA dance, city Park dance, church dance, elementary school dance, high school dance, Homecoming dance, or Prom that we ever went to: did a girl talk to you in school or in the neighborhood that had never really talked to you before? Did a girl tell you that she'd see you at the dance? (That had to be a signal, right?) Did a girl look at you (or you at least think she may have looked at you) at the previous dance? Did you get a new outfit (which now gave you confidence you didn't have without it?) Did you stand along the wall like a lump of coal waiting and waiting, trying to muster up the nerve to ask a girl to dance last week but the timing was never right so you vowed (all week long) that you were definitely going to ask this particular girl to dance (and she either didn't show or picked up a new boyfriend the night before)? Did you dance with a girl at the previous dance but thought you should've asked her out, but you chickened out, but you were gonna make up for it this week? Did you work on some new dance moves which upped your confidence and irresistibility? Did you finally have your hair looking absolutely perfect?

Amazingly all of those factors and many, many more really impacted how much most of us enjoyed our time at the dances; at least in the beginning. When we were young, we allowed every outside stimulus you can imagine to make or break us, but as we got older we just plain didn't care and it's amazing how many good things can happen when you just don't care about what people think. When we were juniors and especially when we were seniors, if we asked a girl to dance and she said no, we would just move on to another one, there seemed to be plenty of girls to go around. If that had happened to us when we were freshmen, it would've been three months before we drummed up enough courage to give it another try.

Our early years at the dances were somewhat pathetic, we stood along the wall jabbing and wrestling around with each other while we watching the girls dance in big groups to the fast songs. It looked like they were having so much fun, but mentally we just weren't ready to join in the fun. Eventually we started sneaking out away from the wall a little bit and made our own little group on the edge of the dance floor; we did what we affectionately now call "The Lawnmower", which basically was us moving our arms in and out like we were pushing a lawnmower. Now mind you, we weren't dancing with girls, it was just a big group of guys (strength in numbers I suppose), and if an upperclassman would walk close to us, we would stop what we were doing and start talking about some random piece of news. We were weak, pathetic, idiots. But around halfway through our sophomore years we started to mix right in the middle of the big girl groups and low and behold they liked us being out there with them. To make sure that we could fit in with them, we began studying *American Bandstand* and eventually *Soul Train*, and then we practiced in our rooms. We would turn on the music (not with other guys in the room, by ourselves usually behind locked doors), watch ourselves in the mirror, and practice over and over again. By dancing amidst the girls during the fast songs, (freestyling, doing the bump, or some of the many line dances) it made it much easier to ask one of them to slow dance with us when the music changed to a slow song. We finally figured out that we weren't picking our future brides; we weren't trying to estimate the matching of our DNA to speculate our future children's success. It was just a dance! And amazingly, when it was just a dance, there was no pressure and our jaws moved freely and we were able to talk, talk like a human being, talk like we did with our friends, and it was kind of nice! It was nice to smell a girl, they even had their own shampoo that was named, "Gee Your Hair Smells Terrific", throw on some Love's Baby Soft or Charlie and a little bit of glitter (that always got on all of our clothes), and you had the complete package. We boys tried to keep up our end of the olfactory battle with English Leather, Brut, Aqua Velva, or maybe some of our dad's Old Spice; and if a dab of it was good, a half pint of it had to be better. I know sometimes the girls could probably smell us pulling in the parking lot.

Once we figured out some of these secrets of nature, our goals changed; dancing with a girl was awesome but we wanted to talk them into going out with us. Now I'm not talking about going steady with us, I'm talking about actually going outside of the building with us. When we boys walked into the dance as a group, it was as if all of us had our own *Mission Impossible* secret operation. "Your mission if you choose to accept it...is to persuade a girl to leave the confines of the dance with you."

Of course for a real, live, breathing girl to leave the dance with any of us boys, the sun, the moon, and all of the planets had to line up; and even though it was our primary goal for all of the 200 or so dances that we went to over the years, it didn't happen all that often.

So when mission impossible was successful, what then? Well, if the dance was at the YMCA (which would have been a dance or two every weekend from September until June) the boy would have rounded up his coat if necessary and waited by the door for the girl. The girl on the other hand would not only have to get her coat but also had to check in with the group of girls she arrived with, in all honesty these girls could veto the whole affair. If they didn't like the boy, (or if he had just went out with one of them the week before) they might tell her that she couldn't go. It could also be possible that a girl was deemed by her friends, too intoxicated to be going anywhere. (In truth it was neat how the girls took care of one another. I could give a dozen stories of how a guy from our group went AWOL for several hours before we even started looking for them.) But if everything was cleared by her crew, out the door the both of you would go; usually given "a look" by the people who took tickets at the door.

The two of you would stroll along the houses of the neighborhood and possibly through some back alleys. Even though we boys had planned and practiced what we were going to say to get girls to go out with us, in the beginning we didn't have much of a game plan after that. (I will say that as time went by, and we became seniors, we had the whole thing down to a science; but in the beginning it was pretty crude.) On any dance night you could easily find teenage couples between houses, tucked in behind garbage cans or parked cars within a two block radius of the Y. You wanted to avoid barking dogs or bright street lights; anything that might bring attention to your secret romantic tryst. I know there was a hammock that was in a guys backyard and I had that pegged as an ideal spot, but after rolling out of and nearly giving two girls (yep, dumb enough to do it twice) a concussion I thought better of the whole hammock thing.

At summer dances at the Big Pavilion, our couples stroll would consist of a trip around the Duck Pond and then slipping off under the Covered Bridge or making your way over to the Little League dugouts. Of course if you had a car, that gave you another option all-together; there were plenty of make-out spots along many of the country roads surrounding town. I will say that I personally had poor luck trying to be romantic in a car; the first day I got my license I got locked in the cemetery with a girl (I had no idea they locked the gates that early), another time I backed up into a ditch leaving the girl's driveway and had to call a tow truck, and still another time... ummm, I can't tell that one but you get my point.

For the most part, nothing really happened between the two of you (well for some people it did, but usually not so much), it would take a long time for the guy to get up the nerve to make a move that seemed clever enough for that first kiss. Most of the time spent "out" with the girl was wandering around trying to find a place to hide in the darkness and establishing that first kiss. Fifteen minutes of awkward, teenage, fumbling around passion later and it was time to go back to the dance. Luckily they allowed us back in without paying or none of us would've ever went out with a girl; it was hard enough coming up with dance money once, let alone doing it twice in one night.

Once we returned, whatever was happening on the dance floor stopped for a few minutes for both groups. The girls group surrounded the returning girl, like a herd of mother lions checking on a cub that had wandered away from the den. But the guys group was a little different, there were always a bunch of high fives, big smiles, and a general feeling of accomplishment; I think we figured it was a success for our entire group of renegades. If someone in our group was lucky enough to go out with a girl, it gave the rest of us knuckleheads hope that we somehow had a chance as well. We didn't spend any time talking about what happened, we knew that there would be a full account of the evening from start to finish once we got back to the car. The stories were usually 80% truth, 10% slight exaggeration, and another 10% absolute fiction.

Most of the time, just being at the dance, being with our friends, and jumping around like idiots was more than enough for us. The music of our generation was second to none as far as getting people out on the dance floor, here a few of the great ones that got us up and moving (songs taken straight off of my phone): *Atomic Dog* George Clinton, *Boogie Fever* The Sylvers, *Boogie Nights* Heatwave, *Boogie Oogie Oogie* Taste of Honey, *Brick House* Commodores, *Car Wash* Rose Royce, *Dancing Queen* Abba, *Dazz* Brick, *Fantastic Voyage* Lakeside, *Ffun* Confunction, Fire Ohio Players, Flashlight Parliament, Funkytown Lipps Inc., *Good Times* Chic, *Groove Line* Heatwave, *Hot Stuff* Donna Summer, The Hustle Van McCoy, *Jungle Love* Steve Miller Band, *Lady Marmalade* Patti LaBelle, *Last Dance* Donna Summer, *Le Freak* Chic, *Lido Shuffle* Boz Scaggs, *Love Rollercoaster* Ohio Players, *Night Fever* Bee Gees, Play That Funky Music Wild Cherry, *Ring My Bell* Anita Ward, *Saturday Night* Bay Coty Rollers, *September* Earth, Wind, and Fire, *Shake Your Booty* KC & the Sunshine Band (you could insert any KC song in here, they were basically all the same. Awesome!), *Shame* Evelyn Champagne King, Slow Ride Fog Hat, *Some Kind of*

Wonderful Grand Funk Railroad, *Strawberry Letter 23*
Brothers Johnson, *Sweet Home Alabama* Lynard Skynard,
Takin' Care of Business Bachman, Turner, Overdrive, *Tear the Roof of the Sucker* Parliament, *Tell Me Something Good*
Chaka Kahn, *We Are Family* Sister Sledge, *YMCA* Village
People, and these are just to name a few.

Every song reminds us of a place we were at when we
listened to that song so many years ago, it reminds of whom
we were with, and what we were doing. Hearing those songs
opens the flood gates of our emotions, emotions that
sometimes were neatly tucked away and often forgotten, but
it only takes a couple notes of those songs, a couple words
from the lyrics, and everything comes back in full color.

Our DJ was great, if there was a high school dance DJ Hall
of Fame, he would be in it. He was great at playing songs
that would get us out on the dance floor. In the first hour of
the dance he would play nothing but fast songs (dance
songs), in the second hour every fifth or sixth song would be a
slow song, and in the last hour every fourth song would be a
slow song, with the last two songs of the night always being
back-to-back slow songs. For a long time his last two songs
were the same, *Always and Forever* Heatwave followed by
Elton John's *Someone Saved My Life Tonight.* When you
heard those songs playing, you knew you had better "S*&# or
get off the pot", because you'd have to wait another week to
get that chance again. But you'd better hurry up because a
lot of people were grabbing their coats and heading towards
the exits and a lot of others were snatching up whatever girls
weren't already on the dance floor. You could've danced
every single song that was played that night, but if you missed
out on dancing that last song you felt cheated. (And
remember my 11:00 p.m. curfew, I knew that *Someone Saved
My Life Tonight* was about seven minutes long, so when that
song started playing, I started my near sprint home, putting
me in the door exactly one minute late. But if I was already
dancing with a girl during *Always and Forever* and she wanted
to keep dancing, well the heck with it, the Old Man would just
have to yell at me; it was worth it.)

When we entered the dance everyone was given a three by nine inch stock of colored paper that had a list of the songs that made the *American Top 40* that week and on the other side were various coupons that were geared towards teenage buyers. By the time we left the dance, those cardstock Top 40 sheets that we had stuck in our pockets were often soaked through. The amount of calories that we burned in a three hour dance was unbelievable; no wonder we were all skinny as a rail.

I don't know how many times I came into the house after a dance, usually in a full sweat (some from the dance and some from sprinting a mile and half to get home), pulling everything out of my pockets (a couple quarters, keys, my comb, and the Top 40 sheet all crumpled up), and then just lay there staring at the ceiling with the music still ringing in my ears, thinking about everything that happened that night, everything I wish had happened that night, and everything that I wanted to happen at the next dance.

A Few Parting Shots

✍ I'm positive that I could keep on writing for quite a long time, but even when you are at the grand buffet eventually you just have to stop and walk away. I purposely tried not to cover historical events; I figure if you want to know about that kind of stuff you can find it in any book. I wanted people to know about us, about how we felt, about what we did; and I can guarantee you that none of us spent time worrying about Nixon, or Patty Hearst, or the Bay of Pigs; we were too busy playing at the time.

I have tried to give an honest depiction of what it was like to grow up in the 60's and 70's. It wasn't all glamorous, as a matter-of-fact it was downright tough sometimes, but we got through it the best that we could, our parents raised us the best that they knew how, and I can't imagine there being any place or any time period that a kid could've grown up in that could've been better than during the 60's and 70's in the United States of America.

Obviously everyone's childhood was a little bit different so many of the items that I wrote about may have been strikingly different than others; all I could really do was write about how it was in my town, in my neighborhood, in my house. Most of the pieces of the story were generalizations about our time period; they could have been describing events from Portland, Oregon to Portland, Maine. When I talk to other people from across the country my own age, yes there are subtle, regional differences, but the story stays pretty much the same.

✍ So what does growing up old school mean? It means that you played outside every day, all day long, from sun up to sun down. It means that if you got hurt you rubbed some dirt on it and you kept right on playing. You did things you weren't supposed to and you probably had some close calls but you lived through it; now those are the funny stories you tell of "remember when." It means that you were expected to eat SPAM and fried baloney (yeah, that's how we spelled it) sandwiches every once in a while. You probably got picked on by some bullies but you probably played plenty of pranks yourself. Gas was under a dollar and your dad would let you sit on his lap and drive the car on back country roads. Your parents smoked, drank, cussed, and beat your butt when you deserved it. We had great music and listened to it played loudly; we danced, and grew our hair long, and lived every day like it might be our last.

Growing up old school meant growing up with respect, maybe that respect was out of fear of what would happen if our parents found out about our squirreliness but it worked. And that discipline shaped us and gave us the structure and foundation that we needed to go out and make a mark in the tough world that we grew up in.

Growing up old school meant learning the value of hard work, the importance of putting in a full day's work for a full day's pay. Elbow grease, putting your back into it, and good old fashioned manual labor were our calling cards. We didn't look down our noses at people that worked for a living.

Growing up old school meant using whatever we had and making the most out of it. We used our imaginations and could turn nothing into anything. We didn't sit around whining about what we didn't have, we made do, and we made it work. That creative can-do spirit helped us be achievers.

Growing up old school meant that you had thick skin and could take it when times got tough. Those tough times might have come from bullies, your own parents, or the lack of necessities; but regardless of the cause, you learned that life isn't always fair, and life is tough, and you better stand up for yourself or you'll be run over and no one's gonna shed a tear for you one way or the other.

✍   Sometimes a smell reminds me of those years: (citronella, chlorine, Coppertone –the Three C's of summer, a fresh rain, or even the smell of fresh cut grass). Many times it's a sound that takes me on a journey back through time: (kid's playing at recess, Emergency Broadcast tests, neighbors calling for their dog – reminds me of parents calling for us, and of course the hundreds of songs of our era). And other times I see things that refresh the memory banks: (drive-in movie screens, roller skating rinks, big groups of kids playing in the street, names scratched into fresh concrete).

Why are we so easily drawn back to those years, those beautiful, innocent, crazy years of our childhood? I believe part of it has to be the sense of invincibility that coursed through our veins during this time; everything we did was at Mach speed, we never slowed down from the time we got up to the time we were forced to go to bed. We had no fear of the future, we certainly didn't recognize our mortality, we played and allowed others to worry about things, worrying about things wasn't our job. Our sense of invincibility was certainly proven in all of the daring stunts we pulled every day, stunts with little to no thought put into them, no concern over potential injury, no concern of potential injury to others, and when you cheat death on a daily basis it became old hat, it became a normal part of our day. Our antics kept us feeling alive; it was only when we were subjected to playing inside that we felt like we were being cheated. Even if we were trapped inside our own homes we still found adrenaline pumping activities to help keep us "alive", like climbing in a laundry basket and sledding down the basement stairs. It was irrelevant that there was no carpet, no way to stop except into a brick wall, various nails stuck out along the course; we were invincible until proven otherwise and those dangerous details didn't matter.

✍ And even though many of us during this era weren't even particularly excited about the possibility of attaining our driver's license, me and many of my friends and guys I knew choose to forego our driver's licenses until we were 17. I know I figured I could walk or ride my bike anywhere in town that I wanted to go and it wasn't like I had a car sitting in the driveway waiting for me anyways so why hurry? I re-upped my permit twice because I didn't feel the need to take the test to get my actual driver's license. But eventually, just like how our bicycles released us from the shackles of our immediate neighborhood and allowed us to ride all over town, cars multiplied our boundaries even further. It opened up more opportunities and allowed us to discover treasures in other faraway places that we never would've been able to get to on our bikes.

Of course the catch with all of this freedom and all of this lengthening of our tethers was the continuous and steady loss of our innocence. Once all of those precious pieces of our innocence were lost... they were lost, lost forever, never to be returned. They were bells that couldn't be un-rung. And even though we were encouraged and allowed to be kids, it had its toll on us as well: we played so many hours and did so many things to "Up the Ante" that it was inevitable that we did things that were regrettable (I was dumb or brave enough to list quite a few of my misgivings), sometimes we never recovered from those regrettable misgivings. Another casualty of growing up with this much freedom is the fact that I don't think most of us were terribly close to our parents, how could we be close, we spent nearly every waking hour outside playing. Our parents didn't get much of a chance most of the time to be a part of our lives; I figure that's why many of us from the 60's and 70's have went overboard trying to do as much as we can with our kids.

✍ Fact of the matter is, I ain't no spring chicken anymore. I can't run ten second hundred yard dashes anymore (but what I would give to feel that rush of wind in my face and feel my feet barely touching the ground), I can't shop for 28-inch pants or size medium t-shirts, I can't do double flips off of the diving board anymore (I was banned from doing any more gainers from the Piqua pool when I turned 48. They didn't assume a 48-year old, 230 pound man could do that safely. Well, a bumblebee shouldn't be either to fly either, but they can !) I wake up with aches and pains that I can't remember having when I was younger, my seventh knee surgery quickly tuned into an eighth, which was a total knee replacement. All of the medical issues that I watched my dad and my friends' dads have are now creeping up on the horizon. I know I used to think it was stupid for people to sit down and plan out a will but I catch myself writing down which kid will get what objects of my possessions. It's not like I feel like I'm gonna die anytime soon, as a matter-of-fact I feel like I'm going to be around a good long time, but being around isn't the same as being alive, and I don't think any of us will ever feel as alive as we did back in those glorious years of our youth. I suppose I could drag the laundry basket over to the basement steps and go for a ride, I suppose I could go out and throw tomatoes at stop signs, or maybe set up a little ramp, tie a bed sheet around my neck, and ramp my grandpa-looking road bike across the driveway, but alas nothing is going to bring back those days. Captain and Tenille just aren't going to have another number one hit, Wolfman Jack's gravelly voice isn't going to greet me on the radio, and the money spent on the Six-Million Dollar Man wouldn't pay for a good relief pitcher in today's world.

So as I step into my Chevelle with the hula girl on the dashboard, peace sign bumper sticker, eight-track kicking out some *Kung-Fu Fighting,* I will hit the high beams with my dimmer switch, get on my CB radio and wish you all a "10-4 Good Buddy." Thanks for taking this journey with me.

✍ Note: Over forty times in this book I referred to my dad as the Old Man, many of the references depicted him as a mean, intolerable, grump and there were certainly times when that was true but I also realize that I probably meant more to him than anything on Earth. Most of the things he did were in an attempt to make sure that I turned out better than him. Without his discipline... well, you've read the book, I probably would have spent my years behind bars. Yes, I did a bunch of dumb, immature things but I always knew where the line was between mischief and felonies. So I don't want anyone to misinterpret my gratitude for the lessons I learned from my parents.

Were the photographers better in the 60's or was I just that good looking? Maybe a little of both.

Second grade class picture. Note the blackeye (bike wreck from ramping a tree root). The photographer tried to hide it by filming the left side of my face, (I am the only one facing left). It almost worked.

Kiwanis Braves coached by Mr. Henry. Second place two years in a row. Lot of Converse, plenty of hair, stirrup socks, three-inch wide belts, and attitude.

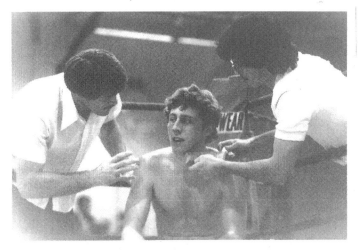

Boxing for that "Free" YMCA membership; only cost me a broken nose. (I was way ahead in that fight too, until I got hit with a random haymaker.)

The Cambridge Municipal Pool in all of its 1970s glory. If I had a dollar for every sunburn that stemmed from spending the day at "The Big Pool", I could retire in The Hamptons.

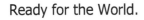

CAMBRIDGE HIGH SCHOOL
Graduation
June 17, 1979

Ready for the World.   17:01 5k road race, pretty good.

First car, 1970 Buick Skylark GS. Would LOVE to have that baby back. Probably would cost more than the $3500 I paid.

Yes, there really was a Gomber Ave.

The old YMCA Mansion. Oh the times we had in there!

Doing The Bump. Disco, catching dance fever. Far Out!

PB's, our teenage monetary system. Paid for a lot of dances.

Me, my cousins, and Grandpa Dadoo. Have Gun Will Travel.

These were our cellphones. We always kept a dime in our sock, just in case we ever needed to make a call. Lot of prank calls, lot of calls to girls or boys then hanging up when they answered, don't ever remember making an emergency call.

Roller Derby, now that'll bring back some memories: Bay Bombers, LA Thunderbirds, Jam, Ronnie Robinson, must be talking about Roller Derby. Another Saturday Morning staple at our house.

Dude! How were these a game for children? Or anyone?

Saddle Shoes.

Pretty basic, but call me crazy, they're kind of sexy.

Girls probably knew that too.

Ah, the technology and beauty of the Etch a Sketch. Still bad.

Schwinn Apple Crate. The Sistine Chapel of Old School bikes.

Cambridge Junior High School, it looks like Arkham Insane Asylum. This photo definitely doesn't adequately portray the despair, dread, and anguish that cultivated inside those walls.

I really hope you enjoyed your journey and it brought back a hundred great memories. Remember to tell your friends how they can re-live their Growing Up Old School days too.

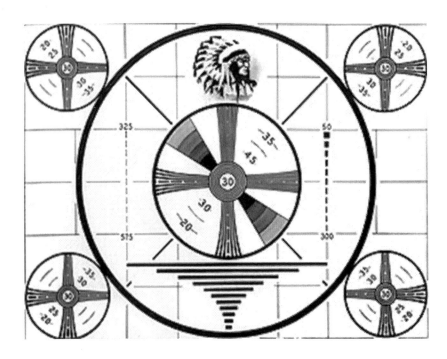

This is G.U.O.S. Growing Up Old School signing off.

★ ★ ★ ★ ★ ★ ★ ★ ★ ★ ★ ★ ★

Oh, say can you see by the dawn's early light?
What so proudly we hailed at the twilight's last gleaming.
Whose broad stripes and bright stars through the perilous fight
O'er the ramparts we watched were so gallantly streaming?
And the rocket's red glare, the bombs bursting in air,
Gave proof through the night that our flag was still there.
Oh, say does that Star-Spangled Banner yet wave
O'er the Land of the Free and the Home of the Brave?

PROUND TO LIVE IN THE GREATEST COUNTRY IN THE WORLD.
GOD BLESS AMERICA

Made in the USA
Columbia, SC
26 July 2024

39389538R00154